CHAIN OF CHANGE

Thoughts On a Dream Deferred

the dream is in the process
and not the outcome
it is found in the struggle
for peace
and not in achieving it
in the working of the artist
and not in the creation
in the sun's rays
and not the sun
in the belief that we can

—Mel King
12/31/79
11:58p.m.

CHAIN OF CHANGE

Struggles for
Black Community Development

Mel King

South End Press   **Boston**

Cover Artist, Sharon Haggins Dunn
Cover Design, Pat Walker

This book was designed, typeset and pasted up by the South End Press Collective.

**South End Press, Box 68 Astor Station
Boston, MA 02123**

to
all of you
who are a part of me
especially the youth

PREFACE

After the Civil War, the government of this country was, supposedly, establishing justice and equality for its citizens. Instead, Reconstruction politics triggered a Jim Crow backlash by white citizens which engrained racism deep into our national norms. Now, after the War for Civil Rights, from 1954 to 1969, we are encountering a similar resurgence of racism. But there will not be a return to Jim Crow in Boston, for people of color are moving toward taking control of their own communities, toward determining their own futures.

Chain of Change is about change and power. It's about how the Black community in Boston has changed—about how these changes have occurred and how these changes in turn have shaped subsequent developments in the Black community. It's about the chain of events that is leading to the empowerment of the Black community. Black power is being forged, as we link together our struggles, as we break the chains of dependence on the white power structure.

Boston is not unique in terms of the progress achieved by Black people, but because this is where I have been, and because so many of the factors that have shaped Boston's development have also affected other cities, I have focused on the Boston experience. Boston also has a reputation of being one of the most racist cities in the country. The racist violence of white people in Boston has been so intense in part because the Black community has taken forceful steps to secure its freedom. The struggle by the community of color has been actively opposed by the cornerstones of white Boston society including the Catholic church, the Brahmin power structure and white politicians. As always, from Reconstruction to present, when people of color threaten to become too effective, violent retaliation is carried out.

The history of the Black community in Boston is important for many reasons. One important reason is so that Black people can appreciate just how much progress we have made. We also need to analyze our experience, to take the time to understand it well, and to decide how we should proceed from here. At a time when Black and poor people see their efforts disparaged, when the few social programs that were institutionalized nationally out of the struggles of the sixties are being cut away by Congress, at a time when we realize that it has been thirty years since the Supreme Court decision that promised us equality, at this time people may wonder whether we have made any gains at all. We have.

Another reason for this book is for our children. Franz Fanon reminds us: "Each generation must out of relative obscurity discover its mission, fulfill it, or betray it."[1] Children naturally follow the example set for them by their role models. We must look at our experience over the last thirty years and see if we are setting the kind of example that we care to have emulated by our young people. They are the future. To meet the future, they need to know all they can about the heritage of activism and effort that has come before them. They must be provided with a "meaning" of the actions upon which they can build. This book is an effort to record the community's experiences for our children who must carry on "the mission."

Finally, for the sake of ourselves as well as our children, for our future as well as our past, we must go beyond our history and analyze our experiences as part of the process of planning our next efforts. What have we learned from our efforts over the last three decades? What can we do differently and better? It is not enough to look back and feel good about our work up to now; we must push ahead, dare to fulfill our mission, challenge this society to fulfill its promise, and pave the way for our young people to fulfill theirs.

ACKNOWLEDGEMENTS

That this book has been published could be a story in itself: first, because of the length of time it took; second, the way it was done; third, the people who were involved in the process of shaping it; fourth, because of those who suffered through the reams of paper and hours of work that prevented contact and companionship; and lastly, what I learned about the process of writing a book, and about me.

What started out in 1969 to be an attempt at sharing information with Judy Wagner about the events and issues in the Black community in Boston over the last twenty years turned into a mammoth data gathering effort and exploring of newspapers, flyers, posters and memos, most of which had been collected by Joyce King. When we soon realized that the chronology of events displayed an interesting pattern or chain that linked together the different struggles, we attempted to see what would happen if we talked about them and the people involved in a way that would tell a story about what went on so that people could learn from it.

The next step was to find a way to get down on paper what was in my head about these events and activities. Given the hectic pace of my schedule, it was quite difficult to get the time to get my thoughts together, and coordinate those times with Judy Wagner who would take dictation and further research the issues involved, as well as to coordinate all this with those people who would transcribe the tapes and type the manuscript. After six years we finally got it into publishable form—only to find out that the 1000 plus pages that we had accumulated were too many for one publisher, while another publisher was only interested in the educational part of it, particularly since in 1975 we were in the middle of the furor over school desegregation. In addition, questions were raised about how much of me was involved in the story—that more of my personal experiences would enhance the readability of the book.

However, for me the importance of this book is to capture how other people came out of these experiences, and to show the connections between the struggles. Therefore, we interviewed quite a number of people involved in Black community struggles, and have quoted extensively from these interviews throughout the book, and have also included an epilogue which includes in-depth answers to many of the questions we asked these community activists.* By way of thanking these people for their support in this undertaking, I want to thank all of the people who have participated in the struggle for human development, for empowerment.

A number of people have provided critical analysis of the book, including Ruth Batson, Byron Rushing and Chuck Turner,which was very, very helpful since they were involved in the struggles over the years and had invaluable insights into the chain of change. I also want to thank Beverly Adams and Connie D'mils for reading the manuscript and for typing the drafts, Charles Miller from Urban Systems Lab at MIT for his research support, Mary Ann Crayton for copy-editing, Martin Gopen for proofreading and indexing and for keeping all the buttons over the years, and Sharon Dunn for drawing the cover.

My sincerest appreciation is to Judy Wagner for her labor of love because she had to have wanted to see this book happen more than I did because she put in the time and the energy that really made this possible. The last acknowledgement has to be for Joyce King who not only collected most of the materials over the past 20 years that were the guts of the book, but then had to put up with my absences on the one hand, and my request on the other that she read every word three times; and although she insists that there is not enough of me in it there's more of me in it than there would have been if it had not been for her incisive comments, and without her love the quality of the expressions in the last chapters would not have been possible.

A final thanks goes to Pat Walker, my editor, and South End Press for struggling with me over two years and six missed deadlines to finally get it together because they believed enough in what we were trying to convey to hang-in and publish it.

---

* The full transcripts of these interviews plus the source materials for the book will be available at the Afro-American History Museum of Boston. Accordingly all excerpts from these transcripts and documents are not footnoted in the text.

CONTENTS

CHRONOLOGY*

1952 New York Streets Targeted for Urban Renewal
1958 West End Demolished for "Urban Removal"
1961 Mel King Runs for Boston School Committee
1962 BAG Sponsors Selective Boycotts
     Residents Reject South End Renewal Plan
1963 First School Stay-Outs
     Boston School Committee Debates Defacto Segregation
     Mel King's Second Attempt for School Committee
     "STOP" Day—Black Community Stops Working
1964 Second School Stay-Out and the "Freedom Schools"
1965 Boardman Parents Hire a Bus
     Operation Exodus
     Racial Imbalance Act Passed
     Mel King's Third Attempt for School Committee
1966 State Withholds Funds from School Committee
     METCO Is Formed
     New School For Children
     Police Riot in Grove Hall
1967 New Urban League
     Roxbury Action Program
     United Community Construction Workers
     Community Assembly for a United South End
     Tom Atkins Elected to City Council
1968 Unity Bank
     CAUSE Takes Over BRA Site Office
     Tent City Demonstrations
     Highland Park Free School
     People's Elected Urban Renewal Committee
     Emergency Tenants Council
     South End Tenants Council
     Route 128 Employment Express
     UCCW Shuts Down Sites Across the City

* This is a chronology of the events and organizations discussed in this book. It is not a complete chronology of events and organizations in the Black community in Boston.

1970 New Urban League and UCCW Win Hiring Quotas
     Black Student Strikes
     BURP Controversy Creates TAB & City Housing Court
     Boston Plan Imposed on Local Construction
1972 Mass Black Caucus First Community Inaugural
     Action Caucus '72
1973 Judge Freeman Upholds Altschuler Plan
1974 Court Ordered Desegregation Plan
1975 Bill Owens Elected First Black State Senator
     Third World Jobs Clearing House
1976 Ted Landsmark Attacked at City Hall
     Boston Marshalls Attack Black Workers
1977 Galvin Plan Narrowly Defeated
     John O'Bryant Elected to School Committee
1978 Boston Jobs Coalition
1979 Mel King Wins 65% of the Black Vote in Mayoral Race
     John O'Bryant Re-elected to School Committee
     Boston Peoples Organization

LIST OF ABBREVIATIONS

AFL-CIO	American Federation of Labor-Congress Of Industrial Organizations
AGC	Associated General Contractors
APAC	Area Planning Council
BAG	Boston Action Group
BHA	Boston Housing Authority
BJC	Boston Jobs Coalition
BPO	Boston Peoples Organization
BRA	Boston Redevelopment Authority
BSF	Black Student Federation
BSU	Black Student Union
BUF	Black United Front
BURP	Boston Urban Renewal Program
CAB	Contractors Association of Boston
CATA	Columbus Ave. Tenants Association
CAUSE	Community Assembly for a United South End
CDFC	Community Development Finance Corp.
CEC	Community Education Council
CEDAC	Community Econ. Development Assist. Corp.
CIRCLE	Centralized Investments to Revitalize Community Living Effectively
CORE	Congress of Racial Equality
CBPS	Citizens For Boston Public Schools
DES	Division of Employment Security
DOL	Department of Labor, U.S.
DPW	Department of Public Works
ETC	Emergency Tenants Council
FHA	Federal Housing Authority
FUND	Fund for Urban Negro Development
HEW	Health, Education & Welfare, U.S. Dept. of
HUD	Housing and Urban Development, U.S. Dept of
IBA	Iniquilinos Boricuas en Accion
LRCC	Lower Roxbury Community Corp.
MAW	Mothers for Adequate Welfare
MCAD	Mass. Commission Against Discrimination
MDTA	Manpower Development Training Act

METCO	Metro. Council for Educational Opportunity
NAACP	National Assoc. for the Advancement of Colored People
NECDC	New England Community Development Corp.
OEO	Office of Economic Opportunity, U.S. Dept of
PEURC	People's Elected Urban Renewal Committee
RAP	Roxbury Action Program
ROAR	Restore Our Alienated Rights
SEPAC	South End Project Area Committee
SETC	South End Tenants Council
TAB	Tenants Association of Boston
TDC	Tenants Development Corporation
UCCW	United Community Construction Workers
UCS	United Community Services
USES	United South End Settlements
WDL	Workers Defense League

INTRODUCTION

Chain of Change is the story of the development of the Black community in Boston over the last three decades. To appreciate this development, it is helpful to understand the nature of the relationship between the Black community and the power structure in Boston, the stages of development the Black community has gone through, and how each stage was manifested in the different aspects of community development.

Accordingly, in this introduction I will develop a framework for analyzing the relationship between the Black community and the Boston power structure from three different perspectives: *the structure of power, the shape of power,* and *the balance of power.* After this, I will develop a theory about the three stages of development that have taken place within these power relationships: *the service stage, the organizing stage,* and *the institution building stage.* In each stage, I will show how these power relationships have changed in four critical areas of the Black community: *education, housing, politics,* and *economic development.*

The structure of power in our community has been imposed by outside agencies which control the resources and define the scope of services available. The image of power is determined by the psychological factors which are largely internal to our community, although the external power structure controls the media and other important institutions that influence our self-image. The balance of power refers to the distribution of power which determines how decisions are made inside and outside our community.

The Structure of Power

During the past century Boston's ethnic neighborhoods, particularly those inhabited by Black people, have been "served" by an incredible number of programs administered in the missionary spirit, by non-community residents serving city, state, federal and private agencies. In retrospect, we can see that the design and implementation of these programs impaired their effectiveness as vehicles for community development. In each instance there were community boards, not only for each program, but for each neighborhood location of a program as well. The South End of Boston serves as a good example. In this one neighborhood there were programs, each with its own board, related to urban renewal, anti-poverty services, community health, schools and social services. Each board was elected at a different time.

Difficulties arose when decision-making boards like that of the Boston University Health Program cut across both the South End and Roxbury. A pattern of multiple, overlapping and confusing boundaries and responsibilities of service programs dominated in Roxbury, Jamaica Plain, North Dorchester and other central city neighborhoods in Boston.

Worse yet, in terms of political confusion, communities with a strong sense of identity were divided up for the convenience of various political power groups. Sections of the South End, for example, were put into five different wards; thus, there was no chance for the South End as a whole to be an electoral entity even though its historical identity makes it a community. Gerrymandering permeated the politicians' game plan and is a good example of how well the power structures' "divide and conquer" tactics have worked. One of the most important structural factors in Boston politics was the decision made in 1951 to restructure the city council from a 22 ward district seat body to a 9 member body elected at-large. That change, made in the name of "good government" reform, occurred when the Black population numbered significantly enough to influence the vote in several wards, and guaranteed that the Black community would not be able to elect its own representatives. The access to city government which has been protected in other cities, i.e., New York and Chicago, through boroughs or ward systems was squarely blocked in Boston at that time.

The programs and political boundaries established by those in power outside the community have consistently been constructed to make it virtually impossible for community residents to take responsibility for the operation of their own neighborhoods. We are then criticized for our "failure" to make things work. This is the phenomenon that William Ryan has dubbed "blaming the victim."[1] A good example is found in the medical services where the professionals from outside the community are actually responsible for the delivery of services, but the community boards are held responsible by the funding source or by the community.

Most of the private agencies in our community were founded by outside church groups and philanthropic institutions, or by individuals who have kept their hands on the steering wheel (and the purse strings) of services to the poor, maintaining a majority of board members from outside the immediate services area. An examination of the membership lists of these boards, from the 1950's to the present, reveals many of the old Boston family names. These boards have influenced the structure of power in the Black community many times.

United Community Services, a social service agency, for instance, used its sway as a funder to insist that community agencies federate into the United South End Settlements, the Roxbury Federation, Dorchester Settlements, and others. This arrangement not only lessened each agency's autonomy but also gave United Community Services much greater influence over the agencies, their programs and how their money was spent. As we shall see, this stranglehold was firm until the late sixties and even then a group like the New Urban League, which finally challenged the way United Community Services made its funding decisions, found very little support among other community groups who feared losing their funding from this outside source.

The structural problem for our community was that the design and external control of so many community agencies actually inhibited community development and the possibility of community control. The constraints built into the structure of these community service agencies obscured the potential of these institutions to contribute to the healthy development of the inner city. If we ask why it was so hard to deal with these structural constraints, we run right into the other two major barriers to community development: the self-image of our community and the power elite of Boston.

The Image of Power

The failure to deal with the chaotic approach to servicing the community of color can be traced primarily to attitudes about the "ghetto" as our homes have been persistently labeled. The problem is both internal and external. To those outside the city, mostly commuting residents, the stereotyped attributes of the ghetto (that is to say, Black people) are negative: crime, drugs, unemployment, poor service and facilities, welfare, and other characteristics considered disruptive to American society. There is a pervasive underlying belief along the "blaming the victim" model that people of color do not have the ability to develop a self-supporting community that can contribute to the larger economy and culture.

According to the press and other media, which are controlled by those outside the community, it is some inherent flaw in the Black community which keeps it in a rundown state. The media perpetuates a self-fulfilling prophecy of despair and hopelessness for people of color.

This persistent message that white society does not believe in the commitment or the capability of the community of color to improve its situation has seriously damaged the self-image of people of color. The constant refrain "There's no way" increases the anxiety and frustration of those who care. So internally, pressure builds and the confidence to proceed with community building and development processes by community residents are inhibited. The late Whitney Young, Jr., former president of the Urban League, once related a story of his travels through Nigeria which illustrates this negative self-image. Upon his return trip, he boarded the plane and walked into the cockpit. The pilot and crew were Black Africans. He was shocked and he had feelings of uneasiness; he questioned their ability to perform in that role. In doing so, for a moment, Young accepted society's notion that Black people could not work for themselves, thereby supporting the criteria of worth, as established by white society. This is genocide—death by exhaustion—which kindles the desperation of those of us whose survival is linked to that of the city.

The strengths of our community, the leadership, talent and energy which are evident there, are seldom mentioned. The racist practices which have created and maintained negative characteristics in our community, such as the high levels of unemployment, are ignored. When I was 17, I was part of the first challenge to the existing fair employment practice laws. Ed Cooper, who was then head of the Urban League, sent me to be interviewed at a number of places. I learned that there were only some jobs which were considered "acceptable" for businesses to offer a Black person. They actually believed that their customers would object so strongly to being served by a Black worker that their business would be damaged. Being relegated to jobs of busboy or floor sweeper helped to reinforce the self-image which then supported the white guidelines. We began to believe that we couldn't do anything better.

Just why was this image, this negative view, allowed to become so all pervasive? A careful evaluation lends credence to the idea that the negative image of our community is most strongly propounded by those who control the economic resources. They have no intention of letting go their hold of the one-way benefits that come through the colonial relationship, in which they have the upper hand. The same people who, today, are ripping off the resources of people of color in Africa and Asia, have also been busy exploiting the resources of the

Black community in Boston for all these years. The controls used to maintain this relationship, both at home and abroad, are psychological and physical. After a while these controls, i.e., a negative self-image, become internalized and those in power have to waste very little effort to stay in power.

Psychological control is exerted by creating, and then exploiting the negative image, and the habitual acceptance of externally imposed definitions. It was not until the 1960's that some of those negative attitudes we maintained about ourselves began to change. The battle continues. The perpetually pessimistic language describing people of color worked to reinforce this negative self-image, as does the condescension inherent in the servce role, "You can't do for yourself, so I'll be kind and help you." We soon discovered how difficult it is to shake this sort of pyschological domination. For instance, during the days Black people were negotiating for the management of the Unity Bank in the mid-sixties, the message of the financial backers and the Boston power structure was that only a white person was suitable for the management position. When we acceded to their pressure, we gave credence to their image of us as incapable. But when the Bank failed (under white management) it was then all our fault. For the white power structure, projecting our negative self-image was an easy way to have their cake and eat it too.

One major reason then that people of color have internalized negative attitudes about themselves is lack of control over the media. The message from radio, newspapers, magazines and the television in the fifties (and right to the present) has always reinforced the racist values of the society. During those years there were no Black people on commercials shown participating in the national economy, no Black families portrayed. The only shows about Black people were of the "Amos and Andy" type. Although some more shows have been developed in the past ten years, they by and large still continue the stereotyping that is at the heart of racism in this country; in addition the production staff and crews rarely include Blacks. The news remains almost exclusively controlled by whites. Although one station in Boston recently hired a Black commentator, and at long last there are Black producers in Boston, none of the stations have Black general managers or board of directors members. It is impossible for the Black community to avoid absorbing the image conveyed by both the exclusion and the stereotyping in the media.

Physical control is maintained by keeping resources scarce to inhibit the community development which could reverse the psychological pattern. These controls are manifested in the funding policies of many of the externally controlled community programs and agencies, and such institutions as banks which refuse to lend money for mortgages. The banks and the other financial institutions practice "red-lining," whereby they draw red lines around Black communities, refusing to lend money and making it impossible for people to maintain their homes or to sell them. Later after the property deteriorates banks finance the reconstruction of the same parcel for white folks who can afford higher rents and mortgages.

Absentee slumlords charge outrageous rents, while simultaneously permitting their properties to deteriorate. Then they blame the Black people living there for creating the slum. Keeping people of color locked into physical conditions that sap their energy and batter their spirit is yet another way that a negative self-image is instilled in our community.

There can be no doubt that the imposition of this negative self-image on the Black community is racist. Racism is the denial of Black humanity and it permeates every corner of society: the industries and unions, the banks and realtors, the school system, and the national, state and city governments, as well as the day to day relationships between white folks and people of color. The racist attitudes and behavior of liberal reformers continue to support these racist institutions, as well as the white people who make no pretense about their racial feelings. Racism is not a mistake. White folks benefit from racism, though humanity suffers, particularly white humanity. Through racism, white people are able to feel superior, to make profits, to stay in power, to take out their frustrations. But not all white people get all these benefits from racist behavior.

The Yankee Brahmins, the white, Anglo-Saxon Protestant males who have long dominated Boston, have cleverly found ways to use racism to keep other white groups in line. The white Irish Catholics were shamefully abused by Yankee industrialists. The exploitation of Irish workers was manifested in both psychological and physical forms and left deep scars. In the fifties the Irish were losing the grip on Boston politics which had come through James Michael Curley's reign. The state economy was changing in ways that made it inevitable that the Irish, once the most despised group in Boston, would now compete with Black people, the newer group available for exploitation. The job that was done on their own self-image keeps the Irish feeling that they are a persecuted minority even today when they still control much of the city budget, union positions, patronage and the schools. After World War II, the Black community posed a threat to that control. The Yankees have continued to encourage a racist norm in Boston as a way of keeping Black people under control and as a way of keeping the Irish politicians too busy fearing they will lose ground to the Black community to challenge the control of the economic system by the Brahmins.

White racism is the denial of the humanity of Black people whether practiced by Brahmins, Irish or any white ethnic group. Given the history of slavery in this country, it is only white people, and mainly white males, who have the power to oppress Black people *systematically*. Black people in this society do not have the power to be racist. Black people may react violently to white racism, but to call this "reverse racism" is to obscure and perpetuate the real bases of racism among whites.

The Balance of Power

Reversing the negative self-image of people of color and restructuring the boundary lines and service agencies to genuinely assist Black community development depends on the reorganization of human and economic resources. Without the power to command the use of resources, it is impossible to change the structure and the psychology of the inner city.

One major external force acting to retard the development of the Roxbury, Dorchester and Jamaica Plain communities is the "Master Plan" for the city. Few people realize that during the early fifties Boston's power structure developed a detailed blueprint envisioning their "renewed" city. Every urban renewal project, each transportation program, every housing development site, was designed to fit the dimensions of this plan. The original vision is filled with huge monuments to the technology that allows skyscrapers to be built and vast business empires to flourish. The Plan's emphasis is on size and institutions rather than on the people of the city and their needs. The plan leans toward the people from outside the city who utilize its institutions for work and business. Highway systems development was emphasized rather than improvement of public transportation. Building construction focused on large downtown business complexes or luxury housing, ignoring the business and housing needs of the urban neighborhoods of Boston. The original plan was revised in 1965; and in many instances, it is right on schedule in terms of consciousness and commitment.

One element of the early plan was the construction of the Mass. Turnpike through the famous and once beautiful Copley Square of Boston. The highway tunneled under the square mandating the demolition of some of the most distinctive architecture of old downtown Boston.

The Southwest Corridor, linking Interstate Route 95, Maine to Florida, through the southwest part of the city was another element comprising Boston's "Master Plan." Initially, the Inner Belt portion of this highway was designated to cut a huge swath out of the heart of the Black community. Although residents sucessfully organized a political strategy in the early 1960's, homes and businesses were leveled before the community realized the impact of the plan and took action.

A major purpose of the Master Plan was to revitalize the residents right out of Boston's inner city neighborhoods to make way for higher income white residents that the plan's proponents hoped to entice back into the city. The West End and the New York Streets section of the South End were demolished without a trace to accomodate the Master Plan. Other neighborhoods were severely altered before residents banded together to demand a role in the decision-making that affected their lives and homes. Even in the areas where active resistance to the Master Plan developed, as we shall see, the struggle to retain the original character of the area and to make urban renewal benefit the original residents is still an ongoing and fierce movement.

Just who is behind this Master Plan? At the inner circle is a group known as "The Vault," the power elite which consists of the chairman of First National Bank, the John Hancock Insurance Company, the other major banks, utility companies, corporations, and investment houses in Boston's business community. This low profile organization of Boston's business, financial and industrial elite has been hostile toward development efforts in the Black community from the very beginning. At the next level of power are the Chamber of Commerce which acts as the implementing arm of the inner circle in many cases, the universities and large churches which own huge amounts of "non-profit" tax-exempt land in Boston, and the Boston Redevelopment Authority (BRA) which has the job of handling the physical changes in the city for the Vault.

It has taken us a long time to realize that the business of racism, power control and ethnocentricity are so deeply entrenched in these elitists that it is impossible to enter into a partnership with them. It has taken even longer to recognize the scope of their power. They have long made up the controlling groups of the United Fund, United Community Services, many foundations, and the boards of the city's major institutions, particularly universities and hospitals. There are endless interconnections among these members of the Vault, the Chamber of Commerce, and all the various funding sources. For instance, Charles Adams of Raytheon was chairman of the United Fund; Ephraim Caitlin of the First National Bank was the next major office holder in the Fund; other famous Boston family names ranked high in the other major institutional and funding postions.

Black Bostonians have repeatedly made the mistake of expecting these people, by virtue of their Brahmin position, perhaps, to be a source of support. We approach them for help even when our experience indicates that they have opposed past projects that might increase the independence and power of the Black community. We have to remember that we are asking support from people whose own businesses operate and thrive on racist practices in South Africa as well as in Roxbury, the South End and Dorchester in Boston.

In the Service Stage, we were just beginning to understand that the balance of power in Boston is based on economic exploitation and racism. We did not clearly understand how the delivery of services, the physical conditions of our neighborhoods, the segregation in the public schools, and the pervasive negative image of people of color all are used to keep the balance of power far from our reach. We began to come to the realization that these factors are all connected, and above all that the balance of power will never be shifted willingly by those who are now in control.

Stages in Black Community Development

My theory about the stages of Black community development has evolved out of my experience with the process of change in Boston's Black community over the past thirty years. The theory is built around a chronological framework, although it is important to realize that the stages of development did not occur at exactly the same time in the different areas of development which will be described in this book: education, housing, politics, and economic development. No evolutionary process is completely smooth; at times events in the community appear to double back on themselves, overlap or reiterate one another. But the theory provides an outline for what appears to me to be the major direction and types of change for our community over the past several decades.

The three stages are the service stage, the organizing stage, and the institution building stage. In the course of these stages, there have been accompanying psychological changes, as the self-image of people of color evolved from negative to positive, from dependence to independence. A similar evolution has marked the power relationships shaping community change. During the period of negative self-image the community was essentially powerless. As the community has moved toward a more positive self-image, its power has increased and it has gained control over more of its own affairs and has begun to demand accountability in terms of both political and economic power relationships. At the same time, one of the most important products of this change process has been the skills which people have acquired. The Black community is acquiring the skills to be able to lead itself and others. Struggle has proven to be one of the most effective means of education; and the acquistion of skills has supported the positive changes in self-image and has contributed to the building of power in the community.

Chronologically, the stages have roughly corresponded to the decades of the fifties, sixties and seventies, with some significant overlap. The fifties and early sixties were the period of the service stage, of being dependent. During that time we fought to have access to the services available to others in the society, pressing to be allowed to vote, to eat and drink where we wanted, to be able to use public facilities, hotels, motels, parks and other resources which had been denied to people of color for generations. The efforts to get jobs, decent education and other basic American opportunities were all focused on the services offered by churches, social service agencies, settlement houses, charity groups and "concerned" business and commercial groups. We did not see clearly the dependence and debilitation which a service relationship creates. We did not understand that as long as we waited for others to help us, we would never be able to take charge of our own lives. We always assumed that our inability to get access was due to our own inadequacies; our schools weren't as good, so our skills were not up to standard, so our incomes didn't allow us to get decent housing, so our family life was inadequate. We did not understand for instance that in many cases it was not our children who were inadequate, but the deliberate segregative and discriminatory policies of the Boston School Committee which kept Black youngsters from achieving excellence.

During the middle sixties we began to organize. We began to see ourselves differently. In this organizing stage, we understood that not only are we *deserving* of services in our own right as members of this society, but we are also *capable* of serving ourselves on our own terms. We were essentially powerless during the service stage, but as we moved into the organizing stage we began to assume some power in the process of working together to make institutions more responsive. Our collective voice began to be heard more clearly than our timid individual pleas for entry, and the political implications of working together began to be obvious.

In the late sixties, with the failure of the federal government's pretenses at building a "Great Society" and the timely diversion of energy from civil rights struggles to the Viet Nam war, not to mention the systematic murder of the leaders of the Civil Rights Movement, the community of color began to build its own institutions. Demanding access to existing institutions naturally led us to think about what we were trying to get into. Did we really want our children to be taught like the average white child in Boston? Did we want to build housing in ways that would require us to exploit others as we had been exploited? We began to understand that the society as it stands will never meet our needs on our terms because our terms are contradictory to many of its basic premises. So we began to develop our own institutions. Some of them were Black versions of the societal norms; but many of them were genuine alternatives. Beyond just getting our share, we were working to change the quality and character of our share. During this period, the transformation of the Black self-image became more dramatic. Black Power was a slogan which electrified Black communities across the country, and we began to explore our heritage in earnest. We began to redefine Blackness, to see its inherent beauty and worth, to understand its strength. We permanently changed the American language; we changed the way we dressed; we changed our self-image and the way others viewed us. And we built models which other groups have used.

The institution building stage began in the late sixties and extended throughout the seventies, a period in which increasing numbers of community groups in the Black community formed to provide services or to carry out development plans for the Black community. However, with the serious economic pressures brought by the Nixon administration's policies in housing and education, and the oil and energy crisis, inflation and a general recession, many of these fledgling institutions perished for lack of resources, and others retreated to an isolated course of self-preservation which has prevented much interaction with other kindred efforts. At the same time, during the seventies, "institutionalization" of many our concerns was taking place in a variety of ways as existing structures had to accomodate some of our demands.

Most importantly, the late seventies were a time when we began to make links with other groups. Our consciousness and perspective broadened and led us to recognize the importance of forging links with groups engaged in struggles qualitatively similar to our own. We were determined to offer mutual support and protection during the battles ahead to preserve the gains we had made and to insist on further changes as we continued to struggle to transform our city. The result of these three stages is the Community Development Process: the empowerment of people of color. If we can get all the community agencies and institutions working together to provide services directly to the community on our own terms, if we can humanize the political process street by street on a day to day basis and build organizing into our work as an ongoing process, we will have the basis of Community Development that will meet basic human needs.

All of the stages discussed have been the steps toward the process of community development which will integrate our lives in all the possible human and political dimensions— individual, family, community, city-wide, state, national, global, universal. As we move further into the experience of building coalitions and more deeply into the process of community (self) development, we will become increasingly powerful and increasingly positive in our view of ourselves and in our ability to lead and work with others. Our experience in the last thirty (or three hundred) years has provided the basis for our visions about what sort of city and society we need to make it all happen. We are ready to use power to build for our future.

Outline of the Book

Part One describes the Service Stage as it unfolded in Boston in the 1940's and 1950's, including some factors which made our participation in a dependence realtionship at first inevitable and, eventually, inevitably intolerable. Part II discusses the unfolding of the Organizing Stage throughout the 1960's, in the areas of education, economic development, housing and political power. Part III portrays the Institution Building Stage in the 1970's in these different areas. Part IV contains a "Vision" which, I believe, is the natural outcome of our experience; and a "Strategy for Community Development," a strategy for building on our experience and seeing our dream come into fruition in the city of Boston in the decade of the 1980's.

At the end of the book there are a series of interviews with Black community leaders who are part of the *Chain of Change*. They share their personal visions and suggest where the resulting chain reaction will lead us.

CHAIN OF CHANGE

2   CHAIN OF CHANGE

PART I

THE SERVICE STAGE:
Blaming the Victim

This is how it was to be powerless and to curse oneself for cowardice, to be conditioned by dirt and fear and shame and signs.
 To become a part of these signs and feel them in the deepest recesses of the spirit...
 To be a plaything of judges and courts and policemen, to be Black in a white fire, and finally to believe in one's own unworthiness.
 To be without books and pretty pictures, without the rationalization of psychology and sociology. To give in finally, to bow, to scrape, to grin, and to hate oneself for one's servility and weakness and Blackness.

—Lerone Bennett, Jr.[1]

The History of the Black Community in Boston

Before discussing the service stage, it will be helpful to briefly review the history of the Black community prior to the 1950's. The first Black people came to Massachusetts as slaves in 1638.

After seizing the Shawmut Peninsula, the Boston merchants stole Black people from Africa to work in their homes and shops. Three hundred and fifty years later the descendants of these same merchants are still taking our land and exploiting our labor. But we fought back then and we are fighting back now.

In 1787, Prince Hall, a Black veteran of the Revolutionary War, petitioned the Massachusetts Legislature on behalf of Black citizens in Boston, "...our children... now receive no benefit from the free schools in the town of Boston, which we think is a great grievance..."[2] Receiving no response from the legislature, Prince Hall founded a school for Black children in his home in 1798. Black children remained in separate schools until right before the Civil War. Also, prior to the Civil War, there were no Black elected officials in Boston due, in part, to the Garrisonian Abolitionist opposition to Black people voting. Frederick Douglas broke with Garrison over the right of Black folks to vote, and to have positions of influence within the abolitionist movement.

After the War, the Black population doubled between 1860 and 1880 as a result of the migration of Black people from the South. At this time, the Black community in Boston lived on the north slope of Beacon Hill, on the opposite side from the Boston merchants. Given their increasing numbers and geographic concentration in one ward, the Black community was able to elect two Black representatives in 1866 to the Massachusetts House of Representatives. As Republicans, Black representatives continued to be elected until 1896 when the districts were gerrymandered to make it impossible for the Black community to elect representatives. Also, the housing on Beacon Hill at this time was beign converted from wood to brick structures, in the process of which the Black community was relocated into the South End of Boston and Lower Roxbury. As a result of the redistricting, and the migration across the city, the Black community was too dispersed to have any political clout in the city. There was not another Black State Representative until 1958.

Beginning in the 1900's and 1910's, there was another increase in the Black population due to the immigration of Black folks from the West Indies, particularly from Jamaica and Barbados. Interestingly, the West Indians came to Boston because they were able to get on the fruit boats of United Fruit (Standard Brands today) coming from Central America and the Caribbean (similarly, the Irish came to Boston because they were able to get on the British mail boats coming to North America). There were significant differences between the West Indians, who had lived under British colonialism and the older Black community in Boston. Many of the West Indians didn't come to Boston to stay, but planned to return to their homes as soon as they had enough money or could retire. Accordingly, they were not that interested in becoming citizens, or developing Black political power in Boston. They were more oriented towards the Black Nationalism of Marcus Garvey and the Universal Negro Improvement Association. The older Black community tended more towards integration and the thinking of William Monroe Trotter.

Throughout the 19th century, and until after World War II, Black workers were confined almost exclusively to either domestic labor, or low skilled manufacturing jobs. For instance, in 1930 of the 11,060 Black people employed in Massachusetts, there were 6,099 manufacturing workers, 5,782 domestics, 88 school teachers, 99 clergy, 49 doctors, 15 undertakers and 38 lawyers.[3]

There was also discrimination within the manufacturing industries. There were no Black workers in Lowell's textile mills, and only 31 employees out of 7,605 shoe workers in Lynn. Steve Thernstrom, in his book *The Other Bostonians* concludes of this period:

> There was virtually no improvement in the occupational position of Black men in Boston between the late nineteenth century and the beginning of World War II. In 1890, 56 percent of the Black males employed in the city were unskilled day laborers, servants, waiters, janitors, or porters; three decades later the fraction was 54 percent, and in 1940, it was 53 percent. As of 1890, a mere 8 percent of Boston's Blacks held white collar jobs; half a century later, the figure was only 11 percent.[4]

As we will see below, after World War II dramatic changes began to take place within the Black community, and in its relation to the white power structure.

The Service Stage

The Service Stage was a time during which the community of color was dependent on the "good will" of the white society for access to its goods, its services, its jobs, housing and schools. Black people were expected to trust that the system would work for them—eventually. The Brown decision of 1954 was, many thought, all that would be needed to assure that people of color would be able to share in America. Meanwhile, the Black community was relying on the charitable programs and serivces of settlement houses, white churches, the white-led Urban League, and the white-dominated National Association for the Advancement of Colored People (NAACP). The relationship between the community of color and these institutions was of a missionary nature: the assumption was that Black people were somehow deficient (heathen) and needed to be converted into acceptable Americans. To help in this case meant to change those being "helped" because there was something wrong with them. All the boards of such institutions had white members from the suburbs, including the Urban League, who played leading roles. As a result, there was always a white person out front to do the speaking, to influence the thinking, to keep control of the situation. White people had apprenticeship programs to get into new job areas, but Black people had pre-apprenticeship programs because it was assumed they didn't know how to act.

During the Service Stage we knocked politely at the door for the most part, and our own negative self-image and the reality of our lack of organization and consequent lack of power (whether collective economic strength or political clout) hindered any impulses to do more than wait for an eventual slow materialization of the "American Dream" for Black people.

Nationally, the memorable names from that era were A. Phillip Randolph, the leader of the Dining Car and Pullman Porters Union, Harry Truman (yes, he desegregated the armed forces), Ralph Bunche of the NAACP and, from a very different view, Paul Robeson. I'll never forget seeing Robeson in Boston in 1948—this striking man who sang, acted, traveled, was an outstanding, lawyer, musician, athlete, linguist and what's more brought a message of dignity and determination to see Black people win a different status, both psychologically and materially, in this society.

And there was Rosa Parks who, in 1957, sat down and declared by that simple act that she would no longer allow herself to be devalued, and that she *deserved* to get the same as any other person. Her statement, which leads us into the next stage, was part of the transition from negative to positive self-image, from the subservience of dependency to the demands of increasing independence.

In Boston, the Service Stage was a time when there was a transfer of power from the Irish domination of Mayor James Michael Curley, who made a career of "taking care of his own", to more malleable representatives of the Yankee power brokers who had sat irritably on the sidelines during Curley's reign. With the election of Mayor John Collins in 1956 came some of the major policy and programs which set the stage for the struggles of the next two decades—massive urban renewal (we always thought of it as "urban removal"), the surbanization of job sites, and the deliberate segregation of Boston's public schools.

In the Black community the Service Stage was marked by diverse efforts to improve our situation by working through the system. In particular we focused on education, trying to find ways to improve our children who never seemed to measure up by white standards. Eventually, as we shall see, our community came to understand that it was not our children who were lacking, but the system itself which made it impossible for Black children to obtain equal education in a racist setting. But in the years before that realization of *our* worth and deserving catapulted us into the organizing stage, we ran tutoring programs and tried through the assistance of settlement houses and other social service agencies to "improve" ourselves.

In the area of housing we saw the first evidence that our

city government would work hand-in-hand with developers to promote the removal of Black, Hispanic, Chinese and other peoples of color out of the potentially desirable sections of the city. Trustingly, we sought "services" to assist the displaced families in finding new housing.

In politics, the Service Stage was reflected in the patronage system: a relationship existing between a few Black people who worked with the white machine to deliver the Black vote in return for favors to their community. In economic development we relied on a few narrow channels into existing job markets.

By the late fifties and early sixties, the Black community, like Rosa Parks, had begun to realize that services which left us standing in the back of the bus were really no help at all. As we gained more information about just what was going on and more insight into the debilitating nature of the dependence on services, we became increasingly prepared to take action that declared our worth and our right to the quality services we deserved.

Chapter 1

GROWING UP
IN THE SOUTH END

I grew up in the South End of Boston. My folks had come from Barbados and Guyana after World War I with the West Indian immigration. There were four girls and seven boys. One girl and one boy died in infancy and the two who were first born were left with grandparents in Barbados.

My folks were very involved with all of us. My mother used to make fantastic pastries and salads from surplus foods. My father would cut our hair, fix our shoes, and other similar tasks. We used to talk about the abilities of the other young people my age. My father would explain that these folks had reached certain goals and that he expected me to compete with them.

My father, secretary for his local union, was involved in organizing workers on the docks. He worked on sugar boats. A lot of the union meetings were held in our house. I used to overhear them talk about the importance of organizing, some of the struggles, like fighting management, the poor work conditions and striking. I'd look at the minutes from these meetings with amazement. I knew my pop was smart and creative, but the fact that he was writing these things down struck me as wonderful.

My parents did a lot of things in terms of sharing. My mother was always looking out for others. When we grew up, she got involved in the Church and women's groups. She was a counselor to a lot of people. Some of my awareness also comes from being competitive in the ways my pop moved me.

I grew up on the one hand feeling positive about being a West Indian and Black; but on the other hand, I had to grapple with the negative imagery of being a Black child in the United States, not wanting to identify with people who were slaves and who behaved in a Steppin Fetchit, Rochester model. Everytime one of those movies was shown, we had to fight the next day in school because someone would come up and mock you.

As far as white teachers and white students were concerned, people who were Black were considered Negro or Colored, but white people were of American or Italian or Irish descent. We resisted that by insisting that we were West Indian. At the same time, folks of West Indian descent resisted identifying with people who were Black and from Africa, because of all the sterotypes and negative connotations. There were people around, for example, called Portugese, who rarely admitted to being from the Cape Verde Islands. It was a long time before they put together the fact that they were African, because their identity was Cape Verdean.

In the 1940's there were around 23,000 Black people in the city, mostly living in the South End and Lower Roxbury. In the South End there were thirty-six racial and ethnic cultural groups. They used to call the Abraham Lincoln School the "Little League of Nations," and, later, when my kids went there, they called it the "Little United Nations" because there were forty-three identifiable groups attending. The South End had always been one of the few neighborhoods in the city with multi-racial, multi-ethnic groups. The West End also reflected that, but most of the other communities had two, maybe three groups at the most, and usually just one. Roxbury, Mattapan, and Dorchester were Irish, Black and Jewish. During the thirties and the forties these ethnic groups co-existed in some places, but in other places they mutually excluded one another.

The focus of activity in the South End was around the churches. There were many different churches in the area. We attended the Church of All Nations. They had different services for different ethnic groups and one main service. In that way most of us grew up in pockets in the church. A lot of the Europeans went to a culture maintenance program after school. Most of the Black kids went to Settlement Houses. So while they were learning their cultural traditions, we were pushed into becoming Anglo-Saxon Americans. The church was central in shaping our identity as Negroes or Coloreds.

The coming together of Black folks happened around people who joined the Marcus Garvey Movement. In those days there was a column in the *Afro-American* newspaper (published in Baltimore) about Boston and two Black newspapers, the *Chronicle* and the *Guardian* which documented activities in the Boston-Cambridge community. But until I came back from college, I didn't have any sense of any mobilization of Black people around these activities. Of course there was the NAACP and the Young Progressives, but both groups involved Black and white people.

However, I was aware of the schools in the South. We used to follow them athletically. I knew about Shaw, Lincoln, Morehouse, and some other schools because of the people from there who were working on their graduate degrees at northern universities in the same way that Martin Luther King, Jr., did. When I was a senior in high school, a close friend suggested that I go to Claflin College, but my folks wouldn't let me go, partially because of Jim Crow and segregation. However, next spring, the football coach from Claflin came North to recruit Tom Queeley, Sylvester Mills and myself. He told my mom that he would take care of me, and finally she consented.

At Claflin College in South Carolina, I began to feel positive about being in the South, even with the segregated conditions. For the first time I was attending schools run by Black people and was made aware of Black people doing things for themselves. I began another process of identifying. I probably did it in a somewhat negative way, such as looking at people who were white, and making some statements about how they were colorless.

While in college I got exposed to the Young Progressives, attended NAACP activities, and had the opportunity to see Paul

Robeson in Boston one year in June. He talked about his vision of what this country could be; and he sang and was a football player and all. He also talked in some ways like my father, about what it meant to be Black and to be the best. He said you didn't take any stuff from people, but that you didn't bother people either. Robeson told us to always stand up for what we believed in. Perhaps more than anyone else except my own father, Robeson was an early influence that got me involved and ready for the work to come.

I liked going to school in the South but saw the problems in it. I liked the times after football games, especially, when we'd come back singing, and I could feel the spirituality and humanity in the group. I learned about the struggles people had, in particular some of the scenes of racist behavior in Charleston and Columbia, South Carolina. I got a real appreciation for that piece of the struggle seeing its conditions firsthand.

I learned quickly enough what the system in the South was, the rules of the culture and the expectations. I stopped going to the theater where Black people had to sit upstairs and started patronizing the Black theater instead. I rode in the back of the bus, once, and it felt so crummy that from then on I hitchiked. My father had told us that you didn't take anything from anybody. If anybody bigger than you hit you, then you had the right to pick up a stick and protect yourself; but you never hit anybody smaller than yourself.

Claflin was good because they recruited a lot of people to bring football back to life. I played football, baseball, and basketball. In my second year I was captain of the football team. The first two years we were all green; but by the time we were juniors and seniors, we had gained confidence. There were folks who had come from all over, but eighty percent of the people in the school came from the South. My involvement in athletic activities provided me the opportunity to travel to places like Columbia, South Carolina, Savannah, Georgia and Jacksonville, Tampa, and Daytona Beach, Florida. I made new acquaintances, especially with players from other teams.

We used to go out with a preacher who was a "circuit rider", which meant he went to different churches each Sunday. We became his little choir. Going with him we would see what the churches were like in rural areas, what kinds of things people were dealing with in relationship to the church, and what their needs were. We observed funerals and the kind of processions and rituals people were involved in.

Eventually, I acquired an appreciation for how much people lived off the land and what they produced. I can remember very distinctly having dinner with one family where everything on the table, with the exception of sugar, salt and pepper, spices and macaroni, came from the land. They ground their corn, had hogs, sweet potatoes—it was just phenomenal how people could make it off the land, what it took for survival and the rawness of life in those areas.

We also got a chance to sit in on camp meetings and religous ceremonies. I could see the differences in the congregations and the types of sermons delivered to them. In the rural areas the church was fundamental, sermons were the hell and damnation, fire and brimstone type. The churches the students went to were more "intellectual," with sermons with a different style message.

After college, I came back to Boston and married. In 1952, I earned a masters degree in education at Boston Teachers, which later became Boston State College. I had trouble getting a job teaching. I asked if this Masters in Education meant I could teach Black people only. Between that and incidents of discrimination in trying to get housing, I had pretty much made up my mind about how I was going to address the issue of discrimination and racism.

As far as I was concerned, people in Boston had real delusions. Early in the discussions on the issues of desegregating the schools, people believed that because it was Boston and not Mississippi certain things could not happen here. Most people were ignoring the fantastic and fanatical racism excluding people of color from total participation in the public schools. There was a sense of arrogance around the fact that this was Boston, but at the same time, the denial of access was much greater here. The failure to recognize this prevented people here from effectively dealing with the hostility and racism that surfaced in the 1960's.

My strategy was to work with the youth in the community; and ultimately focus on institutions and institutional change. I knew there was nothing wrong with me.

Chapter 2

CREATING THE GHETTO

What is the culturally deprived child *doing* in school? What is wrong with the victim? In pursuing this logic, no one remembers to ask questions about the collapsing building and torn textbooks, the frightened, insensitive teachers, the six additional desks in the room, the blustering, frightened principals, the relentless segregation, the callous administrator, the irrelevant curriculum, the bigoted or cowardly members of the school board, the fairy tale leaders or the self-serving faculty of the local teacher's college. We are encouraged to confine our attention to the child to dwell on all his alleged defects. Cultural deprivation becomes an omnibus explanation for the educational disaster area known as the inner-city school. This is blaming the victim.

—*Bill Ryan*, Blaming the Victim[1]

The Schools

After getting my degree from Boston Teacher's College, I taught at Boston Trade High School for a year; later, I taught at Boston Technical High School. However, I left that position to become Director of Boy's Work at Lincoln House, a settlement house in Boston's South End, because I knew my brothers and sisters were on the streets and the schools offered no outreach programs to attract them. I also remembered the fantastic influence an older man had on me and my friends when we were on the corners. Also, in my own experience it was effective to work with kids in their own territory. I also took the job because there were no other Black people working in any of the nearby agencies, and I had the feeling that the Black kids would have a hard time believing that they could be and do what they wanted, unless they saw some of their own people working in such positions.

Not long after, I became involved in a new field, called detached work, or working with gangs on street corners. In the middle fifties the "bopping gangs" were the big thing, at least in the press, with their jackets and other symbols that identified them and their turf. Our objective, basically, was to change the way those young people spent their leisure hours, which meant we reduced conflict between themselves and the rest of the community. It was through this work that I began to put together some of the pieces of how to work in a community.

Working with Gladys Guson and Ed McClure, we decided to try and get the kids involved in football, basketball, and baseball, but we learned one important thing very quickly: if we really wanted to do something with the kids from thirteen to seventeen, we had to do something with the young adults from nineteen to twenty-five. So we began with a football team which developed into a pretty good organization. By 1954, we had a half-dozen teams in the neighborhood. A real community spirit began to develop and before we knew it, we had the Ravens, the Raven Juniors, and the Ravenettes. Eventually we began organizing club groups which got kids involved in a problem-solving process: they learned to deal with getting organized, raising money, developing football teams, or whatever else they wanted.

Some very perceptible change began to take place. A priest walked by some kids on the corner and reported to me later with amazement, "You know, I could hardly ever walk by those guys before, with all their bad language, and today they were talking something about doing a, 'Single Wing T Formation' ." On one level our solution to the problems was quite simple. A group of kids in a housing project had the neighbors really upset with all their antics: jamming elevators, urinating in the halls and elevators, and raising hell until late at night. We started working with them every afternoon after school with football, afterwards they were so tired that they went home and went to bed. Some of the resources which we could offer participants were a gym, space to hold meetings, and coaching. We helped to solve the most immediate problems that they were causing in the community, but we began to realize that it all went much deeper.

In 1958, the staff at United South End Settlement conducted a community survey that revealed that 85% of the kids in those gangs, both Black and white, were dropouts. They needed advocates, people to open some doors; but when we tried to get them jobs we ran into some frustrating discrepancies.

The kids had a rigid, if vague, idea of the sort of jobs they wanted, which were along the pressed-shirt-and-tie, pencil-pushing, $2.00 an hour line. Their aspirations did not match most employers' image of high school dropouts with "no skills." All we could find for them were jobs they had already found undesirable: dishwashers, pushing racks in the garment district, shippers, etc. Not only did we have a lot of kids who had not graduated from high school, but also maybe 50% of the kids had not even received an eighth grade certificate. Their options were extremely limited, to say the least, so we began trying to answer the questions: how do we get them to stay in school? How do we get them the skills they need? We fell headlong into the trap that most people do and saw the problem as primarily with the kids. This was compounded by the feeling of many of their parents that their own failure was keeping their kids from making it. We were basically assuming that the kids needed to know how to make it in the system as it was, and therefore we had to change the kids.

So we began a series of tutoring programs and other kinds of educational enrichment, and at the same time we began trying to encourage some kids to go on to college. We developed a motivation fund which managed at first to get two or three, then six, then fourteen, and then forty to fifty kids going beyond high school. The emulation theory we had been operating on was clearly at work here. Once kids began to see their friends or older brothers and sisters going on successfully, they decided they could do it, too.

Initially, I thought we had to concentrate on getting the kids to learn to read write and compute better. (I must have been very naive because I had learned to do all those things and couldn't get jobs myelf). But as we began trying to work with school programs and the counselors, we consistently came up against some very fundamental and difficult things, especially the attitudes and expectations of the teachers and staff about the kids in the areas. "These kids are no good!" These barriers, combined with the impact of exclusion on a broader societal scale, e.g., few Black people on TV, drastically reduced the kids' motivation, and hampered the development of their self-esteem. In the area of employment, we had to deal with the severely limited access to jobs as well as the kinds of qualifications required.

My co-workers and myself finally began to realize that the root of the problem wasn't the kids; it was the fact that there was no access or very limited access to resources. The youngsters we worked with were just as bright as any others; their problems had much more to do with the school than any deficiencies they may have had. The guidance system, the curriculum, and the teachers' attitudes, were all ways to deter them from achieving what they wanted, deserved, and were capable of achieving. It became very apparent that we needed to get into the positions of power where decisions were made.

On the one hand, we were up against an archaic school system filled with people who were not accountable to the city as a whole and to the Black community specifically; and on the other hand, we faced the spectre of social and institutional racism. Some Blacks, myself included, were naive enough to think that because we were in Boston, the "cradle of liberty," the folks in charge could be counted upon to change and deal with the problems once they were pointed out. We soon learned. We also began to understand that simple service can't accomplish major overhaul of a faltering system.

Housing: Urban Removal

Segregated housing is the other side of segregated education. The mechanism for institutionalizing the struggle for space has been urban renewal—faithfully carried out by the Boston Redevelopment Authority (BRA). Urban renewal appeared in Boston during the late forties and early fifties. Elaborate plans were designed to renew the downtown area of Boston. The real intent of urban renewal could be seen in the experiences of inner city neighborhoods.Residents of the West End, the South End, and Roxbury endeavored to make their neighborhoods viable communities while the city planners sought to remove them.

Urban renewal in Boston began in the South End. The history of the South End of Boston is representative of the plight of many inner city ethnic neighborhoods. Its first rapid development came in the 1820's when it became a fashionable area for the new commercial class; by the 1840's, however, a building boom crowded in around the large family homes and brick row houses were built, for which the South End is still known.

After the crash of 1873 much of the South End's real estate was foreclosed and then bought up by speculators who became absentee landlords. The South End became the "port of entry" for the many successive waves of immigrants, first Europeans, then rural Black folks. A large number of old people, mostly male, who had come to the city hoping to "make it" but failed to find work, settled into the increasing number of rooming houses that supplied cheap housing. One of the South End's neighborhoods was the New York Streets, an area which came to be know as the model of urban renewal initiative among the nation's major cities:

> New York Streets was Boston's first redevelopment project. Planning for it was initiated in 1952. The New York Streets was the city's first effort to assemble enough land for private industry to build efficient, modern structures. It represents the thinking which characterized the inception of renewal throughout the country. Its genesis was in the problem facing industries seeking new locations in the city, namely, finding in one downtown spot parcels large enough to build a modern factory. Industry could not afford to buy numerous parcels, clear them all and still construct a

factory on which investment capital could derive a profit. This undertaking is proof that renewal can serve as a vehicle for private industrial and commercial development. This is the classic partnership of city officials and private interests aimed at improving the economic base of the city.[2]

The New York streets, so called because all the streets in the area had the names of New York State cities that were named after Native American tribes, were in an ideal location for the light industry and commercial uses visualized by the planners to be so essential to revitalization of the city. It was between two major downtown thoroughfares, close to the railroad tracks, adjacent to the projected Southeast Expressway, and near the Fort Point Channel.

This area, which already had a couple of lumber yards and other light industries, was acquired when city officials in conjunction with the local press began an attitudinal "briefing" campaign. When I was away at college, my family sent me a series of articles from the *Traveler* which called the areas Boston's "skid row." I was surprised because I had always called it home. But there it was, right in print.

Let me tell you what I remember about the New York streets from my childhood. Up and down Harrison Avenue there were shops and stores of all descriptions and families who lived over them in apartments upstairs. On the corner of Seneca and Harrison there was an Armenian store with olives in barrels out front, and a fish market next door. The next block down on the corner of Oneida was Leo Giuffre's bakery, I think. There was a synagogue on Oswego. Bikofsky's bakery was on the corner of Lovering and Harrison, and Saroka's Drug Store a block down on Davis Street. The only liquor store in the neighborhood was on the corner of Gloucester, Golden Liquors. On Dover Street the popcorn man would set up business. Across the street were Green-Freedman Bakery Co. and Derzowitz's Deli.

The Andrew School, where we all went through the fourth grade, was in the block between Rochester, Genesee, Albany, and Harrison. We used to play ball in the area between Albany Street and the Fort Point Channel, which was also a great place to watch the drawbridges and the tug boats. We would swim at the Broadway Street or Dover Street bridges. The lumber yards, also between Albany and Fort Point Channel, provided some of the best fires a kid could ever hope to see.

On Seneca Street, where I lived with my parents, there were also Irish, Portugese, Albanians, Greeks, Lithuanians, Armenians, Jews, Filipinos, Chinese, and a few (very few) Yankees. Across the tracks were Syrians and Lebanese and a larger number of Chinese. Although our buildings were pretty well sorted out by color and ethnic backround, the street belonged to all of us. There was a street baseball team and when the Armenian twin sisters down the block had a double wedding, they washed down the whole street for dancing and celebration.

Some years later my family moved across the way to Florence Street, where they lived until I finished college. In 1953, they were informed by city officials that the "slum" was going to be "renewed" and they must relocate. They were given minimal assistance and faced higher rents.

The *Herald-Traveler* series which described the Dover Street area as "Skid Row" was an important factor in the "renewal" of the New York streets. Labelling those streets as slums depersonalized the issue, and blocked out any understanding of the impact urban renewal would have on the lives of the people, like my family and friends, living there, and provided a rationale for replacing "undesirable" elements of Boston with less troublesome "light industry." The fact that the *people* living in the area had significantly fewer options than other groups by virtue of their color, national background, and economic status was blotted out. Those articles helped reinforce the attitudes that allowed the city to come in and raze my family's house.

The New York streets were cleared and stood empty for several years until the city could find developers. Ironically, the New York Streets were relaced by Herald and Traveler Streets and the *Herald-Traveler* became one of the area's primary tenants.

Some years later when I was running for School Committee, I met with the editor of the *Herald-Traveler* and mentioned that we were neighbors. He asked if that meant I had a house in Danvers, Massachusetts where he lived. I explained that his office was on the site of my old home on Seneca Street.

In the middle fifties I was working at Lincoln House coaching kids in the South End. I could trace the movement of families from one neighborhood to another by the route I had to go to pick up the kids I worked with. As one area was demolished, families were forced to move on. From the New York streets families generally moved to Castle Square; from there, when it was renewed, most white families went to South Boston, Dorchester and Jamaica Plain. Black and Portugese families moved to Washington Park, Lower Roxbury, and North Dorchester. Some families have had to move four and more times in the face of renewal pressure.

The New York streets were followed by the West End, a Jewish and Italian immigrant neighborhood which was renewed into a set of high-rise, high-cost apartment buildings before anyone understood what was happening. Of this accomplishment the BRA reported,

> Charles River Park (the garden apartments that replaced the West End neighborhood) represents an effort by city and private developers to make it possible for those people who have means and desire to do so to live close to downtown. The apartments are convenient to the new Government Center, to the Financial District, to retail outlets, to historical points of interest, to restaurants...[3]

Herbert Gans, in his book, *Urban Villagers,* cites another series of articles in the *Herald-Traveler* which called the West End a "cesspool" and ended with the rousing thought that if readers were to, "...come back in ten years....you won't know the city."[4]

By 1960, two years after the West End was demolished, official Boston had established the Boston Redevelopment Authority along the lines of the "integrated planning and execution agency" recommended by the Boston Chamber of Commerce in 1956 to undertake the "broader and larger range approach" to renewal.[5] As a whole, the urban renewal program executed by the BRA has never been, and was never intended to be, a neighborhood program. It had its origins in the large scale planning envisioned for the city of Boston by its businessmen with a focus on downtown revitalization. The program has been consistently obsessed with size: the towering Prudential Center

Building, the mammoth Government Center, the grandiose Christian Science Center; and has apparently found it difficult to turn its attention to neighborhood needs.

The Black Machine

About the same time I became Director of Boy's Work at Lincoln House in 1953, I also started to get involved in electoral politics. At that time, the first real political organization we had in the community was taking shape. Shag and Balcolm Taylor ran the Lincoln Pharmacy on Tremont Street which served the South End and Lower Roxbury, and which was the center of political activity.

The Taylors initiated old fashioned ward politics in the Black community. They were, surprisingly, Democrats. Influenced by Roosevelts's liberal policies during the Depression, the Taylor's broke with the tradition of supporting the Republican Party, a tradition which the Black community had upheld since the Civil War and Reconstruction era.

The Taylors would set up meetings for Curley, the Irish machine mayor, in the Black community, run ads in the paper for him, and use the favors that folks owed them to pressure people into supporting white candidates in the Democratic party. One of the things Shag and Bal got in return was to be elected to the National Democratic Convention. Another concession that the Taylors received was that police seemed not to notice that the Pioneer Club, a private club run by the Taylors, ran after hours as a bar. Through their contacts at the Pharmacy and the Pioneer Club, the Taylors became the hub of political activity.

In the early days, the Taylors were able to use their influence to get Black candidates appointed to local judgeships. As time passed their power increased along with the increase in the Black population. Between 1940 and 1960, the Black population increased by 40,000. As a result, enough folks lived in Ward Nine, the area the Taylors were located in, to make it possible to consider running a Black candidate for the House of Representatives. The Taylors used their party connections and their influence in the community to get Lincoln Pope elected in 1958 to the House. Linc was the first of their successful proteges.

The Taylors were able to provide some jobs and services from the City and the State, in return for which they delivered the Black vote. However, their power and influence was more illusory than real. The limited patronage they were able to dole out was based on their good behavior and the approval of outside forces. They were able to provide as long as they played the game. The service stage was represented in the political development of the Black community by the approach of looking for individual solutions, rather than questioning the system; by taking the white power structure's handouts rather than organizing the community to demand satisfaction of Black needs.

Creating the Ghetto

In order to understand the nature of the Service Stage, particularly why people of color were caught in the position of dependence, and why it eventually became impossible to keep us in that position, we need to look more closely at the factors at work within and outside the community of color during this period.

Economically, the 1950's brought the rebirth of the Massachusetts economy. After fifty years of decline and stagnation, due to the flight of the textile industry to the South, and the flight of Boston capital to other regions, and to Central and South America, the economy began to turn around with the advent of high technology industries along Route 128. Route 128 is the beltway that encircles Boston. It provided the location after World War II for firms specializing in the commercial adaptation of the spinoffs of MIT and Harvard war research. These new technologies offered the promise of high enough returns to lure Boston capital to invest in the state once again.

However, textiles and other manufacturing industries such as the shoe industry continued to move South and eventually to other countries, to exploit the inexpensive labor of poor people, and people of color. I had personal evidence of this trend the summer of my junior year in college when I came back home to work at Pritzer's, a clothes factory. When I went to tell them where to forward my last paycheck, the foreman said, "Oh,

Orangeburg, South Carolina, we're setting up a new shop there this year." But while these manufacturing jobs declined in number, professional jobs within the state tripled between 1940 and 1970. Based on the increasing demand for electrical components, space and war research, and more recently for computers and communication equipment, Massachusetts was able to build a competitive edge nationally, and even internationally.

The growth of Route 128 in the 1950's was accompanied by the growth of the suburbs, and the further decline of the inner city. Between 1947 and 1959, employment along Route 128 increased by 27,600 jobs, while in Boston the total number of Jobs decreased by 17,500.[6] The white suburbs, built in part with F.H.A. homeowner loans, provided the labor supply for these outlying suburban industries as the inner city labor force remained trapped in the few industries left.

During this period, the Black population increased fourfold to 104,596, to 16% of the city population. Black skilled laborers, however, only increased from 5% of the labor force in 1940 to 11% in 1970. In other words, given that the number of skilled jobs tripled during this period, Black workers held relatively fewer skilled jobs in 1970 than they did in 1940 while the size of the Black population quadrupled.[7]

The pressure from the increasing supply of Black workers and the decreasing job opportunities, was compounded by the growing Puerto Rican population and the rising number of undocumented workers settling in Boston. These factors assured an excess supply of workers of color who were competing for minimal wages in unskilled jobs.

As a result of these changes in the local economy, stratification developed within the Black community. The majority of Black incomes stayed at the poverty level or below while a small Black middle class formed among those folks employed in the few professional jobs open to Black workers. Black professional earnings rose to be 63% higher than the earnings of Black unskilled workers.[8]

During the forties and fifties, the Black community faced increased segregation on all sides. Excluded from the suburban jobs and housing, Black workers were relegated to unskilled, and for the most part, service sector jobs within the city. This job segregation was reinforced by educational segregation as witnessed by the fact that the average Black educational level in 1940 was 93% of the city level and that figure increased only 1% thirty years later.[9] By the late 1950's, the Master Plan for Boston had begun its job of forcing Black people out of the South End into Roxbury and Dorchester in order to accomodate the commercial and residential needs of Boston's banks, insurance companies and, of course, MIT and Harvard. This housing segregation went hand in hand with the gerrymandering of the Black population in such a way as to assure that they had no political voice. This systematic denial of jobs, housing education and political representation by the Boston power structure came to full development in the creation of the "ghetto," for the image of the ghetto allowed the ruling elite to blame the Black community for what they had systematically imposed upon us. By blaming the victim, they could assume full missionary zeal in their efforts to provide services to the Black community which served to further perpetuate their control and domination.

But within the "ghetto" the humanity of Black people was not to be denied. We were beginning to understand that we were not the cause of our problems, and we were beginning to organize to confront the power structure that sought to dominate us.

PART II

THE ORGANIZING STAGE: Black Power

The Organizing Stage encompasses most of the decade of the 1960's. The moment Black people began to awaken to their own potential and to state, "We are deserving," the process of organizing ourselves began. No longer were we content to wait. We demanded our rights. The Black community in Boston was of course dramatically influenced by the Civil Rights movement which spread from the South to our own neighborhoods in northern cities. The March on Washington in 1963 was echoed by "The March on Roxbury," organized that same year to dramatize the same issues. I'll never forget hearing the small son of a friend say, after hearing people involved in the civil rights struggle in North Carolina speak in Boston, "Daddy, I'm no longer ashamed to be a Negro."

From a negative self-image we moved to the concept of "Black is Beautiful." Our African heritage was reasserted by the artists and leaders with vision such as Leroi Jones (later Imamu Imiri Baraka). Nina Simone sang, "I Wish I Knew How It Feels To Be Free;" Aretha Franklin sang, "Young, Gifted and Black." We changed our dress, hair styles, and the English language. We also began conscious changes in our values toward sharing, community, and the redistributing of resources. The celebration of Kwanza, the African ceremony of community and kinship, become a tradition in Boston's Black community.

The War on Poverty and the Voting Rights Act, passed and instituted in 1964 after John Kennedy's death, were not enough to prevent the explosion of Black anger and frustration in Watts; Black communities across the country watched as Watts burned. We also watched the bitter struggle of Black parents to gain control of the public schools in the Oceanhill-Brownsville section of New York City. We listened to Malcolm X and Elijah Muhammed who exhorted us to wake up the sleeping giants of our heritage, our pride, and our power. The Black Panthers brought a new level of consciousness and a new tone to political community work. And in 1967 Stokely Carmichael electrified the country with the phrase that summarized and asserted the fundamental change in our self-image: Black Power.

The Organizing Stage was also mightily affected by the decision to escalate the War in Viet Nam coinciding with the peak of Civil Rights activism. This decision also conveniently distracted national attention away from the issues Black people were raising. It is no accident that both Malcolm X and Martin Luther King, Jr., were killed at the points in their careers when they began challenging U.S. imperialism and began to gain an international consciousness about their work. They had also both been very successful—too successful—at getting people of color to "Be somebody."

In Boston we focused on the issues of education in much of our organizing. I ran for School Committee three times (1961, 1963 and 1965) in an attempt to gain some direct decision-making power over the education of Black children. There were various attempts by parents to do for their children, and themselves, what the city government and the society were clearly unwilling to do. Community initiated busing and boycotts of the schools are examples of these efforts.

There was also considerable organizing activity on economic fronts through selective buying campaigns and even a work stoppage. In the area of housing we began to take direct action to change the relationships of tenants and landlords and to take greater power over the housing development and management. In 1967 I moved to the Urban League of Boston and we began a period of intensive organizing on all these issues taking charge of our own community development through community control. And in 1967 and again in 1969 we marshalled our resources to elect Tom Atkins to the Boston City Council.

The Organizing Stage culminated earlier in the areas of education and housing, but efforts to organize politically and on economic development issues extended into the late 1960's and even early 1970's. It was during this decade of organizing that the community of color gained a tremendous range of skills which we would apply to the next stage, as we went beyond organizing, to develop our own institutions.

Chapter 3

THE SCHOOLS:
Stay Out for Freedom
and the Racial Imbalance Law

In 1962 the thrust for Boston's Black community development was formulated around the issue of segregation in the public schools. In subsequent chapters, we will see how the Black community organized to defend its rights in other areas as well—economic development, housing, and politics.

Just about the time we began realigning our sights and perceiving that the school system was the culprit rather than our own children, several things happened at once. A group called Citizens for Boston Public Schools (CBPS), founded around 1960, began to consider running a slate of candidates for School Committee. This coincided with the interest of those of us in the community who were looking for ways to get people in the community (particularly parents) directly involved in school issues.

The Citizens were deeply concerned about the way the Boston School System was operating, particularly the serious administrative and management problems including not only graft, but also the lack of education for the children the schools were supposed to be serving. The Citizens organized to attend School Committee meetings, researched educational issues, and asked the School Committee some searching questions. They soon realized that their approach was too low key and the only way to get results was to get a majority of votes on the School Committee itself.

The need for us to be involved at the decision-making level prompted me to find out more about the Citizens' activities. When I learned that they were ready to run some candidates for School Committee and that they were planning a meeting in the South End, I spoke to Rev. Royden Richardson, a minister at the Tremont Methodist Church, and a member of the group. I told him I had some thoughts about what needed to happen in the schools and would be very interested to talk to people about my ideas. Herb Gleason, the President of CBPS and Paul Parks came from the group to have a talk; we realized we had seen each other around. I had been involved in a lot of campaigns, particularly since I worked with young adults and sports teams. We talked about the issues as I saw them at that time: drop-outs, the curriculum, Black representation, Black teacher an l administrator role models, and vocational education. On the basis of that discussion I went before the Citizens to be interviewed. Interestingly enough, one of the other candidates they interviewed was Louise Day Hicks, whom they decided not to endorse. At that point she had not yet made her famous "You know where I stand" pitch on busing.

The Citizens did endorse a slate of four: Arthur Gartland, William O'Connor, Nathaniel Young, and myself. It is safe to say that our candidacy did not excite any great interest in the South End and Roxbury; in fact, the largest number of votes I received in any area was West Roxbury which is not a predominantly Black area. We didn't know the realities of running a political campaign at that time, but we did use the race to educate people regarding the problems in Boston's schools.

One of our primary goals was to motivate the residents to realize that the failures of the Boston School system were affecting children all across the city, not just in isolated neighborhoods. All of Boston's children, except for an elite few, were being cheated. We contended that a connection existed between the failure to deal with the cause of drop-outs and the problems of welfare and crime. We also began to talk about de facto segregation as one of the major issues the school system was going to have to confront. It is interesting that at that time I was labeled by some teachers and others as a supporter of busing, an accusation prophetic of the misunderstanding and emotionalism the busing issue would generate, and continues to generate until this moment.

1963: Stay Out for Freedom

An extraordinary level of activity in Boston was generated by the work of the Education Committee of the Boston branch of the NAACP. On June 4, 1963, the Education Committee called for a public hearing before the Boston School Committee to discuss the priority issue—de facto segregation. On June 11, the Education Committee presented its case to protect the well-being of the children in Boston's schools. Forty other religious, civil rights, labor and community groups supported the presentation, some contributed testimony before the School Committee. At that point we were operating as a coalition. The School Committee was unimpressed however, and our requests were met with stolid inaction.

The next day, June 12, Cannon James Breeden, Chairman of the Citizens for Human Rights, announced a Stay Out for Freedom to protest de facto segregation. The NAACP negotiators insisted that none of the school system's important problems could be solved without public and official recognition of the de facto segregation condition; but the School Committee argued that they could not recognize "segregation" because it did not exist.

Boston's newspapers published some alarming facts while the negotiations ensued:

Forty per cent of Boston's public school pupils attend classes in buildings 50 years old or older; 5 of the 192 schools in use in Boston were built before 1885; only 5% of the pupils attend schools less than 10 years old; all predominantly Black schools except two are over 50 years old; of 8 schools with classes in basements unfit for children's uses 7 are in predominantly Black schools; Boston spends approximately $240 per pupil in predominantly Black schools, and $275 per pupil on a city-wide basis; of Boston's 2,800 teachers only 10 are

Black, and the Black administrators number exactly 4,
all in assistant positions ...Four of the predominantly
Negro schools were recommended for abandonment in
a 1962 study and...eight of them were recommended
for renovation. The Garrison School, intended for an
enrollment of 690, has 1050 students. The Ellis, with a
capacity of 640 children, has 823 enrolled, both schools
are predominantly Black.[1]

We tried changing the wording, but no matter what we said, the
School Committee simply would not, could not, admit that they
had contributed to anything so wrong. "There is no de facto
segregation in Boston," said Mrs. Hicks dogmatically at the very
first mention of this controversial term in the NAACP statement. "Kindly proceed to educational matters..."[2]

Perhaps the most important source of pressure on the
school committee was the community's highly visible support
for the NAACP negotiators. "While the hearing progressed in
the chambers at 15 Beacon Street," reported the Boston papers,
"more that 800 Negroes assembled outside the building and at
City Hall, where they sang the songs of protest that are being
sung in the Southern Civil Rights battles."[3] The work of
Melnea Cass, Ruth Batson, and Tom Atkins enabled the Black
community to pressure the School Committee in the streets as
well as the negotiation table.

Public opinion was fanned to a higher and higher pitch. The
emotions roused by the frustrating meetings with the powers in
charge, coupled with the impact of parents discovering their
children were bright and eager and capable, produced a powerful and volatile source of energy. Finally, we decided that a "Stay
Out" was the sort of short-term demonstration that could capture and channel all that energy to dramatize the concern and
determination of the Black community, and to present the hor-
rifying facts to a wider audience. The presence of officials, on
the other side, revealed the effectiveness of the tactic.

Governor Endicott Peabody, in a last minute effort to avoid
the Stay Out, stated that de facto segregation was a reality and
government agencies should take the responsibility to change

the condition. Governor Peabody "declined to be specific on his personal feelings regarding the situation," reported the Boston papers, but he "said he hoped the boycott would be avoided."[4]

The police commissioner was on special alert, and Superintendent Gillis was to meet with President Kennedy at the White House Wednesday where he said, he would "insist that Boston public schools are integrated."[5] Attorney General Edward Brooke was called on again by Mrs. Hicks to "inform Negro leaders of state laws concerning compulsory education and to take steps to insure attendance by Negro pupils tomorrow."[6] Brooke himself is reported to have "brushed off" charges by Mrs. Hicks that a number of white children, including girls, had been threatened with violence if they refused to join the boycott. "This talk of violence comes from alarmists," the papers reported him as saying. "This is not Birmingham or Jackson. This is Boston."[7] To complete the series of public reactions, the local Juvenile Court Judge warned parents via a newspaper legal ad that they could be jailed or fined if they allowed their children to join the protest. Louis Lyons reported on the day of the Stay Out that there were varying estimates of students out of school—5,000 according to one source, 3,000 according to the Christian Science Monitor and Associated Press and 2,000 from the Globe, using unofficial figures. "By either figure," Lyons said, "an extraordinary demonstration for one organized within a few days largely by newer, younger leadership."[8]

"Vote on Tuesday!"

It was painfully clear during the 1963 elections for School Committee that Bostonians generally were not aware that the entire school system operated on an elitist basis which worked against the vast majority of students. The operational biases were epitomized in the attitude of Jospeh Lee of the School Committee, who commented that, the people in Charlestown (a largely white working class area of Boston) were only interested in working the docks, so there was certainly no point to worrying about sending those students to college. Once again we concentrated on using the election for the education of the voters and to dramatize the issues facing all Bostonians concerned about the quality of education available to their children.

The Citizens for Boston Public Schools endorsed another slate of candidates (Willian O'Connor, Arthur Gartland, John Carney and myself), and we set out across the city. In their endorsement statement the Citizens tried to clarify some of the misunderstandings which had arisen in the course of the protests. They carefully pointed out that the NAACP had never made a demand for large scale busing, a notion which seemed to terrify voters and which the School Committee did nothing to dispel. The Citizens' pamphlet explained that instead of massive busing, the NAACP rather "demanded that district lines be re-drawn and new schools located so as to diminish racial imbalance. "

As a candidate, I tried to clarify the critical points: the time had come to lay aside our prejudices and to work toward overcoming the terrific loss of human resources that was built into the Boston school system. I talked about the need to help Black youngsters feel as though they were a positive part of the society, and to assure them that they were no less valuable as people than any other children. There was evidence that irreparable damage in terms of gaining a positive self-image had already been done to the Black child, in a white-controlled, all Black school by the time she or he has reached high school age. There were a number of specific suggestions to improve our schools:

1) Decentralize the school system to have programs geared to the needs of the varied communities, greater parent involvement;

2) Improve communications between the school and community;

3) Round-the-clock community schools for public use;

4) Improved selection and utilization of instructional educational media equipment and materials.

Two days before the primary election, a "March on Roxbury," organized by the NAACP, took place to express support for Civil Rights efforts in Birmingham and elsewhere, to dramatize the poor school conditions in Boston, and extend the challenge proferred by the March on Washington on August 28: "To build an integrated society." Ten thousand people, Black and white, marched to the site of the Sherwin School, an atrocious example of the dilapidated, outmoded facilities relegated to Black use. Orzel Billingsley, Birmingham attorney and member of the Baptist church in which four little girls were murdered by a bomb, declared about the school, "I don't see how it could be used for Negro or white education." In a speech to the demonstrators, I reminded them, "If we do not march on the voting polls like we have marched here today, we will never see the end of de facto segregation in Boston."[9] The following day the Sherwin School mysteriously burned to the ground.

On Tuesday, the vote reflected the feelings and fears stirred by the protests and actions of Boston's Black people. The five incumbents took the top five slots, with Louise Day Hicks in the overwhelming lead. Gartland, the only incumbent endorsed by the NAACP and Citizens for Boston Public Schools, lagged a poor fifth, only 2,000 votes ahead of the sixth place candidate and nearly 38,000 votes behind Mrs. Hicks.

I, too, found the vote a demonstration of widespread anti-Black feeling in Boston, in spite of its reputation for a liberal viewpoint. In all, I felt the election provided us all with a pointed reminder about reality. Boston was not responsive to the plight of Black people, educationally, financially, nor psychologically. The re-election of the School Committee made it abundantly clear that the hardest work lay ahead, and we were forced to abandon our naive notion that Boston whites wanted integration. Although the election temporarily deflated the momentum from the mounting waves of activism and the increasing awareness of the Black community's situation, we began girding for the next round. We had ample evidence of the opponent's resistance and we laid our plans accordingly.

The Racial Imbalance Law

During 1964 the germs of protest and action sown hastily in 1963 came to fruition, more dramatically, deliberately and explicitly than ever before. The momentum generated by several activities—the Stay Out for Freedom, the STOP Day (Chapter 4) and the memorial for Medgar Evers (Chapter 4) was somewhat stymied by the election results in the 1963 School Committee race. However, the NAACP, still spearheading the drive for equal education, initiated a new strategy. Plans for a new school Stay Out for Freedom were underway by January, 1964. Canon James Breeden, of the Episcopal Church, requested the support of the NAACP and after lengthy debate—local vs. national NAACP positions—support was unanimously given.

Community groups and local leaders took sides for and against the tactic and purpose of the Stay Out. The Massachusetts Civil Liberties Union found no legal irregularities in the plan particularly in view of the School Committee's failure to take action on the matter of de facto segregation.

"Under these circumstances," read their press release, "resort to a stayout becomes a reluctant but legitimate attempt to emphasize the importance and the urgency of the issue of school segregation. We see no legitimate basis for objection to the choice which the organizers, parents, and children have made."

Cardinal Richard Cushing expressed his disapproval, but other church groups, including students at Boston College, voiced their support. The first ruling by State Attorney General Edward Brooke that the Stay Out was illegal caused much consternation and heightened the morality versus legality conflict.

Just before he left on vacation, February 14, Brooke made a second ruling on the responsibility of parents and "boycott" leaders which laid primary responsibility on parents rather than Stay Out leaders. But the ruling left substantial uncertainty about actual liability of reprimand procedures stating that the matter finally rested in the Supreme Court.

In the meantime, support, much of it generated by clergy, mounted in the suburbs.

In my personal capacity as Chairman of the N.E. Commission on Social Action of the United Synagogue of America, I urge all my fellow-citizens, regardless of

faith or race, and especially my fellow-Jews, to act in
support of the School Stayout for Freedom on February 26th.

Dr. Steven S. Schwarzchild[10]

Literature circulated urging parents to keep their children out
of public school February 26, emphasizing the similarity of the
Stay Out objectives to demands made 115 years earlier, by a
group of Black parents to the Boston School Committee. This
Stay Out was specifically aimed at getting recognition of de
facto segregation, for though the 1963 Stay Out had yielded
some small advances in the number of Black counselors and
Black teachers, and the acquisition of new textbooks, no progress had been made toward trying to get at the root of the
problems.

> Segregated schools tell our children, 'You are Black,
> you are different, you are inferior;' and the white child-
> ren, 'You are white, you don't have to know about
> Negroes, you are superior.' Our children carry this lie,
> and the hurt it causes, with them into high school,
> where it affects their work, their relations with others,
> their chances of going on with their studies, and their
> chances of living without segregation. And they carry
> this hurt and this battle with them throughout their
> lives, as we do.
>
> —Stay Out Handout

Plans for protests similar to those staged in Boston were being
forged in 10 other cities, four years after the famous sit-in at the
Woolworth's lunch counter in Greensboro, North Carolina. In
spite of the momentum of the controversy, "More than 20 per
cent of Boston's 92,844 public school children missed classes
today as the second boycott in eight months hit this city," cited
the Evening Boston Globe.[11] An unexpected 9,000 students
including 1,000 pre-school children, attended Freedom Schools
throughout the city of Boston.

Superintendent Wm. H. Ohrenberger claimed, "Today's demonstration was a success for no one. It was a regrettable loss to all those involved..." "Real freedom," he maintained, "is manifested only through obedience to the law...Unhappily due to boycotts and other events of late, a color line is being drawn now that never before existed."[12]

Surprised by the number of students who stayed out, the media tried to downplay the day, "The boycott did not measure up to the expectations of its leaders whose goal was to get most of the 92,844 pupils to stay away from school," failing to mention the Freedom classes.

To those of us in the middle, however, the view was somewhat different. As "principal" of the South End House, I saw kids everywhere, excited, aware that they were directly involved in changing the schools which shaped so much of their time. And it made an enormous impact on the children to watch their parents caring enough to make this sort of massive effort to communicate to those in power. The parents worked to make things happen and the children imitated their spirit and determination. A great amount of political and cultural education took place for students and parents alike.[13]

The Stay Out showed us all that there were a hugh number of resources in our community, many of them underutilized. For example, the churches got a look at how they could use their facilities more than one day a week. The Stay Out demonstrated more clearly than any other activity that the community does have the capability to get organized and to act in its own behalf—a fact that would pay off somewhere down the line.

As an instrument for arousing awareness, focusing attention, and getting people involved in community action, the Stay Out proved to be successful. There was no question, moreover, that the Stay Out raised consciousness outside the community, because the issue was stated in religious/political terms which forced a lot of people, including some at high levels of government and clergy, to take a stand.

The Stay Out also prompted on-going classes in Black History after school and in the evenings; it brought to the surface some of the more sympathetic teachers in the school system; and, in the long-run it helped create the atmosphere in which the 1965 Racial Imbalance Law could be considered and passed in the Massachusetts State Legislature.

We're Comin' Out

..."Again," stated the staff report of the 1966 hearings before the Massachusetts Advisory Committee to the United States Commission on Civil Rights regarding segregation in Boston Public Schools, "no significant results were obtained." The judgement may seem harsh in the light of the positive effect of the Stay Out on the community, but by and large the Stay Out failed to loosen the School Committee's unyielding position. The advisory group appointed by the School Committee as requested by the NAACP was unacceptable, so other routes— predominantly legal—were chosen.

Several other significant events in 1964 prepared the way for intensified activity in 1965-66. In early March, 1964, the State Board of Education and the Commissioner of Education, Dr. Owen B. Kiernan, appointed an Advisory Committee on Racial Imbalance and Education. The Committee was "asked to examine the racial composition of the public schools in Massachusetts, to determine whether or not there is racial imbalance, and to consider ways in which school systems can deal constructively with racially imbalanced conditions."

By July, the Committee had concluded that segregation did exist in 78% of the public schools in Massachusetts, (that is, 78% of public schools have none or less than five percent nonwhites) and that racial imbalance was detrimental to sound education in no less than six ways:

> 1) Racial imbalance damages the self-confidence of Negro children. 2) Racial imbalance reinforces the prejudices of children regardless of their color. 3) Racial imbalance does not prepare the child for integrated life in a multi-racial community, nation, and world. 4) Racial imbalance impairs the opportunities of many Negro children to prepare for the vocational require-

ments of our technological society. 5) Racial imbalance often results in a gap in the quality of education in our society. 6) Racial imbalance in the public schools represents a serious conflict with the American creed of equal opportunity.[14]

Significantly, the Kiernan Report proposed a series of steps to begin alleviating racial imbalance, among them, busing, where necessary, to exchange students in grades 3-6, in order to equalize Black and white enrollment. The Committee also recommended State legislation to cope with racial imbalance by: 1) charging school committees with the task of eliminating imbalance; 2) preventing further construction of schools that would be imbalanced; and 3) withholding state financial aid to communities with imbalanced schools.

For my part, I found the report lacking in specific provisions for community involvement which seemed to me crucial to implementation. The proposal did not recognize the importance of parent participation in selection of administrators and teachers. Additionally, provisions for parent input in curriculum development and choice of books and materials to be used in the schools were ignored. It did not alter the power relations between parents, community, and the administrators and teachers in the schools.

In the meantime, a group of parents with children at the Garrison School were informed that their children were being transferred to the Boardman School in the fall. The children would have to walk past heavy construction on both sides of the street to a school with conditions no better than those they were leaving. The parents brought suit against the School Committee to halt the transfer and to have their children bused to another school, because of the hazardous conditions. On September 13, 1967, the injunction was denied and the suit dismissed. Appeal was filed, but no action was taken. As a result, the "Boardman Parents" made the decision to hire their own bus to transport their children to the Peter Faneuil School which they proceeded to do with the help of funding from numerous private sources. The Boardman parents initiated busing in Boston and paved the way for more extensive community sponsored busing in the following months.

As early as 1963, Rep. Royal Bolling, Sr., had submitted a bill, only 14 words at the time, which was to prohibit communities with racially imbalanced schools from receiving state aid. The bill was killed in 1964. In 1965, he refiled the bill, but was so certain it would be killed that he did not even appear at the public hearing.[15] In the spring the effects of the Kiernan report, which made a similar recommendation for legislation to withhold funds, were being felt, and as a consequence the bill was revived and combined first with one from Education Commissioner, Owen B. Kiernan, then with bills submitted by Governor Volpe and Sen. Cohen from Brookline. The bill covered such items as the responsibilities of school committees to move against racial imbalance, the conduct of schools in regard to racial matters, prohibition of state aid to racially imbalanced towns, and annual reports to the legislature on the efforts to abolish imbalance. In four months, the signing ceremony took place and the first such legislation on racial imbalance in the country became law. The bill was notable for the large number of community organizations and individuals who participated in the drafting and lobbying process.

The time, at long last, was right for the passage of this law. I attribute its being passed to three major factors: good organization, the atmosphere set up by the demonstrations of the community, the behavior of the Boston School Committee, and the fact that the bill was non-threatening to enough of the state legislators to get it passed. The organization was largely a coalition of Black people, Jewish people, and other white liberals, particularly the suburban Fair Housing groups who had succeeded in pushing legislation on that front.

The Kiernan Report had a strong influence on the climate of the times. This was also the height of the Civil Rights wave of activism across the nation, which was at least temporarily stirring, prompting, activating the conscience of the nation. Dr. Martin Luther King's visit to the Boston Common in the spring of 1965 helped to emphasize the fact that many onlookers were drawing comparisons between Boston and the South—which may have been too close for comfort for image-conscious legislators. It also helped to have Reverend Vernon Carter literally camping on the doorstep of the School Committee with picket signs until the legislation passed.

Many legislators, I suspect, looked upon the bill as a means to control the Catholic groups which had run the school system and the city for so long. Many of the bill's supporters were from suburbs or areas of Boston that would be little affected; besides, the bill contained a "voluntary" clause that made it impossible for busing to be mandatory.

Most Black people, I think, looked at it as a step toward the attention their children needed, but suspected it would not be enforced, and were bothered by its one-way implications (bus *Black* students, not white). I testified at the hearing on the bill that unless it required two-way busing it would not work. As written it fostered the prejudice that white children were better than Black children. I also questioned the "voluntary" clause about busing, since all other aspects of schooling are mandatory regardless of parental biases.

The law's impact was twofold: immediate increased pressure was placed on the Boston School Committee members; though in the long run it served to disguise further de facto segregation. In actuality, the School Committee was able to dodge its pressure simply by refusing to agree to its definitions. It had an immediate and disastrous effect on the next School Committee election: A. Gartland, the one voice of reason and compassion, lost. In and of itself, the Racial Imbalance Law was not enough to create meaningful change within the public school system.

The School Committee was adamant and rejected a proposal to transport students from the crowded Gibson, Endicott, and Hyde-Everett schools to schools in largely white areas, a practice which was not entirely new for the school system. The only alternative, Ohrenberger announced, was double sessions, a state of affairs that many parents could not tolerate, financially or educationally. Parents banded together and talked about a temporary busing program to dramatize their plight and get their children into better schools. By September, they had obtained a list of vacant seats (it had to be "stolen" according to Mrs. Ellen Jackson) and Operation Exodus was born to transport 475 children, increasing to 976 children by 1966. The money ($65,000 a year) was raised through mothers' marches, community events, and various benefactors. In the tradition of the Boardman parents' effort, Exodus tried to solve a community problem, imposed by the external powers, by rallying community resources and taking the initiative from the officials blocking their requests through "proper" channels.

The 1965 School Committee race was an astounding example of voters refusing to deal with the mounting evidence of incompetence, political opportunism and outright fraud on the part of some members of the committee. The race quickly grew heated as the Citizens' group hammered away at the major issues: fiscal responsibility, outmoded courses (particularly vocational), condition of school buildings, teacher recruitment, and racial imbalance.

The facts were incriminating. Of the 5,000 students leaving the school system each year, 1,500 or more than 25% were dropouts. What better indicator of "no confidence" in the school system? As a counselor, I had talked to numerous kids to whom I could offer virtually no options. It was always a shock to realize that a kid of 17 was unemployable and possessed obsolete skills due to the lack of training he or she had received in school. The majority of children were in schools older than their own grandparents; the schools loomed dark and dreary as prisons, but no jail would have been allowed to have cracks in the wall or crumbling plaster, broken windows and decayed woodwork.

The primary voting exposed the vast distance between the voters and the issues. We tried to be optimistic because all Citizens' candidates made the final election (John Gaquin, G. Parker, Arthur Gartland, Velia DeCesare and myself). Our theme was "We're Comin' Out." I actually came in sixth and closed the gap between myself and other candidates, and for the first time in the city's history a greater percentage of Black voters than whites went to the ballots in a primary election in an off year. But the fact remained that Louise Day Hicks pulled almost 90% of the votes cast; one in three voters apparently voted *only* for her.

In the last round we challenged Mrs. Hicks head on, charging that she in particular was using the fear-laden issues of busing and race for her own political advantage; sidetracking parents from understanding the failure of the system under her guidance. In a televised interview of candidates, George H. Parker of the Citizens' slate stated bluntly: "There are people who would rather see this city torn apart by racial strife than face the issues." Even Boston's Chamber of Commerce chastised the School Committee's actions in fear of "serious economic harm" to Boston's financial state. The Greater Boston Labor Council refused to endorse Mrs. Hicks, terming support for her a "mockery" of their principles. Nevertheless, her victory in November was definitive. Though voices were raised to deny that the vote was racist, the evidence was clear that almost three-quarters of the Boston electorate were touched by the incumbent committee's blatant apeal to bigotry. Mrs. Hicks exemplified this bigotry when she said,

> ...these industrious children (the Chinese, listed as non-white in the school census) don't want their school racially balanced. I don't think they enjoy being called, in effect Negroes.

It was inconceivable that the voters elected Hicks and company for their educational achievement. If nothing else, the Citizens' slate had made the choices distinctly clear. We also learned that in a city-wide election Black voter solidarity was not enough to swing the balance against the entrenched racism. Arthur Gartland lost, marking the last attempt to form a city-wide coalition on School Committee elections.

These years were a period when increased awareness and information about the situation in Boston's schools pushed parents to action. Parents took the safety of their children into their own hands through the formation of Exodus; the community rallied behind the NAACP Education Committee's challenge to the School Committee over de facto segregation, holding the two dramatic school Stay Out days. The cause was taken up legislatively through the Racial Imbalance Law. Three times we attempted to get a liberal slate onto the School Committee.

Although some of the results from this period of intense activity were disappointing, and even foreboding, there were other outcomes. The Black community was fully warned about the deeply entrenched resistance of whites. The community had gone too far to turn back. The battle lines were drawn and we knew we would continue the struggle as long as necessary.

Chapter 4

ECONOMIC DEVELOPMENT:
Black Boycotts and the Police Riots

Shortly after we realized it wasn't the inability of our children to learn but the schools which were the problem, we saw that the reason Black workers were unemployed was not the result of poor training but rather the racial discrimination sanctioned by employers. Historically, the primary approach to increasing income for Blacks in Boston had been the traditional training programs. Most "manpower" programs focused on fitting the person to the available job, without questioning the job opportunity structure or the requirements. Very often the increment of change in wages was particularly negligible (from welfare to minimum wages, for instance), and the fact that the gap between Black and white average incomes had increased absolutely, was not taken into account in planning and training.

Over time a substantial number of agencies, including the NAACP and the Urban League, decided to start screening entry level training services, particularly when federal legislation made funds available. But as early as 1962 community social workers and organizers, and an assorted group of college students, mostly white, initiated a drive that demonstrated some other approaches to the problems of getting jobs and raising

47

income levels. The Boston Action Group (BAG) was formed to apply direct pressure on individual firms that apparently were closed to Black workers. The process utilized by BAG is worthy of detailed study. It is an example of direct action to affect economic conditions.

The Boston Action Group (BAG)

The decision to engage in direct action was influenced by the success of a group of ministers in Philadelphia who had told their congregations not to buy from companies that operated with discriminatory practices. The selective buying approach produced enough pressure to obtain a number of new jobs for Black people. Similar selective patronage boycotts had been sponsored in New York by the Northern Student Movement. A Babson student named Al Rosanes, who had participated in that effort, began to organize college students in Boston. When that group began to fail, some of the people involved at Saint Mark's Social Center, including Donald Shaw, Tony Williams, Bill Strickland and Noel Day revived the effort into the Boston Action Group (BAG). Noel Day remembers that:

> We got big maps of the community and set up a kind of program where everybody met around 9:30 or 10:00 Saturday morning. Everybody got assigned certain blocks. We were at that point doing a survey trying to find out what kind of products the Black community was buying and at the same time using that survey to acquaint the community with the concept of selective patronage campaigns, (and) trying to find block captainson every block—who we would give leaflets to, and other information, (to)...distribute on their block, so we would meet every Saturday morning and we would role play with interviewing and rapping with the people; we would have coffee and donuts for all the volunteers; we would assign them in teams of two people to a block; and then we had it set up so that they canvassed for a certain number of hours and by 2:00 everybody was supposed to be back. They handed in the completed questionaires, their block got crossed off the map so that every week the organization could

see what it was accomplishing, (then) we had more refreshments, usually wine and stuff like that. Everybody got debriefed; if there were any questions that they brought back from the field, they took down the name of the person that had asked the question and we would give them a follow-up phone call the next week.

BAG printed leaflets including one which depicted a large club made of dollar signs with the caption: "This is the money you spend; it's the club you can use to get what you want."

Crucial to the BAG approach was that initial four month information and education stage during which BAG workers knocked on doors explaining selective buying, citing statistics about the economic status of the average Black worker (at the time Blacks made 52% of the average white worker's wage and one out of three Blacks made under $2000 a year), and organizing block captains for future distribution of information.

The first target was Wonder Bread. About 12% of the company's sales was made in Black areas of Boston. A meeting with the personnel manager verified that of its 250 workers, the company employed only eight Black people. All eight workers were production employees in the baking plant, with no one in sales, trucking, office demonstration or other customer relations work.

One month after the first meeting, BAG approached the company again, this time with the specific demands that the company hire twelve Black people (five driver-salesmen, one long distance truck driver, four clerks, and two bakery plant production workers) within thirty days. The company protested that it had no jobs available. At the end of thirty days another meeting was held at which it was learned the company had hired Rommie Loud, a Black athlete, to do sales promotion, but it had not filled any of the other positions demanded. This was another example of the institutionalized tokenism that was to become the way out for numerous businesses in the coming years.

Then the mobilization began: on the next Saturday, ministers throughout Roxbury, the South End and Dorchester (all areas with strong Black populations) urged their congregations to boycott Wonder Bread; leaflets were distributed through the neighborhoods asking people not to buy "Jim Crow" bread;

letters were sent to all the block captains asking them to notify their neighborhoods of the boycott and urge them to join; ministers, students, housewives, social workers, and others joined a Saturday picket march through the community to raise consciousness about the boycott; store owners were asked to cancel their Wonder Bread orders and were picketed if they refused; press releases were used to tell the BAG story across the city.

"We asked them how many Black employees they had," remembers Noel Day, "and they were quite open about the number that they had. They had some bakers but no bread truck drivers or anything like that. They said they couldn't find anybody who was qualified for those jobs." Sarah Ann Shaw, a BAG member, recalls,

> ... We marched down through Dudley Street from Townsend Street.. with signs saying "Boycott Wonder Bread", "Don't Buy Wonder Bread" and we stationed ourselves at several stores. We went in and asked store keepers not to take Wonder Bread, and the ones who refused and said they were going to continue to sell Wonder Bread, we stationed people in front of their stores handing out leaflets and explaining to people why we didn't want them to buy wonder Bread. And finally the Wonder Bread people got in touch with Noel who was chairing the group and said they wanted to talk and miraculously they found some jobs.

Within 29 days the company hired eight Black people and made promises to employ others, with a "progress report" meeting slated in six months. At one point, Noel Day remembers, the Wonder Bread people sent a Black lawyer from New York to meet with the BAG people,

> He came up and tried to deal with us legally, and essentially we told him to go back to New York; and a couple of weeks later the Wonder Bread people called us and they admitted they were losing $15,000 a week in the Black community and agreed to make hires. At that point I think we made a grave tactical error... We opted for a postion of security and said, "your job is to hire people. if you can recruit white people you can

recruit Black people and we won't send people to you."
I think in retrospect it would have been smarter for
BAG and the other organizations to have recruited the
people, because the people who got those jobs had no
sense of responsibility or commitment back to the
community or to any organization.

In spite of the short-comings now evident, BAG proved beyond
a doubt that selective buying could mobilize enough financial
pressure to change the policy and hiring behavior of a company.
The effectiveness of the campaign was in large part due to the
thoroughness of the research and the exhaustive community
organizing and educating. The target was well chosen and the
organizing produced an ad hoc coalition broad-based enough to
support the boycott.

Not long after the BAG campaign, CORE (Congress of
Racial Equality) launched a similar pressure for jobs against the
prestigious First National Bank of Boston. This time limited
sucess was obtained because of the potential damage to the
bank's image as well as its pocketbook.

"We never even got to the point where we had to boycott,"
Noel Day related about the First National Bank experience...

After some pressure (the picketing of Dudley, Ken-
more and the main offices), the V.P. said, 'these
gentlemen are talking about power and we understand
power, don't we? And... we will hire twenty Negro
tellers by next Friday and I don't care if we have to hire
two white men to teach everyone one of them how to
count; they will be on the job.'

STOP—Time to Reconsider

In June of 1963 the tactic of boycotting was excercised on a more
general level of demonstration against economic and other conditions for Black people in Boston. Just a week after the first
School Stay Out a group of social workers led by Hubie Jones,
Noel Day and myself, scheduled a general work stoppage to
dramatize the plight of Black people in almost all aspects of life.

The purpose of STOP was straightforward,

> To appeal to Negro citizens and sympathetic white
> citizens in our community to refrain from *work*, buying,
> amusements and use of mass transportation on June
> 26th in non-violent protest against the following racial
> injustices inflicted upon the Negro in Greater Boston:
>   1) Discrimination in hiring Negroes
>   2) Police Brutality inflicted upon citizens in Roxbury
> and the South End.
>   3) De facto segregation in the Boston School System
> with the accompanying deplorable conditions in the
> schools, inadequate supply of books, dilapidated build-
> ings, etc.
>   4) Discrimination in public and private housing.

The word STOP was intended to convey several messages:

> It says to the discriminating white community, *STOP*
> inflicting various forms of racial injustices on Negroes.
> It says to the Boston Negro, *STOP* denying the condi-
> tions that exist and mobilize yourself to join others to
> effect changes. It says to the Civil Rights Organiza-
> tions, *STOP* the state of competition and lack of coordi-
> nation that exist so that we can work together STOP
> has come to say that a city that only looks at its
> strengths and not its weaknesses is in danger of des-
> troying itself. We have too much invested in the life of
> the Boston community to stand by and see that
> happen.

Some Boston Black leaders, including the NAACP which had
supported the School Stay Out, were sufficiently uneasy with
the scale of action planned by STOP organizers and initiated a
memorial service to Medgar Evers on the Boston Common the
same day and urged people to attend the memorial rather than
the STOP march. In the end,both the rally for Evers and the
STOP day took place on June 26. In a gesture of solidarity in
spite of disagreements with the NAACP and others, the STOP
organization sent an estimated 1,000 people to join the other
several thousand gathered at the Common in tribute to Evers.
For some the march had a deeply moving significance:

Negroes who are in the higher financial brackets dropped their social standing—joined hands with their brothers and sisters—black and white, Christian and Moslem—and marched down Columbus Avenue to the Boston Common clapping their hands and singing FREEDOM, FREEDOM, AND WE SHALL OVERCOME. The spectacle was so heart shaking that many grown men were touched and broke down and wept. In the downtown office buildings all of the windows were filled with white faces surprised, even amazed at what they saw!!!...this was Boston, Massachusetts, we thought the Negro already had his freedom here.

The caption below a picture in a community newspaper read:

STOP followers arrived in the Boston Common singing "We Shall Overcome." When the group, numbering over 1000 arrived the crowd of over 3000 broke into uncontrollable applause... each person catching the 'freedom now' mood.

STOP Day had a number of ramifications—mostly signs of things to come. The large scale boycott plans aroused anxiety and resistance among many leaders who didn't want to participate in such visible protest. Some important differences in approach and commitment (or self-interest) began to be evident between Black people and whites in organizations like the NAACP. STOP also initiated the dialogue between Black workers and the Association of General Contractors (AGC). The STOP pickets concentrated on the Prudential site (a large business, office space, high-rise luxury apartment complex that towers over the Boston Hub) then under construction, demanding jobs for minority workers. AGC tried to blame the unions in a preview of the buckpassing that was to come, and eventually a half-dozen or so workers were put on the job.

Job (Mis)training

The beginnings of activism by BAG, CORE and the STOP movements led some of the existing "direct service" community agencies in a circular fashion back into training and job placement. Once some of the pressured businesses began to make jobs available, the community had to provide a mechanism to fill them. The years between 1962 and 1966 were spent in a prag-matic effort with the few resources available, to find the type of manpower programs that would really meet the needs of the inner city work force.

Federal legislation and programs had a significant impact on this search since much of the money available for manpower training came from federal sources. In 1962 the first version of the Manpower Development and Training Act (MDTA) was passed with a focus on institutional and on-the-job training primarily for workers (unemployed, disadvantaged youth and older workers), and to set up some new programs. Money for all these programs was passed out to the Division of Employment Security (DES) and the State Vocational Education Department which could contract for on-the-job training with local agencies. The MDTA legislation was followed by the Civil Rights legisla-tion passed, in an aura of guilt, in the wake of JFK's death.

The problem with these programs was two fold: first, the narrow definition of just who was to be served; and second, chan-neling money through the DES and the Vocational Department ultimately meant relying on training provided by Boston Public School system. The inevitable result was that children were stuck with training not designed to meet their needs. One young man who wanted to get machine shop skills quit school because the equipment was of museum vintage (belt-driven machines) and he wanted to know how to run newer, more sophisticated precision tool and die equipment. He went to the DES for counseling and was told about the "new" MDTA machine operating course. When he signed up, he was assigned to the same school, the same old machines, and even the same teacher. The MDTA money was being spent from 3:00 to 9:00 by the same people who failed the students from 9:00-3:00. The young man dropped this course, too, and is permanently recorded as a two-time drop out. Newer machinery was sent to a few schools. But at the Daniel Webster School in East Boston, the Brown and Sharp Precision machines remained in their packing crates because the teachers didn't know how to run them; the floors were too weak to sustain the weight; and the power supply was inadequate.

These school-based programs had some other troublesome characteristics, too, such as the selection of courses and the location of the classes. Courses were taught with no relation to the demands of industry. Woodworking is taught faithfully altough there hasn't been a demand for woodworkers around Boston for fifteen years. When questioned about this discrepancy, Joseph Lee of the Boston School Committee replied that "woodworking teaches traditional Yankee values," a rationale which has questionable relevance to a Black student in Roxbury or the South End.

Location of MDTA courses took on an insidious pattern: the courses for accounting, dental technicians, forestry and computer operation were held in outlying towns such as Salem. Black people were consistently referred to programs in building maintenance(janitorial work), upholstery, short order cooking and the like, which were taught in town. One instructor for a baking course flatly told the United South End Settlements Youth Training and Employment Center not to send any more Black referrals—they were too hard to place!

This declaration pointed out another flaw in the MDTA based training—the programs made no attempt and had no power to loosen the tight-fisted control of local customs and the local unions over most skilled trade jobs. Even if trained, many Black and other ethnic workers could not get close to the jobs that might be available. The DES and the State Department of Vocational Education had done nothing to take an advocate role against discrimination in union hiring and control of apprenticeships. At that time, it was policy for Employment Services to accept white only job orders.

All things considered, the MDTA service programs were not serving the people who needed training and assistance getting jobs. By 1965, Martin Gopen, then a counselor for the MDTA funded South End Youth Training and Employment Center, wrote a blistering open letter to the Division of Employment Security citing case after case of bureaucratic mishandling and insensitivity, and the numerous ways in which the MDTA programs served to dehumanize and discourage applicants with intimidating tests, misinformation and general incompetence.

With government funding and DES or school system personnel clearly not the answer to the manpower needs of Boston's inner city work force, community agencies and concerned individuals continued to seek and develop other alternatives. One such effort was Jobs Clearing House, a program started by Tom Brown, who was involved in the NAACP's Labor and Industries Committe, to assist Black college graduates in finding executive and middle management positions in downtown Boston. When the scarcity of college trained people became evident, the Clearing House moved to working with high school graduates. This program, like many of the other service programs that were developed in the effort to offset the disastrous results of the established training channels, served to skim the top talent, and sometimes moved the same skilled folks from job to job, rather than meeting the needs of the masses of unemployed or underemployed people. Nevertheless, by October of 1965 the Clearing House had found over 900 jobs for community workers and processed 3500 applications since its beginning on Labor Day of 1963. Businessmen started coming to the Clearing House. Tom Brown felt that the old stereotypes were being effaced, "The white man believes the Negro labor pool is largely unskilled; the Negro, in turn, doesn't know or doesn't dare believe that the 'off limits' sign has been yanked down in most places." He cited established testing for applicants as a major block for Black workers—an issue that was to become a focal point for action a few years later.[1]

A somewhat different approach was also tried in 1964 when the Clearing House and several of us from United South End Settlements Youth Opportunity Center teamed up with Dr. George Rohrbough of the Chandler School for Women and some Boston businessmen to run an unusual free summer session for any jobless Black women who wanted to sign up and obtain marketable skills. The session was a resounding success and became something of a community effort with the spouses, children and neighbors of the enrolled women helping out with the household affairs until the women finished the rather rigorous schedule for twelve weeks. Special efforts were made to place all the graduates in jobs as quickly as possible. The efforts of CORE and other civil rights groups had loosened up the business community to the point of general willingness to hire the available trained women. Community initiated service programs such as these sought to fill the skill and training gaps.

The Police Riots

At the same time that the Black community was trying to acquire the "training" necessary to break out of its entrapment, it was also fighting for adequate welfare for the families of those who were being denied meaningful employment. Mothers for Adequate Welfare (MAW) was begun by Black mothers who clearly realized that their welfare payments were not enough to support a family. Their organizing began to expose an important factor in the economic development of many poor areas. Welfare recipients were unable to get sufficient amount to live on, yet working jeopardized any sort of support. The War on Poverty began to provide some new horizons through community aid programs which hired welfare mothers to work in schools and other institutions, but the general role of the state welfare system was to perpetuate a condition of poverty. However, the Welfare Mother's demands for decent treatment and adequate welfare payments in 1965 set the scene for the confrontations to come.

They pressed forward seeking rent subsidies and other types of support. In the summer of 1966 a delegation of Mothers met with Massachusetts Governor Volpe after staging marches at City Hall and the State House. Their spokesperson explained that they sought a measure of human dignity in the way they were treated, not simply more money. On Thanksgiving 1966 forty women gathered at the Boston welfare office to protest the lack of food tickets for the holiday season to supplement their ordinary checks. They were informed that if special checks were issued, there was no guarantee that the amount wouldn't be cut from their next regular payment.

By early summer of 1967 the Mothers took more drastic action and began a sit-in at the Grove Hall office of the Welfare Department in Roxbury. They stated that they were "tired of being treated like criminals...of having to depend on suspicious

and insulting social workers and at being completely at the
mercy of a department we have no control over."[2] The demonstration was nonviolent, but on the second day, spectators who
had gathered at the scene were suddenly charged by "club-
swinging" policemen who had decided to clear the hall. The
melee, in which a number of people were injured, precipitated
further sporadic incidents of looting and fires which gutted the
Grove Hall area along Blue Hill Avenue, one of the main
commercial strips in Boston's Black community. Eventually, to
the annoyance of the Boston police, all charges against the
"rioters" were dropped.[3] The incidents, called the "Police Riots"
by Black residents, prompted some answering chords from
other groups and a rally of some 1,000 welfare recipients, from
across the state, was held on the Boston Common several weeks
later.

Chuck Turner, who was involved in organizing the Mothers, commented afterwards,

> When the *Banner* talked about a "Police Riot" it pulled
> the covers off the police and everybody had to look at
> the reality. I'd have to say it was tremendously signifi-
> cant.

The Kerner Commission on Civil Disorders didn't even
mention Boston's Police Riots, which were actually a fore-
runner of the more severely violent situation in Newark and
Detroit a month and a half later, but some of the Commission's
recommendations on welfare could have been quotes from the
MAW demands. The Commission Report summary states,

> Our present system of public welfare is designed to
> save money instead of people, and tragically ends up
> doing neither....for those included, the system pro-
> vides assistance well below the minimum necessary for
> a decent level of existence, and imposes restrictions
> that encourage continued dependency on welfare and
> undermine self-respect.[4]

One of the Commission's overall recommendations was to
revamp the welfare system "to provide, for those who cannot

work and for mothers who decide to remain with their children, a minimum standard of decent living, and to aid in the saving of children from the prison of poverty that has held their parents." The report goes on,

> This is our basic conclusion: Our nation is moving toward two societies, one Black, one white—separate and unequal....Discrimination and segregation have long permeated much of American life; they now threaten the future of every American.[5]

The Police Riots underscored some of the frustration of members of the Black community with the lack of positive growth and development in their part of the city. The country as a whole appeared to be moving toward prosperity, but conditions in the Black community were predictably worse than mainstream America. Black male unemployment was estimated from 15-30%. Indignation was beginning to rise in Black communities across the nation. By 1966 the emphasis of economic development efforts in the community was clearly beginning to shift from a simple training program appraoch to more comprehensive efforts at internal economic development. Negotiations were underway to bring three major industries into the Black community, AVCO printing, Polaroid, and Edgerton, Geurney-hausen and Grier electronics. A consortium of Black contractors was hired to do the construction work for the AVCO plant, some members of the Black community promoted internal development of the Black community as an alternative to being dependent on the outside power structure.

The New England Community Development Corporation (NECDC) began planning ways to redevelop the Blue Hill Avenue business thoroughfare through Roxbury. Archie Willians, who became invo1ved in NECDC out of some of his work with the NAACP and the Veterans Administration, describes NECDC as,

> a corporation set up by a group of guys, predominantly white, who had formed a real estate corporation called the Roxbury Development Corporation. They were Harvard professors, architects, who were moved by the Civil Rights Movement. They formed the NECDC

because once they got into the housing, they discovered that there was some social work needed—not in
the traditional form, but innovative social programs
around housing that would allow the people in the
neighborhoods to improve their general life style. And
out of this came the Hilltop Day Care Center.

The idea for NECDC's Concentrated Economic Development Program was to take thirty-five blocks in the Grove Hall
area of Roxbury and initiate as many programs as necessary to
directly increase income. The area contained 275 families with
26% on welfare and 40% unemployed or underemployed.

The proposed program had several major pieces: intensive
job counseling for residents and enrollment in training programs; adult education programs for welfare recipients; subsidies for a few families so that less of the family budget had to be
spent on essential items such as fuel oil and food. One of the
most outstanding features of the NECDC program was its
insistance from the beginning that all programs be designed to
lead to complete community control. Position papers stress
NECDC's basic philosophy,

All of the programs developed by NECDC are designed
to maximize the control people have over those institutions and decisions which have a major effect on their
lives. For too long the centers of power have remained
aloof and unresponsive to the dilemmas and demands
of the poor.

Each program was to provide new skills and power for community residents, and program development was based on a thorough survey of the area to assess its needs. NECDC had
already successfully tried such a policy in its Hilltop Daycare
Center which became a hub for the other activities NECDC
generated.

Unfortunately, like too many programs designed to transfer power or spread around the economic wealth of the nation,
the NECDC Concentrated Economic Development Program
was not funded. Archie Williams comments about the struggle
for funding:

The whole plan of matching housing and social services was essentially thrown askew by the fact the Housing Innovations (the housing component of the program) got money much more readily because they did have assets to put up as security, while the social program—which was to be an expensive program—had a great deal of trouble getting any kind of money. We managed to get funds from Permanent Charities to maintain salaries, but we never could get any money to match the various programs.

But the NECDC idea was to take root and grow elsewhere and the frustration of not being funded provided the impetus for yet another enterprise. The need for technical expertise and an economic base for supporting economic and community development programs was never clearer than with the rejection of the NECDC plan.

Centralized Investments to Revitalize Community Living Effectively (CIRCLE)

A small group of people who had been deeply involved in the continuous series of early economic development efforts in the Black community began talking in 1966 about ways to pull together the resources of the numerous community agencies. The original concept was to create an organization of organizations which would pool efforts toward community development and initiate joint projects designed to stop leakage of Black capital from the Black community. Members of most of the key community agencies or organizations, including the APACs, Unity Bank, Bridge, CAB, and various businessmen's groups attended the initial discussions, focusing on the idea of centralized buying for all the agencies and programs designed to meet the economic needs of the community and community agencies. Central purchasing and a similar idea for a centralized computer information system were never realized, as the group, CIRCLE, became involved in an energy-consuming effort to get a large federal grant for community development from the Office of Economic Opportunity (OEO). CIRCLE, Inc., a consulting and research organization grew out of the need to make some money to put into development efforts.

As CIRCLE evolved it eventually needed a vehicle for handling tax exempt money. CIRCLE Board members negotiated a merger of its board with that of NECDC. Archie Williams recalls that,

> The basic idea was to find some way to coordinate the ever increasing duplication and/or to attempt to move the movement in a specific, coordinated direction. CIRCLE developed and grew. At about this time I believe we were talking about minority economic development. AVCO came in, CIRCLE got a contract with them, and that contract provided some funds for CIRCLE. CIRCLE then got an Executive Director, and then started pursuing other funds.

CIRCLE represented another breed of community institution, a bank of human and financial resources to invest in internal community development. The members of CIRCLE were striving to form a collective leadership and to mount a collective effort to utilize and direct the actions of community agencies to the best interests of the community as a whole. Having recognized the problem of resource leakage from the Black community, CIRCLE set its goals: to plug holes, to overcome the negative image of Black business, prompt new entrepreneurial development, and build a sense of unity in the process of building a community-based economy.

The Boston Model Cities First Year Plan stated CIRCLE's philosophy succinctly:

> One of the fundamental faults of the conventional programs of manpower and economic development programs, in the estimate of CIRCLE, is that they have ignored the need of such communities to lessen their dependency and to increase the capacity of local citizens to affect and control the economic, social and political institutions within their communities. Such programs have generally been unwilling to confront honestly the issues of power and control because of their failure to appreciate the role which social and psychological factors play in maintaining poverty.

In the area of economic development, the community moved in one decade from street organizing for selective buying boycotts to obtain increased numbers of jobs, through training programs to improve wretched educational and government programs, to confrontations over inadequate welfare payments and then to efforts to develop comprehensive approaches to community development such as the NECDC program. Some of these proposals were sophisticated forerunners of many of the approaches we have developed since then. CIRCLE and NECDC were models for community development which recognized the interconnectedness of jobs, housing, and education, as well as the social and cultural structure of our community. The difficulty these programs had in getting funded was not a reflection of their weakness, but of the strong threat they posed to the existing economic structures. What we realized during the efforts to put together these institutions was the foundation of future ventures.

Chapter 5

HOUSING:
Community Assembly
for a United South End (CAUSE)

Community development is impossible without decent and affordable housing. When the New York Street residents and their homes were desolated by the Boston Redevelopment Authority (BRA), as we saw in Chapter 2, the Black community began to realize that the "ghetto" was not due to their neglect and supposed inferiority. The "ghetto" was an image put on the Black community by the the city, banking institutions and realtors, reinforced by cutting off resources to the area, thereby causing the deterioration of the buildings and streets. Consequently, these same individuals and institutions came in and physically demolished the buildings, displacing the residents, and making way for light industry. The community, however, began to demand that the existing housing stock be rehabilitated, and that the temporary relocation of residents and the rehabilitation be undertaken by local neighborhood agencies and contractors.

In 1961, a committee of South End "neighborhood representatives," local business and institutional leaders and the Boston Redevelopment Authority South End project team, endorsed a series of meetings with various neighborhood clubs and associations. This set of meetings had a decided slant in favor of homeowners as there was very little tenant representation. The debate focused in large measure on whether the South End plan should be directed toward the needs of the people already living in the South End, or whether the plan should be designed to encourage higher income people to move into the project area.

Realizing that Federal urban renewal funding guidelines required the approval of the community and investment of local homeowners, the BRA was reluctant to sponsor extensive privately financed rehabilitation that would favor higher income residents. During the four years of negotiations that went on to get citizen approval of the South End plan, existing residents made two things clear: 1) they wanted to rehabilitate existing structures rather than tear down their neighborhood; and 2) they wanted to stay in the South End.

The first plan developed by the BRA in 1962, featured a green belt down Shawmut Avenue. This scheme was opposed by the many shoppers and residents who realized it would "belt" them right out of existence. The green belt would have for all practical purposes separated the low-income housing projects for families and the elderly from a cluster of planned community facilities.

The second plan was begun in the fall of 1963. This time the BRA made a greater effort to ask residents what they desired in the new plan. Community organizing was limited, and once again, the BRA listened mostly to homeowners rather than tenants who made up two-thirds of the South End population. The plan that was eventually settled upon focused on the large-scale rehabilitation of the existing housing stock with an emphasis on housing those who already lived in the area. Over 3000 structures were scheduled for rehabilitation and over 3000 new private rental units were to be constructed with aid from the Federal Housing Program. Nineteen percent of all South End households (3500), two-thirds of them low income people, would be displaced under this plan.

The Boston urban renewal program was the largest in the country in terms of both cost and number of units affected. In the Castle Square area of the South End residents won a reduction in the amount of land scheduled for light industry (in the style of the New York Streets), and an increase in the number of new low-income units to be constructed. Residents were to be given first priority in new housing.

The South End plan necessitated attention to relocation on a larger and more comprehensive scale because of its emphasis on rehabilitation. In 1966, the plan estimated that around 1730 families and 1820 single people were living in the sections of the neighborhood to be closed. About 69 percent of these households needed one-bedroom or equivalent units. The BRA expected almost three out of every four families to move into private rental housing, and one out of five to move into public housing. Almost two out of every three households were eligible for low-rent public housing, but surveys had shown few residents other than elderly people desired that relocation option.

Overall residents were mixed in their reactions. They knew that conditions had to be improved and that they had, with this effort, stemmed the tide of total demolition and displacement evident in the New York Streets. The efforts in Castle Square resulted in a small victory: two-thirds of the land would be for housing and the displaced residents would be given priority to return. However, residents were apprehensive about what the outcomes would be. There was no cause for celebration, as they would soon learn.

I was an early advocate for getting the relocation process out of the city bureaucracy and into the hands of neighborhood service agencies, who had been working closely with families for years. At the City Council hearings on the second South End Renewal Plan, I argued that the residents of renewal areas had to get a bigger piece of the action, both in terms of access to the benefits of renewal, and in terms of contracts to build and to service the needs of people affected by renewal. We did not want to develop new housing services and jobs for someone else to move in and enjoy.

The BRA agreed to contract with some of these agencies for relocation services with interesting results. Agency workers, like myself, were among the few people who knew the possible results of relocation. We had followed our clients from the New

York Streets and other "renewed" areas. We saw first hand what problems families had finding affordable replacements, and what dreadful conditions they sometimes ended up with. In that sense, agency workers were the most knowledgeable about renewal problems and the needs of their families; furthermore, they had a stake in keeping their clients in the neighborhood. They were also the most indignant, with the exception of those displaced, at how people were treated during the renewal process.

During the New York Streets relocation (if it could be called that) there was very little awareness of the hardships caused by the forced move, except among the agency workers who visited the families with children. In that sense we were too knowledgeable and in the end many of us raised embarrassing questions and wound up organizing the people. We were expected to "renew" quietly, with no fuss.

In Castle Square, with a big push from residents led by Bill and Katherine Croke, we worked hard to see to it that residents would get first priority for moving into the new housing, and also that existing agencies such as the settlement houses got a piece of the relocation action. We saw relocation as an opportunity to provide a full range of services to people who were frequently ignored and whose many housing problems were closely related to many other interlocking factors, such as income, education, and family stability. Housing provided a convergence point for a number of issues.

The transition from servicing people to organizing people, as a method for insisting on and assuring human/individual rights, proved successful when Castle Square residents questioned the role of United South End Settlements (USES). Could USES serve both the needs of its clients and the interests of its contractor, the Boston Redevelopment Authority? These issues gained momentum as people demanded control over the services in their neighborhood. Residents began to acquire the political skills to change the way they were being served.

Community Assembly for a United South End (CAUSE) was in many ways the turning point from the dominance of the service-oriented agency. At this time, it was necessary for an agency to function as an organizing catalyst, and ultimately as an action-oriented group united in common interests. It was the failure of USES to provide strong, active leadership that created CAUSE: a much more direct step toward informed community control.

The reasoning behind CAUSE was that there were many cities and towns with a much smaller population than the South End's 29,000 residents that had independent governments and a certain amount of political power. "What is needed in the larger urban areas of this country," stated a proposal explaining CAUSE, "is the division of cities into neighborhood governments which would make the decisions affecting their own area. This would also provide the means for true representation in matters which affect the entire city."

CAUSE was a "vehicle for self-control and self-expression" and would "involve the residents of the community in the decision-making process in matters which affect that community. "A stated purpose of CAUSE was to provide one organization that would not become homeowner-dominated, a characteristic common to other South End organizations: the South End Businessman's Association, the South End Federation of Citizens Corporation, the Citizens' Urban Renewal Committee, and the sixteen neighborhood organizations. The by-laws specified that the membership consist of 60 percent tenants.

In the eyes of members of the Assembly the most critical issue for the South End's low income tenants was whether they would be permanently displaced in favor of a "one-class community." The Boston Redevelopment Authority proposed to bring in the new middle and upper income residents and to supply standard housing at affordable prices for all those people who were displaced, yet desired to remain in the South End. CAUSE stated that the BRA plan for the South End promoted physical renewal instead of rebuilding the existing community. "Residents justifiably feel as though they are being shuffled about to accommodate the monetary interests of a few," particularly Black residents, who had been repeatedly forced to pull up their roots and "start all over again." BRA really stands for "Blacks Run Again." remarked the CAUSE proposal.

CAUSE expressed a strong stand on the displacement problem, calling for a halt to all BRA relocation, demolition and land acquisition. Also, CAUSE leaders attested to the need for relocation housing to be renovated before people were forced to move; they also supported the re-evaluation and rewriting of the plan to include the direct input of community members, especially tenants, and the involvement of residents in the plan via jobs associated with renewal. Along with this explicit challenge to the BRA, CAUSE intended to commence a block by block, building by building, organizing effort to inform tenants about the possible impact of the BRA on their lives and to provide a vehicle for people to express their views.

The CAUSE organizing plan was based on a multiplier effect idea; if tenants felt the need for a tenants organization, given the information CAUSE could supply, the CAUSE organizer would take on the role of a technician, providing resources otherwise unavailable to the group. As more tenant groups were formed, CAUSE continued to broaden its base, rotating the roles of leadership and sharing whatever powers it had with as many residents as possible.

Within a few months of its initiation CAUSE had generated a number of subcommittees to study such key issues as education and jobs, but housing soon took permanent dominance. A report by the housing committee of CAUSE stated adamantly that:

> Housing should be the main thrust of CAUSE at this juncture. Obviously, we must deal with other problems that cause the resulting housing patterns such as unemployment, poor education and the like. However, if we do not attack housing first and foremost there will be no community left here to improve, we shall all have been moved out into another ghetto and will have to start all over again.

CAUSE began to actively support and be supported in turn by a number of tenant organizations in the South End. Two of these groups—the Emergency Tenants Council and the South End Tenants Council—are good examples of the kind of tenant organizations that formed during the period when the struggle for control of the land was beginning to take clear form. As we shall see later in Chapter Eighteen, both groups have evolved over time toward becoming neighborhood development institutions.

The Puerto Rican Community began to develop in Boston during the mid-1950's. In the late 1950's, as part of the outreach work of the USES-South End House, we became involved with a number of Puerto Rican people, dealing with social, economic, recreation, and employment needs. However, the migration from Puerto Rico began to increase significantly by the mid-1960's. The Puerto Rican people coming to Boston realized, similarly to the Black community, that if they were going to protect themselves, maintain their own cultural identity, and develop their own resources, they were going to have to live in the same area. At the time that the Puerto Rican community began to increase significantly in the area between Tremont Street and Washington Street, primarily Parcel 19, Boston real estate developers and bankers began to develop their own plans, through the BRA, for the urban removal of the Puerto Rican community.

Ironically, it has been the fight over housing which has caused the Puerto Rican community to come together as an important cultural and political influence in Boston. With the support of the Episcopal Church and Rev. William Dwyer and community organizer Carmelo Iglesias, the Emergency Tenants Council (ETC) began to organize tenants on Waltham and Pembroke Streets against the proposed demolition plans of the BRA, and for better housing services from the landlords who owned the buildings. Campaigners wearing badges that said, "No nos modaremos de la Parcel 19" ("We shall not be moved from Parcel 19"), went from door to door to get tenants to fight for their rights.

As the struggle with the BRA intensified, ETC through its discussions with the Lower Roxbury Community Corporation (LRCC) realized that the Puerto Rican community had to take control of and develop its own housing. ETC developed a plan for redeveloping Parcel 19 which included mixed income housing, on-site relocation and a public plaza recalling the outdoor gathering spaces of Puerto Rico. Eventually, with the full support of CAUSE, and of Puerto Rican groups from New York and Chicago, the BRA was forced to name ETC as the developer of Parcel 19.

Not far from Parcel 19, the South End Tenants Council (SETC) was being formed to organize the tenants on Rutland Street and W. Newton St. In this area, one slumlord owned over 60 buildings, and held second mortgages on a good many more. SETC chose this landlord as the focus of its organizing.

One of the first things it did was to take several busloads of tenants and supporters out to another landlord's house in the suburbs. The next step was to demonstrate at the Bar Mitzvah of that landlord's son. The Council had found out that the Parcel 19 landlord came from a very religious Jewish family and held the position of Cantor in a local synagogue. A rabbi in the Council suggested that the tenants bring their case to the Rabbinical Court. The Rabbinical Court, we found out, had the power to excommunicate a Jewish person if that person did not try to make peace with those who were in conflict with him or her.

Ted Parish, one of the founders of SETC recalls,

The Rabbinical Court caused Mindick (the landlord) to come and sit down with us. We had already tried individually as a tenants organization to sit down with Mindick to try to work out the differences between ourselves, and he gave lip service to things and essentially said that everything was the tenants' fault. So we felt we were getting nowhere.

The Rabbinical Court helped both parties to commit to paper what we felt was a workable agreement—that was the landlord/tenant lease and grievance procedure, and they helped set up the mechanism that would work to arbitrate any disputes that came out as we tried to implement the agreement we had drawn up. Later on in addition to those kinds of things, I think the Court used their good office to help make contact with people in Washington when it was pretty clear that Mindick was not living up to his end of the agreement, and we went on rent strike. They helped by enforcing the agreement which gave the tenants' council a fairly good chunk of money that we were able to use to buy up the buildings.

SETC, similar to ETC, soon found its role in tenant organizing expanding into housing development. SETC decided that one of the best ways to keep the South End in the hands of the people who lived there was to develop as many houses and housing complexes as possible, all over the South End. They executed plans to develop 400 housing units. Both ETC and SETC began by organizing people who were living in buildings owned by people who were not providing services. Challenging the owners led to their becoming the developers of housing for low-income folks in the South End.

The second organizing effort of the CAUSE group was with tenants on Columbus Avenue. The process used to develop CATA (Columbus Avenue Tenants Association) was a very good example of how agencies and people can come together. By working directly with the tenants we kept people from fleeing the threats of the USES relocation program. The effort resulted in a relationship between those tenants, MIT, and the New Urban League. CATA picketed various sites and finally obtained the option to rehab 100 units under the Federal 236 Program. Tenants selected the management and construction companies and obtained almost $200,000 in tax shelters from the depreciated housing they sold.

Thus far, we have focused on the South End of Boston because I am most familiar with that part of the city. During the same years that the South End was coming of age in housing, moving from the services, to organizing, to institution building, there were some other events that had an impact on housing in the South End and across the city. Some of these events were internal to other communities—mainly Roxbury, North Dorchester, and Washington Park—while others were initiated by federal policy or city programs. All of these events were indicative of the clash between class and cash which is inherent in our American system and shows up most blatantly in people's struggle to get shelter.

Boston Urban Renewal Plan (BURP)

The urban renewal plan for Washington Park, in spite of articulate questions raised by activist groups during the early days of the program, contained no provisions for low-income housing. Dennis Blackett, Director of Housing Innovations, recalls participating in a survey about the relocation required for renewal of the Washington Park section of Roxbury:

> We surveyed the folks in Washington Park who were about to be relocated to see if they knew they were going to be relocated and to see if they knew what was happening. We found out they didn't know a thing. The people who were poorest and were going to be hurt the most knew the least...
>
> ...I have in my mind an image of going down Bower Street and going into a house where on the first floor there was a family about two months up from Mississippi in a two or three bedroom apartment with about ten people, and a whole lot of trouble, and never heard of urban renewal, didn't know that the apartment was going to go zap, and paying some incredible amount in oil for the winter for three or four stoves. And up on the second floor was an old Boston family where the dude was a hunter and a fisherman and he had trophies hanging up on his walls and he had an immaculate apartment—it was just beautiful—and he said, "Oh yeah, we know that, and we're planning to buy a house here and we're going to do this and we're going to do that." The contrast was just out of sight.

In spite of the general failure to alter the Washington Park renewal program in the first planning stages, the issue was not closed because a few advocates continued to raise questions about the scarcity of housing in a low-income price range. As the BRA's first big push in the Park was coming to an end toward the beginning of 1967, the nation's lone Black U.S. Senator, Edward Brooke, issued statements highly critical of the operation of the Department of Housing and Urban Development (HUD), particularly the failure of the Federal Housing Authority to commit money for mortgages to inner city neighborhoods.

One response to the criticism leveled at the Department was the designation of Boston as a test site for a massive FHA-financed housing rehabilitation program. As part of the overall Boston urban renewal program, HUD contracted to rehabilitate about 2,000 units of low-income housing, most of which were located in the Grove Hall section of Roxbury. The units were to be used primarily for residents who would be displaced in the process of the redevelopment of their neighborhoods.

Early in 1967 HUD began behind-the-scenes negotiations with twelve of Boston's large-scale developers to rehab buildings at a federally-provided mortgage ceiling. Eli Goldston, president of Boston Gas Company, was made aware of the availability of FHA money for the rehab project and immediately saw the potential for multiple benefits to his business.

The Urban Observatory history of the project relates:

> The president of the gas utility, who had played an important role in the conceptualizing and negotiating of the project, had two major private objectives: to increase the consumption of his product and to reap a positive public relations image in the larger community.[1]

To further these objectives he formed a limited partnership with the largest of the developers approached by the Federal Housing Authority and offered to provide some of the capital necessary to start the project. "In return," states the Observatory report, "he was able to specify the use of gas for all appliances in the rehabilitated units. The new business would gain $450,000 a year in income plus a tax benefit in real estate depreciation."[2]

All of these machinations were well out of public view in order, rationalized HUD, to avoid speculation at the news of available federal dollars. But the secrecy began to have troublesome ramificaitons in Washington Park and the other communities where BURP operated. For one thing, no Black developers or workers were invited to participate. Also, the ceiling per unit costs meant that the buildings which most needed repairs were bypassed as too expensive. But the treatment of the people involved raised the most public ire. The behavior toward the tenants and toward workers was equally outrageous.

The great rush to complete the project during the winter of 1967 allowed the developers to take a great liberty, particularly with relocating tenants on Humboldt Ave. whose units were to be renovated. In many cases tenants were not even informed of the program; they were forced out by ruthless tactics, such as shutting off the water during one of the coldest days of the year. With inches of ice from burst pipes covering the floors, tenants had to evacuate apartments with no idea where to look for other housing. Heat was also shut off as a way to "encourage" tenants to leave. Even those tenants who learned about the rehabilitation project were not informed of their rights to move back into the buildings after completion. No effort was made to contact residents systematically through the many available community agencies. The BRA was unable to coordinate relocation services on such short notice during the winter holiday season, and the large number of low income tenants who needed to be placed in subsidized units complicated the process. As a result, the tenants were shunted aside in the interests of making money on the project.

The treatment of the residents working on the project was equally blatant. After some pressure to comply with federal regulations specifying the hiring of residents for such projects, the developers hired over 100 local men recruited by various community agencies to work as construction laborers. It was only a matter of weeks before community agencies began receiving complaints that these men were being laid off, a few at a time, and being replaced, it was discovered, by inexperienced whites, many of them Canadians. Suddenly, on November 8, 1967, 64 men were fired at once with no explanation. The rest of the story is the history of the United Community Construction Workers (UCCW) recorded in Chapter 8.

The reaction of the governmental and private institutions, involved in the BURP program, to the community criticisms, was varied. The president of Boston Gas issued statements committing financial resources to serving the Black community; several of the developers, including Maurice Simon and Sidney Insoft, who were the object of an anti-discrimination suit instituted through Mass. Comm. Against Discrimination, by Black workers, agreed to institute training for 300 Black workers through United Community Construction Workers (UCCW); FHA added Black developers to its list of BURP contractors, providing them with bonding and construction financing. In January, 1968, HUD released the extra funds required by the BRA to undertake the adequate relocation program, and on February 2, 1968, the five BURP developers deferred all relocation efforts to the BRA and agreed to notify affected tenants of the BRA service.

Another group that crystaized around the BURP issue was a tenants organization known as TAB (Tenants Assocaiton of Boston) which solidified in the early days of January, 1968. When TAB was formally incorporated, it had developed a model lease based on the lease developed by the Roxbury Multi-Service Center and Hubie Jones, which was used for the negotiations between the BURP landlords and their new tenants. The developers resisted an agreement until January, when they signed an agreement with TAB to use such a model lease. TAB played a continuing role in the aftermath of the BURP experience, particularly when some of the rehab work done in the BURP buildings (rehabbed with $2.4 million of Federal money) was found to be so faulty that many of the buildings needed repairs within a year. TAB led tenants in rent withholding and, along with UCCW, asked Urban Planning Aid to document the poor quality of the rehabilitations, including the consistent failure to meet contract specifications.

Alajo Adegballoh (nee Leroy Boston) fondly recalls TAB as a,

> ...little old neighborhood group, you know; people who had never done anything, people having problems with their gas, their hallways not being clean. When I say little people, they weren't no community organizers or nothing. We used to get out and do our leafletting. We had a pattern. If we found a house that had a problem, we'd leaflet for two nights and the third night we'd go back, a sister and a brother, and the sister would talk

and get the door open and then we'd go in and talk with the person. We'd pick a person in the house...and we say "could we have a meeting in your house?" and she'd say "yeah" and we'd sit around and talk and the people themselves would talk. They didn't need too much help. That's where I really began to develop basic organizing skills. I recognized what you got to do to get people involved. You got to tell people, then you got to have some things convenient for them, then you got to get out of their way.

The BURP experience had impact far beyond Washington Park and its other specific sites, particularly in the institutionalization of Black developers and Black workers on projects in predominantly Black communities, as well as justifying the birth of the Boston Housing Court. The BURP story demonstrates that if a vacuum exists in some areas of advocacy or around particular issues, leadership will form and fill the void. There were no advocates for low-income tenants at that time in Washington Park, but when that overlooked group was seriously threatened by those who thought they could exploit that void, a new set of spokespeople appeared.

The largely home-owning group at Freedom House in Roxbury and similar groups who had worked so closely with the BRA in the early stages of the urban renewal program no longer spoke for the constituency. As in the South End, tenants and workers began to protect their interests themselves. Residents rejected the procedures and standards accepted by the local developers and the federal officials and rather than capitulate, they formed new institutions to meet new needs. UCCW and TAB in particular have served as prototypes for citizen involvement across the nation.

During this period, then, the community went through a series of experiences which revealed the deliberate plans of the BRA to displace people of color from the city, and the incredibly vicious actions that landlords would take against tenants, when profit was involved. It became clear to us at this time that federal housing programs actually encouraged and supported some of this irresponsible profitseeking. The answer in each case was to take action.

CAUSE was a model, before its time, for representative community planning and decision-making. Tenant groups began to assert their rights and, as we shall see in Chapter 10, soon went much further in their insistence that the people participate in the physical development of their own comnunities.

Chapter 6

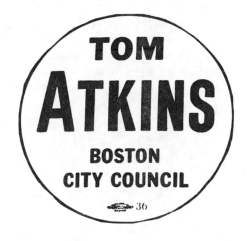

TOM
ATKINS
BOSTON
CITY COUNCIL
36

POLITICS: Why Vote?

Whether in education, employment or housing, the Black community became increasingly aware that no appreciable changes could be made without gaining political power in the city and the state. The development of Black political power meant first of all breaking our dependence on the Democratic party ward machine

As we saw in Chapter 2, Shag and Balcolm Taylor were pretty much in charge of electoral politics in the Black community. The first challenge to the Taylors' control over the political process in the Black community was made by Royal Bolling, Sr. The Taylors' grip started to slip in the late 1950's due to the physical deterioration of Lower Roxbury on the one hand, and due to the increased growth of the Black population in the Franklin Park area, Ward 12. Royal ran for state representative in 1960. Until that time, no Black person had run for office without the backing of the Taylors. But this all changed with the growth of the Black population in Franklin Park. Royal ignored the Taylors and the Democratic ward machine as well; he ran his own campaign and won.

In 1963, John O'Bryant, Reginald Eaves, Ed Texeira and

myself realized that if we were to represent the real needs of the Black community, we had to challenge the Taylors' approach to Black politics. We formed the New Breed. This was our first attempt to focus the Black community on the political process. We wanted people to start looking for change in the system, not for more payoffs and power brokering. We wanted Black people to use the political process to get their needs met.

At the city level, we tried to get people elected to the school committee and the city council. Only one Black person had ever been elected to the city council, and he had to go to court before he could be seated. However, that was back in the 1940's, in the old council, where representatives were all elected by districts. Not surprisingly, shortly after Lawrence Banks was seated, the district system of representation was changed to an at-large city wide election system. Changing to an at-large election process was similar to the way the Black district on Beacon Hill was gerrymandered at the turn of the century to include a majority of ethnic whites in the district and thereby make it impossible for the Black community to elect its own representatives. In an at-large system for the whole city, the Black vote is eclipsed all the more by the white majority.

In 1959, Ruth Batson ran for the School Committee and lost. As we saw earlier, I was a candidate in the 1961, 1963 and 1965 school committee elections and lost each time. Black candidates ran for the city council in 1959 and 1963 and lost. Though we were able to get solid support from the Black community, we were not able to gain representation through the at-large electoral process. The at-large system always favors the largest voting blocks, predominantly the Irish, who were consistently able to elect their candidates, who in turn controlled the schools and the city services available to the Black community.

Although we lost these campaigns, they were nonetheless successful as forums in which to press for the needs of the Black community, and as a way of bringing folks together. When Noel Day, head of the community program run by St. Mark's Church in Roxbury, ran against John McCormack, who was Speaker of the House at the time, McCormack didn't even bother to run a campaign—he won by a landslide. Though Noel never had a chance, he set up action offices throughout the community and pushed hard to let people know the effects that urban renewal was having on the community. After the election, some of these offices stayed in action and became the Boston Action Group (BAG) which was responsible for the Wonder Bread boycotts described in Chapter Four.

At the state level, we were somewhat more successful because of the district election of state representatives. Lincoln Pope was elected in 1958, and Royal Bolling, Sr.was elected in 1960. Since that time there have been a number of Black representatives including the Alfred brothers, Franklin Holgate, Rev. Michael Haynes and George Johnson.

Another success for the Black community in the 1960's was the election of Edward Brooke as the first Black U.S. Senator since the Reconstruction era. In the early 1960's., Brooke realized that the Democratic Party had never run a Black candidate for a statewide position and decided that the Republican party was the only possible way to get elected to a statewide or national office. In 1962 and 1964, Brooke won the Republican party's nomination for Attorney General and won the elections. In 1966 the Senate seat became open as Senator L. Saltonstall, a former Massachusetts governor, stepped down. Brooke, an astute party man, was able to come out on top of the scramble for the party nomination, and ran against another former governor, Endicott Peabody. Though Black folks constituted only 2.2% of the Massachusetts population, Brooke won by a half million votes. Byron Rushing, director of the Afro-American History Museum describes Brooke's election,

> If Black people had said that they didn't like Brooke, he never would have gotten elected. White people were electing him because it was a big thing for them to elect a Black man, a Negro Senator. The liberals and liberal Democrats switched over to vote for Brooke, a Republican, because he was Black.

The Black and white liberal alliance was the key. As a senator, Brooke pressed civil rights issues, blocked reactionary appointments on the Supreme Court, and protected low-income tenants. However, he never worked at providing leadership and organization in the Black community. Despite the fact that a lot of people crossed over to vote for him, he never helped develop a base within the Black community. Although he was more attached to the Republican party than to his community, in later years, he was part of the movement to get rid of Nixon, and, moreover, the Black community rallied to his support when he was under attack from the reactionary press and lost his reelection bid in 1979.

Throughout the 1960's, whether in city, state or national elections, there were no effective Black electoral organizations. All organizing took place on a candidate by candidate basis. If a candidate lost, their organization, if they had one, usually went down with them. However, even though there were no formal organizations, we had a lot of people who had developed political organizing skills. These campaigns and the skills we developed at the beginning of the 1960's formed the basis for the political institution building in the late 1960's and early 1970's.

Although most Black candidates were Democrats, because the Democrats had a monopoly in the state, Black candidates did not have any leverage within the party. Party affiliation was of limited importance as evidenced by the massive switch over vote to elect Black candidates when they were Republicans, as in the cases of Brooke and of George Johnson in 1969. In fact, experience in the legislature showed that on issues of concern to the Black community, you couldn't tell the difference between Republicans and Democrats because of their joining together on issues which affected the Black community adversely.

The Black community raised its voice and won a city council seat and a U.S. Senate seat. However, we were not able to build an on-going Black political organization to hold candidates accountable to the community, and to use each electoral campaign to further the community's development. In this organizing stage, however, we were able to break out of the docility of the service stage, and force people to recognize the needs of Black people—needs determined by Black people.

In 1967, Tom Atkins, then serving as the Executive Director of the Boston branch of the NAACP, ran for city council at the height of the Civil Rights Movement. As Royal Bolling, Sr. observed, "The timing was right. Mr. Atkins had the Black community rallying around his campaign. He also had white supporters in the outlying wards of Boston." In his campaign, Atkins stressed city-wide issues trying to pull together the Black community, white liberals and other communities and constituencies which were not being represented. Atkins was elected with 71,482 votes. He was the first and only Black person to this day to be elected to the at-large City Council.

Atkins did a good job on the Council. He increasingly gained support from around the city for his efforts. For instance, Paul Parks recalls,

> I remember in West Roxbury there was a question about some trucks going to the dump, and there had been some problems about that. And Tom took a position in favor of the citizens, and went out and took part in that issue, which was a very hot issue in West Roxbury at that time. And he got a fairly decent vote out of West Roxbury for this effort.

Atkins won two terms as Councilor and in 1971 he ran for Mayor. There was a significant effort throughout the community to launch this campaign, but Atkins could not win. The run-off that year was between Kevin White and Louise Day Hicks. Solid Black support was decisive in defeating Mrs. Hicks.

In all, there was a considerable amount of electoral activity in the Black community during the early part of the organizing stage. It had been clear for a long time that the geo-political structure of elections made it extremely difficult to get Black people elected. Still, we did see the election of the first Black U.S. Senator since the Reconstruction era. For two terms we had the most effective representation possible from Tom Atkins.

Atkins won in large part via the skills the community developed in other campaigns for other candidates. At the New Urban League we received national funds for voter registration and voter education, a project headed by Bob Phillips. We developed a very good approach to organizing people in public housing through church groups and community-based housing, such as Marksdale Garden and St. Mark's Church. This resulted in a good team for Atkins' campaign, a team so effective that he came in second in the city in 1969.

The importance of the Black vote was finally given city-wide recognition with the defeat of Mrs. Hicks. A sense of power had developed in the Black community but unfortunately, no group stepped in at this time to use this power as a delivery machanism, to hold the city accountable. The community bargained away its political power to the Mayor and became sidetracked in its effort to get control of city services.

Chapter 7

COMMUNITY CONTROLLED EDUCATION

In the second half of the sixties, the Black community was frustrated by its inability to change the public schools through School Committee elections. Community residents developed a number of innovative approaches to gain control over the educational system including: community controlled busing, renaming schools in the Black community after well-known Black people, fighting to increase the number of Black principals hired, and starting community controlled private schools.

Community Controlled Busing: METCO

By 1966, the parent leaders of the Exodus program had decided to keep the buses rolling as a serious option, not just a temporary dramatization of needs, to get children out of crowded, deficient segregated schools and into classrooms elsewhere in the city system. Zealous fundraising efforts of every imaginable description were launched to keep the program alive efforts which continued for five to six years.

Exodus was soon joined by another "busing" program, but this one with a suburban rather than a Boston orientation. The Metropolitan Council for Educational Opportunity (METCO)

was in many ways an outgrowth of that urban/suburban, Black/
white coalition struck up during the lobbying for the Racial
Imbalance Law. METCO evolved from an offer made in
November of 1964 by the Brookline Civil Rights Committee to
the Boston School Committee to accept some Black children
into Brookline public schools.

After the discouraging 1965 School Committee elections, it
became clear to Black and suburban community leaders that the
Boston School Committee was not going to deal with the segregated school system. The Massachusetts Federation of Fair
Housing and Equal Rights, a collection of suburban human
rights committees that had been instrumental in getting the
Racial Imbalance Law passed, began organizing a voluntary
program to bus Black children from the city out to the suburban
schools.

The METCO bill was signed into law after a year of negotiations and intense lobbying, making it possible for children to
attend schools in cities and towns other than their place of
residence. This move effectively extended the Racial Imbalance
Law beyond the boundaries of any one school system. Funding
for the program came from the State, and from the U.S. Office
of Education under Title III (Experimental Programs).

The diversity of the METCO program has been and continues to be received with mixed feelings. METCO relied upon
the suburban school systems rather than forcing the Boston
School system to do the job it was supposed to do. METCO
involved one-way travel, and places the burden of the solution
on Black parents and children, while servicing only a few
hundred children. In its first year, METCO placed 220 children
in seven schools, and by 1967, 425 children were attending 16
suburban schools.

At the Massachusetts Advisory Commission to the United
States Commission on Civil Rights hearings in 1966, Ruth
Batson was asked if she thought METCO was the answer
to Boston's racial imbalance problems. "No, I don't," was her
answer. "I think racial imbalance is so deeply rooted that the
taking of 220 children will certainly not do anything for the
large number of children left in the Roxbury area and I for one,
am very concerned with what is happening with the children

who are still in the community."[1]

METCO harbored the danger of distracting energy and attention from the larger and deeper solutions needed for Boston's problems; it also explicitly reinforced a sense that only white schools could be "quality." The Legislature would never have appropriated $100,000 to parents to improve the neglected schools serving Boston's poor—Black and white. Neither the U.S. Office of Education nor the foundations would have granted funds for a program that was not administered by a white suburban school system. The psychological stress involved for Black children was also enormous and uncounted.

The fear that METCO and Exodus would not get to the root of the racist system in Boston was soon borne out. The School Committee voted "in favor" of the METCO program, but approval was contingent on one condition: "Provided that this program shall not require the expenditure of funds by the City of Boston." METCO was actually saving the city money, as much as $500 per child, but Boston paid nothing to the suburban systems which took in Boston students.

METCO found funds to pay other schools to educate the children that Boston was obligated to provide for and which, in fact, Boston taxpayers were already paying for. And, in an accounting/bookkeeping practice that almost defies belief, the City counted the METCO children as part of its "compliance" plan for the State's Racial Imbalance Law.

Community Control of the Public Schools

The Exodus and METCO experiences contributed to the gradual thrust towards community controlled education. In the next two years parents and community groups organized, in rapid succession, to assault every front blocking community control of the schools.

Toye Brown Lewis, Education Director for the New Urban League of Boston, explained:

> The change from integration to control shows a change in tactics rather than a change in goals. The goal of our community has always been one of quality education But three to five years ago, it seemed that the strategy to achieve the goal had to be integration.

We cannot leave our so-called racially imbalanced schools which are predominantly Black, in the hands of predominantly white staff because even with the Civil Rights Act and all the Federal aid to education, we have lost twelve years of kids.[2]

The urgency created by this waste of our children was one of the factors that prompted Boston's New Urban League in 1967 to begin a concentrated effort at parent education programs and to provide "direct service" to parents and children, including accompanying them to schools and helping to resolve confrontations with principals and counselors. The League also put a great deal of emphasis on organizing parents to "control" the schools their children attended. In the final month of 1967, Operation Exodus and the League joined forces to call an educational conference for all the agencies and groups involved in education in the Black community. The response was excellent, 100 representatives attended, and a strategy was mapped out to apply pressure for changes in the educational opportunities available to Black children. The first pressure point was the new school construction designated for Humboldt Avenue in Roxbury, ultimately to be known as the William Monroe Trotter School.

In the 1966 Civil Rights Hearing staff report, the Humboldt Avenue school was optimistically viewed as a positive experimental asset to the community. It was intended to improve the racial balance situation by being a "magnet" school, and provide a laboratory for progressive elementary education. Unfortunately, the School Committee insensitively named the school for the father of School Committeeman Joseph Lee, one of the most persistent, outspoken and illogical opponents of integration.

At a public School Committee meeting, the Community Education Council (CEC) presented a petition and engaged in lengthy argument to name the new school after the famous Black Bostonian William Monroe Trotter. The next day a community dedication ceremony was held to proclaim the school duly named for the Black hero. We nailed our own name signs over the doors of the school, and a crowd gathered on the sidewalk to join in the christening.

Eventually, the School Committee grudgingly voted to support the community's chosen name. With that psychological victory, parents turned to the issues of power and control. The Boardman parents, who had long been well organized, informed the School Committee that the Trotter School, which was in their area, should be turned over to them and the model subsystem program operative in the Boardman should be instituted in the new school. With fierce determination, the Boardman parents fought off all other comers, their children were admitted to the Trotter, and the old Boardman school was closed down.

Further conflict developed over which other children would be enrolled in the school, and the choice of principal. The Boardman parents formed an active group with the white parents whose children were allowed to enroll. Some of the same white parents who had asked the New Urban League for help in setting up parent education courses in the suburbs brought their children into the Trotter School.

The Trotter is currently considered a working model of a "magnet" school which promotes voluntary integration. Unfortunately, the Black community learned that "magnet" schools still cost them more than their fair share, since so many places are reserved for white children bused in from outside the neighborhood. Here, in the shiny new schools, the Racial Imbalance Law is enforced. But in the decrepit schools to which Black children are traditionally relegated, the Racial Imbalance Law is never fulfilled. The irony, of course, is that to be racially "balanced, "the new school had to exclude many, many children from the immediate community. They walk or ride past the Trotter in which almost half the seats were reserved for white youngsters. Considering the long standing failure of the schools to offer opportunities for Black children elsewhere, it is not easy to settle for having one of the few decent schools in the Black community only partially accessible to Black children.

The issue implicit in the Trotter School case are among the most complicated and difficult for people to comprehend, much less approach. The catch phrases and scare words, "separatism," "reverse racism," quickly arise when Black parents express their frustration at being expected to welcome whites into the few decent schools within reach of Black children. It is a fact that

Black children have long been given disgracefully deficient educational opportunity. To equalize the damage already done to Black children, extraordinary steps—compensation, if you like—need to be taken. It is no wonder that Black parents look askance at sharing scarce new facilities and programs with white children who have access to such opportunities elsewhere, when Black children are incessantly "opportunity deprived" to make room for them.

Similar conflicts arise over rehabilitated housing which attracts middle class whites to promote a supposed economic integration. In effect, lower-income Black families who have no other options are pushed out. This conflict will not soon be resolved unless enough pressure is brought to bear on centers of power and influence, such as the Boston School Committee, to carry out the plans which they have long since been instructed to implement.

Until the resources are adequately distributed and released to the people, with concentrated effort where needed to rectify past deficiencies, the bitter competition will continue with all its accompanying misunderstanding and insecurity—the breeding ground for racial conflict.

The Gibson School, which had also become a center of controversy, was another story. The efforts to get a Black principal met such resistance from the incumbent superintendent that the concerned parents of the Gibson School felt compelled to stage a sit-in. This action closed the school for two months, and prompted parents to initiate the Gibson Liberation School. Several of the teachers joined the strike with the children in their classes, and walked out with them in a rare gesture of solidarity. They were fired and went to teach in the Liberation School at Hawthorne House, an abandoned parochial school.

Parents were protesting the lack of opportunity to participate in the federally funded Title I and III programs at the Gibson School, the lack of curricula relevant to Black children, and the lack of participation in the principal's selection. The principal replied, "I am not paid by the community, I am paid by the City of Boston and will not resign."[3]

The difficulties of sustaining such "rebellious" actions were monumental. Many parents were uneasy about boycott action, and organizers found them unwilling to join in overt protest activities. They felt the Liberation School lacked security (in terms of acceptable academic credentials) for their children and questioned sharply the educational quality possible in an emergency operation. To be effective, such action would have to be sustained over at least a two year period. In two years, most children had moved on to high school, and all momentum was lost.

The New Urban League, which was accused of disrupting the school (mainly because one of its staff members headed the Concerned Parents' group), simply could not provide the magnitude of constant support required to gain full control of the school. Other community agencies could not or would not support this effort. The level of sacrifice was too high a price for people to pay. In early 1969, a League staff member, reviewing the situation, noted the quiet demise of the Community Education Council and later of the Association of Afro-American Educators. She wrote, "Frankly, I don't know where we go from here."

The community people who had become involved in tutoring, fighting for the Racial Imbalance Law, and the School Committee elections came to know the problems of the schools first hand and became expertly qualified to design an alternative and then to seek other experts from outside the community (especially in the universities) who could provide services to the experimental efforts. Most important, parents who once thought something was wrong with their children had the opportunity to investigate the school system and consider other approaches.

"Roxbury has a great need for a showcase school that can show parents and show the public schools what a really good school is all about," said one involved woman, "for as long as the Boston Public Schools fail Negro children so badly, it is up to the community to provide them with some alternatives."

Community Schools

The New School for Children, conceived by the group of parents involved in an uproar over Jonathan Kozol's firing at the Gibson School and parents from the Mackey and Hurley Schools, ushered in a new stage: the development of indigenous community schools.[4]

For the first time, on the basis of their accumulated experience, their outrage and their growing confidence, parents were organizing on a whole new level, not just for "sporadic demonstrations," but for the very basis of power which the School Committee had for so long blatantly misused. Slowly the spotlight of blame was being swung off the children and refocused where it belonged: on the dehumanizing methods, approach and environment of the public schools.

The New School for Children opened in September, 1966, enrolling fifty children in grades kindergarten through six. Without significant outside funding, the New School had to charge $250 tuition. As a result a large number of students were from outside Roxbury, and generally from families with higher incomes, although a limited number of scholarships were made available. The curriculum was based on the interests and experiences of the children, and community folks were involved in the school as teacher assistants. Most of all,the school operated in such a way as to show the parents of Roxbury that they could provide quality education for their children through their own resources.

The sense of frustration over community control took different forms for different people. A group of parents who had taken their children out of the Gibson and started the Liberation School at Hawthorne House joined with some of the veteran leaders from the 1963-1964 Stay Out days, including Jim Breeden and Harvey Cox, and opened Highland Park Free School. This school, like the New School for Children and the Roxbury Community School, was another attempt to replace the dysfunctional existing system with new institutions wholly conceived, operated and directed by the community.

The Highland Park Free School began in September 1968, in the Highland Park area of Roxbury. Luther Seabrook, the first Black Director of the School, describes it this way:

First, and foremost, an urban school. The community

dominates its decision-making process; the community has selected the staff; the community helps to support the cost of the school; the community provides much of the staff and the focus for much of the curriculum; the community's *total educational needs* are served by the school; the school is concerned with, and involved in, all the social, physical, political, and economic factors which contribute to the community's educational health. Secondly, it is an experimental urban school, with as profound a commitment to seeking new solutions to urban education problems through constant experiment and innovation as to the concept of a community school.

The school was for preschool and primary school age children who lived in the Highland Park area. One indication of its success compared to other "free schools" was that of its 117 students in the first year, 96 of those students came from families with incomes of less than $1000. The parents of the children decided to make the school non-graded, and tuition-free. The curriculum was designed to deal with problems brought to the school by Black youngsters living in a white society, as well as the problems brought to the school by white youngsters living in a white society. The curriculum was to help children become alert, capable thinkers who could make positive contributions toward the betterment of humankind. In addition to eight certified teachers, there were "community teachers." The community teacher was to bring the vast resource of urban sociology to the classroom. Every classroom had one community teacher who worked not only in the classroom but also with parents and other community groups to foster the maximum feasible community participation in the school's life, and, in turn, to maximize the school's participation in the community's life.

Today, the New School for Children and Highland Park Free School are closed, and the Roxbury Community School, another alternative school, is in financial trouble. These schools were an invaluable way for people to learn to develop and to implement educational programs. They also helped people get good credentials in teaching and in educational administration.

People have seen what excellence in education is, and that Black people can run good schools. We have learned the kinds of programs needed and what turns kids on and off. Even with the determination to improve the educational environment for all students in all schools, another difficult lesson has been that it is not easy to redirect and remotivate a messed-over kid.

But there was a basic error common to the community schools: the attempt to run them as if they were parochial, that is, as if—like nuns and priests—faculty and staff required only a small income. When the need for income was felt, money was raised outside of the community, creating a dependency relationship. The community failed to support the schools and the schools failed to support the community, as there was no built-in requirement for such mutual support. Parents and other concerned community leaders rarely behaved on the assumption that the educational value of these schools was worth paying for. To finance a community school, resources must be shared with the community so that it becomes incumbent upon the community to support the school.

The flexibility, creativity, and willingness to experiment were all present, and some good education has taken place as a result of the existence of these schools. What was missing was an establishment of priorities followed by a commitment to those priorities on the part of parents and other community leaders. Schools must determine the value of support from the community and the communtiy must determine the value of these schools to its development. Then, the community and the school must accordingly spell out roles and tasks accepting the responsibility to fulfill these expectations.

Chapter 8

UNITED COMMUNITY
CONSTRUCTION WORKER

The last few months of 1967, and the first months of 1968 are inextricably bound together by a chain of events which had been developing over the past few years. Although creative attempts at Black economic development were still being initiated by individuals and groups such as the New Urban League and Grove Hall Development Corporations, it was clear that one of the major barriers impeding the change necessary for successful development lay within the unions, particularly Boston's building trades.

Federal money was pouring into Boston at an unprecedented rate; Model Cities was designing its building program; the City of Boston was getting federal support for schools, public facilities, and the extensive rehabilitation work of the BRA program; and the federal Department of Housing and Urban Development (HUD) announced a massive rehab program in Boston to offset the scorching criticism of that Department by Massachusetts Senator Edward Brooke. Highway construction was peaking, the airport was expanding, universities were building facilities with HEW funds at an all time high rate.

All of these programs had two things in common: federal financial support which necessitated the veneer of "equal opportunity employment," and a continuance of the notoriously racist partnership of Boston building trades unions and contractors associations. In the face of these two conflicting factors, the community soon found itself deeply embroiled in conflict with both the unions and their silent partners at the local and federal enforcement levels. The eventual outcome was United Community Construction Workers (UCCW), the first Black union in modern times, and the "Boston Plan" which was the Department of Labor's method of subverting the direct action tactics of Boston's Black community.

The story of the formation of UCCW details the complexity of relationships involved at the federal, local and industry levels. The conflict that created UCCW was only part of a long struggle that was to encompass every major construction project in the Boston area that utilized federal monies or land under the control of urban renewal plans. The events in Boston shaped the reaction of the industry and the federal agencies, and affected the entire country as UCCW set a model for community militancy to get a fair share of the federal "plunder." Federal officials chose the Boston "Hometown" plan to be implemented in cities across the nation to offset such militancy an solidify "institutionalized tokenism."

The controversy that generated UCCW was plans for one of the largest housing rehabilitation packages ever undertaken in this country. The Federal Housing Authority (FHA) contracted with Insoft Realty and Teri and Penn Simon Construction companies to rehab thirteen apartment blocks containing about 2000 units of low-income housing. Ironically, many of these units were scheduled to be used for people displaced by the Boston Urban Renewal program as we saw in Chapter 5.

In order to satisfy the federal contract requirement that local workers be hired on the job, community groups including the Apprenticeship Information Center, United South End Settlements, the Neighborhood Employment Center, and the Roxbury Multiservice Center helped recruit over 100 men. Before long, however, the contractor laid off all these men. The contractor cited such reasons as lack of technical knowledge, poor work habits among the Black workers, and lack of qualifications, but he showed his hand by replacing experienced Black people with inexperienced Canadian workers who often turned out to be kin to the foremen. Ellsworth Fletcher, for instance, a carpenter with 33 years experience, was laid off and replaced by the foreman's teen-age cousin.[1]

As we saw in the last chapter, on November 8, 1968, 64 Black workers were fired all at once on the Contractor's assumption that there would be no objections from the community or federal officials. By noon the next day the angry group of men who had been laid off vowed to shut the construction site down. Although the head of Teri Construction Company agreed that some mistakes had been made in the firing, he refused to negotiate a solution.

Banding together at Freedom House, a community center in Roxbury, the workers finally hammered out a statement of their grievances and demands, including the termination of the current project supervisor and replacing him with four Black foremen; and rehiring the Black workers on the basis of seniority.

After several non-productive negotiation sessions with Simon and filing a formal complaint with the Massachusetts Commission Against Discrimination, the New Urban League mobilized a group of workers to go to the Grove Hall Boston Urban Renewal Program office with the list of demands for the rehiring and training process and confront Simon, Insoft and their lawyers. The police and it's K-9 corps were called but retreated when they saw the number of men they were up against, and we presented our demands. In response, Maurice Simon threw the papers we offered to him on the floor, at which point the group indicated that we intended to take more drastic action against the project starting right in Simon's office, right that minute. He capitulated, and signed "I agree" to each one of the demands.

By the next Monday the rehiring process was underway. Back at Freedom House that evening, the group that had been rehired first proposed an extraordinary plan for those who had to wait to get back their jobs: they offered $40 of their own pay to help support the others until their job status was settled. As a New Urban League member who lived through it all summed it up: "Today what is being built at Insoft's is more than apartments. Men are building men; men are building a community: and men are building power."[2]

The building was just beginning, however, and the men involved with Simon and Insoft knew that the pair had not changed their villainous ways as the result of one confrontation. Together they owned 1800 of the 2000 units in the Boston Urban Renewal Program plan, having apparently let them run down to the point of needing extensive rehabilitation, and then obtained the BURP contracts for the rehab work. They offered no relocation for tenants occupying the buildings before rehab began, and Insoft forced some tenants out by turning off the heat during a particularly severe winter. One very elderly lady called for assistance when her water pipes burst creating two inches of ice on her living room floor. Insoft was severely fined (with the highest fine ever imposed on a landlord) for failing to provide tenants with heat.

In 1971 a fire in one building killed a child, but neither BURP nor Insoft was cited with criminal liability for failing to provide a second fire exit required by Massachusetts law. In fact, they obtained more money to "correct" the abuses built into the rehab, and in some cases used the money to breakup apartments into smaller units. In 1972 Simon and Insoft received a grant of over $5 million to rehab the rehab.

The need for an ongoing, strong organization to protect the interests of Black workers and their community against the practices of men like Simon and Insoft was clear.[3] The men who had been laid off the Boston Urban Renewal Program project applied for a charter as United Community Construction Workers, the first Black construction workers' union since Reconstruction. These men were united in the common interest of Black workers in all crafts and in the welfare of their community rather than in one particular trade area.

United Community Construction Workers vowed to seek jobs for Black workers without sacrificing accountability to the community or quality work. They refused to participate in the building of new slums for their brothers and sisters. (When some of the workers involved in the original Simon/Insoft confrontation realized how persistent and deliberate the shoddy work of the company was, they quit the Boston Urban Renewal Program jobs.) United Community Construction Workers described its purpose as being "to establish a community based organization to represent the local minority construction worker" and to "make available a vehicle by which they can secure employment and training in the building trades."

To begin with United Community Construction Workers renewed the meaning of unionism: "1) A uniting or being united/combination, 2) An alliance for mutual benefit." United Community Construction Workers was founded on the premise that no one, i.e., white union bosses or shop stewards, can represent the Black worker as well as the Black person him or herself, and the Black union was determined to facilitate the growth of whole Black people with self knowledge, wage earning skills, and survival skills.[4]

To help Black people obtain those skills, United Community Construction Workers pressured Penn-Simon Construction Company into training 12 sheet-rockers, and negotiated training through contracts with the Boston Model Cities program and Wentworth Institute. After gaining recognition as an independent hiring hall in its own right, United Community Construction Workers has continued finding jobs for Black workers and in some cases has helped them gain entry into other unions according to their trade.

United Community Construction Workers was an inevitable link in the Chain of Change: existing white unions and training processes simply did not work for the Black man. The men of United Community Construction Workers met the challenge by forming a parallel institution designed to meet the specific needs of Black workers and to revitalize the meaning of unionism.

Barely a month after the confrontation with Simon and Insoft, HUD Secretary Robert C. Weaver arrived in Boston to dedicate the first of Boston's Urban Renewal Program units which were earmarked to be rent-supplemented housing for low-income residents. A group of community people met with Weaver to express their dissatisfaction with the way the community had been bypassed during the planning and development of the BURP project. George Morrison, of the American Friends Service Committee, who attended the meeting stated: "Nothing happened. It was so difficult to communicate with him that we had to ask at one point if he was hearing us...He said to write him a letter."[5]

At the dedication luncheon, Bryant Rollins, a New Urban League staff member and spokesperson for four other community groups, interrupted Mr. Weaver's speech to charge that the BURP program was a "robbery" which favored profit-making developers who practiced racial discrimination and provided inadequate relocation provisions. It was pointed out that the Federal Housing Authority's approval for the project had come in two weeks, while community non-profit groups and local developers were subjected to long delays on their applications.

In answer to Weaver's comment to send him a letter, after the non-productive private audience, the New Urban League published an open letter detailing the issues involved in the BURP controversy and the general practices of HUD. The BURP program, said the letter, "works as a message to other slumlords across the country that HUD repays their immoral, racist practices with enormous rehab contracts while simultaneously providing rent supplements which allow them to make a profit through Federal largesse." Within the year all the fears expressed in that open letter and more were to be realized.

Chapter 9

THE ASSASSINATION
OF MARTIN LUTHER KING:
The Black United Front

Late in December, 1967 another link in the chain was started when Stokely Carmichael visited Boston. Chuck Turner remembers that,

> Stokely came into town on December 28, he came up to the YMCA...It was 1967...before King was killed, and (he) brought back the whole concept of the United Front...SNCC was the organization that hosted that session. He came back saying that he had traveled around the world and what people had told him in various countries...was that the radicals in this country—the Black radicals in this country —were at a very critical point in the movement and that the repression that was coming down on the community because of the rebellious activities in the northern cities was going to create the kind of climate where the activists were going to be taken away and no one was going to say anything because the activists had allowed a gulf to become established between themselves and the more conservative elements of the community. He was really, in a sense, that first day, speaking to the people who were activists, saying unless the activists

across the country can build a bridge back into the more stable elements of the Black community, we were going to find ourselves wiped out in a year or two. He suggested that what activists throughout the U.S. should do is form United Fronts and appeal to the self-interests of the activists by saying it is the only way you are going to survive the crunch that you can see coming. He stayed in town for awhile and talked to the Guscotts; I don't know if he talked to the Snowdons; he talked to Rheable Edwards and O'Ray Edwards, and talked to some others, so he created a climate both among the activists and among the more conservative people of the Front.

There was a series of small meetings among some of those people who had heard about Stokely's challenge. Alajo remembers how "a few fellows, five, six or seven," would gather at the Pewter Pot Muffin House downtown on Boylston Street on Sunday mornings,

> ...talking about the dynamics of a United Front, how are we going to bring it about, the impact it would have on the community, all the things that organizers usually talk about. There's no set pattern, you just talk about people, places, and tie them to things and what kind of philosophy (we) were going to espouse, where we would meet, all kinds of things.

There were about four public meetings held between January and April 3, of 1968, after those first small gatherings, where the shape and role of the United Front was hammered out among the disparate, yet, interested parties.

1968—Year of Retribution

1968 was a year of reckoning for America. The fires and snipings of the ghetto riots during the summer of 1967 still singed the memories of white America, the Kerner Commission's report on civil disorders was stinging the national conscience, and then Stokely's predictions became a reality: Dr. Martin Luther King was assassinated. In the convulsion of guilt that came after his death in April, Boston's white community, like most of white America, "fell all over itself" to "assist" the Black Community.

The assistance came in the form of new programs, a sudden (and limited) surge of new job openings, leverage brought to bear on institutions such as the Transit Authority, and for the first time a little money without strings attached was allocated for the Route 128 "Employment Express." Meanwhile, federally sponsored programs, i.e., Model Cities, were getting underway, and active community groups redoubled their efforts to pressure for the opening of the construction industry. Individuals and organizations had new, although short lived, access to resources and opportunites leading to the establishment of some of Boston's most innovative Black ventures.

For one thing, King's death galvanized the United Front into reality. "Prior to the riots on King's assassination," remembers Archie Williams,

> (the United Front had been having meetings with various organizations. Chuck Turner was playing a key role in bringing this all together. The NAACP through Rheable Edwards was too...I didn't attend those meetings...(but) I'm sure there were people from the Roxbury Federation, because the United Front was supposed to be all the civil rights groups and all of the social service groups.

Chuck Turner feels those early meetings accomplished their purpose well. "History is a Mother," says Turner, remembering how the Front unknowingly held a meeting the evening of April 3,

> We had a meeting April 3, at the Multi-Service Center and I think it was filled to overflowing. There was an incredible cross-section...The discussion was whether they were going to accept a certain formula for the steering committee: The whole question about inclusion, exclusion, and they gave the directive to the temporary steering committee ... to go back and pool thoughts and come up with a better structure. The next evening King was assassinated. I'm not sure who called the meeting up at the Y and somebody said, "This is the time for the Front to assume its responsibilities."

"After the assassination of Martin Luther King," relates Archie Williams,

> we had disturbances.   We set up headquarters for rumor control or whatever we could do to control the police to keep things from getting out of hand, or whatever we could do to help people who had been put in jail or whatever else. We had a direct line to city hall; and while the Multi-Service Center was the center for that activity, it also became the center for the intensification of the effort to form the United Front. Therefore numerous meetings were held at the Multi-Service Center, some lasting all night. But the result was that it (the Front) was finally formed.

Although there was considerable debate about the Front's "mandate "and authority, especially since all the steering committee members did not appear at the emergency meeting April 4, the ultimate consensus was that the situation demanded swift and unified initiative. There was a dizzying surge of action, recalls Alajo,

> We moved from the "Y" over there (The Roxbury Multi-Service Center) and—I guess we felt we could meet longer hours—and we did meet, days on end, two and three days; man, people didn't go home, didn't eat, *law* was made there. People would listen, then they would transfer into rules and guidelines that would then get heard in the community. We had a direct line to city hall to keep in touch with the kind of things they were doing down there to us...*Everybody* was there. It's the one time, when everybody was there at that long table, that long room.

Not *every* agency joined; the NAACP was one that refrained after a day long board meeting to debate the issue. But it was an impressive coalition, nonetheless.

Alajo considers this time one of the most positive experiences he's ever had,

> I say the most important (experience) community-wise for me was the period around the assassination and what happened to the people...how the people...didn't

Political Platform: Boston Black United Front

The Boston Black United Front believes Black people everywhere must unite or perish. We must begin here in Boston to build a New Black Nation. We believe the first steps are: Politically organizing the community; Culturally educating the masses of Black people and providing for the protection and defense of Black people through the establishment of a Black National Defense Fund. However, the Boston Black United Front believes we cannot build a nation until we control: 1. Our Land: The cornerstone of any nation is control by the people of the land and its resources. 2. Our Politics: A nation must be able to make all decisions internally that affect the lives of its people. 3. Security: A nation must be able to protect itself from crimes against its people and invasion of its land. 4. Administration of Justice: A nation must have its own courts and codes that place human rights above property rights. 5. Schools: A nation's future is built through the processes of educating its children. 6. The Economy: A nation's businesses must be morally responsible for the welfare of its people. 7. Housing: A nation must be able to assure its citizens of healthy housing at rates they can best afford. 8. Communication: A nation must be able to positively project the images of its people and provide factual information for them.

The Boston Black United Front is now attempting to build this nation.

Are you ready to help.

Unite or Perish.

lose their head at all, they just got together. That short period of time we were the people's government; Roxbury was unto itself. We developed a police force, we developed a government, we developed elected officials, and we functioned based on that. For whatever time period that it was, I don't care if it wasn't for a month or for six months...that to me was the most significant time—contemporary time—in the community so far as basic organizing and pulling together was concerned. You have other, of course, but to me that was the most significant.

One of the first things that the Front did was to make a list of issues to be dealt with, and demand a meeting with the Major. Alajo remembers how it was organized so that,

each person would deal with a demand. I think there were 19 people—I counted them, I'll never forget that—there were 19 people and there were 21 demands and somebody had to deal with two of them....It was very well done.

One of the key demands was that 100 million dollars be raised for Black business and community development. Archie Williams recalls,

Going down to the Mayor followed the Martin Luther King assassination and the disturbances and at that time minority economic development was becoming an issue. So the United Front went down and made a demand that the Mayor either give or donate or raise a hundred million dollars for various things including economic development in the Black community. It was at that point that the Mayor formed the Urban Foundation using the same initials, i.e., United Front, and attempted to raise the money through that. Their goal was TEN million, however.

Alajo puts it a little differently,

...The Mayor was slick though. He sat down and listened attentively, and the next day he came out with his own Boston Urban Foundation, same initials as the Black United Front, and he had his thing going which never really did anything.

Chuck Turner feels that the Front and its role in the community were deeply marked by that first set of demands,

> Some people within our community were scared by the uncompromising tone of the original 21 demands and the preamble. In addition, Mayor White tried to scare off Black support by saying he wouldn't deal with the Front. Thankfully, Tom Atkins, then on the City Council, called the Mayor a fool for taking such a position.

Looking back on it, he feels that the initial set of demands, which contained a strongly worded preamble about the exploitation of the Black community and included demands that white businesses should be turned over to Black control, "was a little strong." At the time the demands seemed urgent and reasonable, but they may have caused backlash that was later difficult to erase. The Front in any case turned its attention to the immediate, concrete demand of money for economic development.

Most institutions were not excited by the idea of control-free money for the Black community. The Joint Center for Change and some Black students at Harvard (several Front members themselves were graduates of Harvard) challenged the University to give 10% of its endowment (100 million) to the Black United Front for allocation to its Investment Fund. The University's response was less than enthusiastic.

The first real response to the demand for money free of restrictions was initiated by Ralph Hoagland, the young millionaire who had established a prosperous chain of discount drug stores in Boston and had been a sponsor of NECDC, and other whites who formed a group called FUND. Fund for Urban Negro Development (FUND) was created as a conduit for the transfer of dollars from white to Black hands. Member businesses paid $1,000 a year in dues which were then allocated to Black development groups to use as they wished.

The self interest in such a project for Boston businessmen was evident—they didn't want to be treated to a Detroit-like riot— and the project was seen as temporary as it performed the transfer of resources. But FUND was a milestone in terms of freeing money for Black development that was not to be shaped by the will of the white donors.

The Black United Front obtained a half million dollars of money to do with what it could over a four year period. There were many negotiations around the conditions accompanying the FUND money. Chuck Turner says in retrospect,

> Looking back at it, their suggestion of a joint Black-white board to invest in Black businesses 90% of the raised, 10% to go to the Front itself wasn't unreasonable; (but) it was unreasonable given the perspective of those of us who were sitting there...The people on the Steering Committee took the postion that the money had to be turned over—no strings attached. Their response was that we can't raise as much money if we have that kind of approach; people won't be willing to invest. All we'll be able to do is get donated money, not investment funds. We said, 'that's all right, money isn't everything.' The Front ratified that position and FUND members eventually agreed with it. We went off to organize and within a month or six weeks—I'll never forget it—I went up to the Somerset Hotel and came back with a check for $75,000.

Alajo who was there says of the FUND members,

> ...they were a group of young whites, and that told me something: that people who are institutionalized are very difficult to get at and I guess that goes for everybody, particularly when you are dealing with the system. When you deal with those old institutionalized whites, you've got a hard way to go getting them to understand, or even to react. But here were young whites and they were told, 'hey, if you give them that money they are going to have machine guns and cadillacs.' It didn't deter them to what they felt was a real need. And they were right. I think as I recall, their idea was, 'We've been supporting Black people for all these hundreds of years! Why don't we do what we're supposed to do and give them the money and let them begin to support themselves?' which I think is the whole ball game. They began to do that. I'll never forget that check, the first check for $75,000 at the Somerset Hotel, that was a Saturday morning. I looked at that check, more money than I've ever seen in my life represented in one place.

Alajo, as I was, felt impressed by the minimal ego involved among the young men we presented the Black community's case to. "I think that's the reason it sticks in my mind so," he relates, "'cause I think (of) all these flamboyant, up front kinds of things, television, radio, press conferences; but that (meeting) happened and it was an exchange, peer level exchange."

"Once the money was received," Chuck Turner reports,

...there was a series of meetings with the Front to discuss how to spend the money. Three categories were set up: cooperatives, community development and business development—within community development there were two categories: grants to organizations that represented a coming together of two or more organizations, and a category of straight grants to organizations. We set up the Front Foundation to administer the money under those criteria.

Discovering the need for the Front Foundation was a valuable experience for the community. Alajo recalls how he realized

that we couldn't go out and spend that money for days. That was just a piece of paper. We found out that we had to have that vehicle to receive that kind of money. Or you just couldn't do anything with it. I recognize that in the community anything we need we got in the community. We just need the motivation to pull around, to function for the need at any particular time. We needed a funding, a non-profit agency or organization to receive that money. We didn't have it; we didn't even know where to get it. So when we held that meeting—that was at the Y also—after due advertisement, and out of the crowd, no pre-arranging, out of the group, would be people who were administrative, the kinds of people that we needed to form that non-profit organization legitimizing that system so that we could take that money and begin to use it for what we said we were: addressing ourselves to community problems.

In the four years of its active life, the Black United Front generated or revived a variety of traditions and enterprises important to the Black community. Among these were Kwanza celebrations (the African Christmas-time holiday), Black Solidarity Day, and the Community Research and Review Committee, which monitored research by educational institutions in the community. Most important it was a supportive umbrella force with eighty-five organizations participating, at its height. "It doesn't mean that they agreed on anything," says Alajo, "but it means that they all had a use for the Front." The Front also played a crucial role in negotiating the Boston Plan as we'll see.

Chuck Turner considers one of the Front's most important contributions as,

> providing a place where people with energy and ideas really could come and get a sense of what was going on—where people out of town and the community could come out: that knew there was an organization that every two weeks would be meeting and could be a source of ideas, discussion; it provided a nesting place for projects.

Eventually the Front fell victim to two decisions: first, the unusual co-chair arrangement was dropped, leaving the head of the Front overwhelmed with pressure and work; second, the Front decided to stay out of politics which carried the organization away from the new center of interest. And, not least of all, the funding sources available in 1968 had all but vanished by 1973.

Chapter 10

TENT CITY

The steamy, explosive summer of 1968 began early in Boston just weeks after the murder of Dr. Martin Luther King, Jr., and the violent, angry reation of Black communities across the nation. On April 26, a group of about 30 CAUSE members took over the BRA's South End site office. The door was nailed shut, to protest the family relocations taking place under the BRA's urban renewal plans. At one point we blocked the path of Mayor White who tried to enter the building. We left together quietly under police escort about six o'clock that evening.

On April 28, a group of demonstrators, mostly CAUSE members, approached the Fitz-Inn parking lot bounded by Dartmouth, Columbus and Yarmouth Streets, directly across from my house. The lot was the site of a choice parcel of land which had been earmarked for development by the BRA. Its sound, handsome brick row-houses had been razed, and the lots paved over for parking, until its resale value would net enough profit to suit its owner. This site was the fact and the symbol of all we had been fighting against for so long.

The BRA bulldozed liveable buildings. One hundred families were forced out, to seek non-existent alternatives. An ugly scar of asphalt remained in the neighborhood, and the owners were making profits, catering to cars rather than considering human needs.

On that April morning we gathered early at each entrance to the lot. We parked cars in each driveway. Where we did not have cars, we had people challenging the suburban commuters who came, blindly, each day to park on the grave of a neighborhood block. We handed flyers to commuters trying to enter and to those sitting in cars backed up along Dartmouth Street. The flyers read:

> Dear Parker—This paper is an attempt to tell you why this parking lot has been closed by CAUSE. It is simple, South End people want to live in decent homes at reasonable rent.
>
> No housing has been built. People have been moved, of course. Housing should be built on this land, so your cars will no longer park here.

We made it clear that this protest was linked to CAUSE's demands for an elected urban renewal committee which would allow for community control of urban renewal plans. The elected committee was essential to changing the policies which had allowed these 100 families to be displaced by a parking lot.

As we stood at one entrance to the lot, one driver became so angry that he drove into the crowd knocking me down. Another demonstrator retaliated by grabbing the car's antenna, and there was the threat of a real fight. For fifteen minutes there was a general uproar and in the process of being shoved into police vans, we at least managed to bring the morning commuter traffic throughout the area to a standstill. Twenty-three of us were arrested.

The arrest of CAUSE members provided a surge of involvement throughout the community. A spontaneous "Tent City" sprang up on the parking lot over night. The people of the neighborhood constructed their own city, complete with city hall, town houses, recreation areas, housing, and cooking facilities. We shared meals and we hammered; students from MIT's architecture department joined us to lend a hand in the construction of our "buildings." It was our way of expressing our sense of community— our vision of what our community should be like. We chose this site because the decent housing that existed there was torn down. Today, after twelve years this site is still used as a parking lot.

The Episcopal Diocese of Boston played and inadvertant role in the dissolution of Tent City. Within their organization, there existed a fund to support change efforts by community groups, particularly change initiated by people of color.

Representatives of the Episcopal Diocese came to the Tent City site and publicly presented CAUSE members with a check for $10,000. Soon after the grant was accepted the site was vacated. It was one of our biggest mistakes.

People who were there struggling were given the impression that we left because of money. In fact, we had been infiltrated by undercover police, and we were uncertain as to whether or not we could maintain security and avoid serious injury to some demonstrators. Conflicts also developed around how the money would be appropriated, though this difficulty was overcome.

From Tent City, we planned a series of similar protests designed to highlight other sites that should be used for housing, as soon as possible, instead of being left idle. It was our intention to keep moving and not get caught in situations we had to maintain. We wanted to highlight and dramatize and keep on the offensive. After each event we planned the next.

About the same time CAUSE initiated a lengthy sit-in demonstration at United South End Settlements (USES) to protest its involvement in the BRA relocation program. We felt, as we had a year before, that USES was compromising its role as a community service agency by working for the BRA. Ted Parrish reflects retrospectively,

> I was working for the USES, and I guess that the reason that a number of staff people felt that the sit-in was necessary was that here we saw the BRA as being one of the key governmental agencies that was removing poor people from the South End and if the USES's mandate was in fact to be advocates for oppressed people, then USES ought not to be involved with the BRA.

USES abruptly decided to sever its contract with the BRA, and CAUSE reported that several new programs of "direct benefit to those suffering from repercussions of the urban renewal process" would be initiated.[1] The BRA also agreed not to re-locate another household that desired to stay in the area.

In early May, City Counselor Tom Atkins, Chairman of the Committee on Urban Renewal, presented a set of resolutions and orders to the Council which focused on how to create an elected resident committee to oversee the urban renewal process in the neighborhoods. The City Council passed resolutions to the effect that:

1) an urban renewal body be elected by residents;

2) the election be an official city election;

3) the BRA be directed to undertake renewal activities only with the approval of the elected body; and

4) the elected body be delegated the power to subcontract renewal functions and to interest itself in all issues of concern to the South End.

Later, the City reluctantly gave its approval as well. Citizen committees were appointed to work during the summer to prepare several alternative plans for the election process and structures of the committee. The City Council hearings on the proposals of the committee conflicted between old-time, old-line community associations and the heretofore voiceless poor tenants. Tenants had turned out in overwhelming numbers; the neighborhood association representatives were appalled at the prospect of sharing their power. "The meeting was, after all," stated a New Urban League press release, "the first time in South End urban renewal history that the poor stood up and spoke. And what they spoke of was democracy, fair play, one-person, one-vote, a right to a voice in how their neighborhoods would be run."

Once they recovered from their shock, the established neighborhood associations submitted a counter-proposal to the City Council which drastically cut the power of the elected committee from decision making to review, and changed the composition to be partly elected and partly appointed by the associations. The age of participants was raised from 16 to 20 years. The proposal was hastily concocted and was not reviewed with a wide or representative group of South Enders.

As a result, the February meeting was hot and turbulent. It was clear that all parties were dissatisfied with the BRA's performance and even many of the community residents on the middle ground were disappointed with the lack of initiative taken by the existing community associations or the appointed urban renewal committee. I stated that the City Council was only willing to listen to organized citizen groups if they were white. Fed up with the Councilors' refusal to respond to questions, a number of CAUSE supporters and I walked out of the chambers.

At length, the City Council passed a compromise plan after a five-hour debate about the extent of power to be yielded to the committee. The compromise, which was endorsed by the Mayor and the BRA, stated that the Council could not instruct the BRA to delegate a specific amount of power to the elected body, that the body be elected by persons over 20 years old, that members would be elected for two year terms from 14 districts with seven other members elected at-large.

The steering committee of CAUSE and other members of the community felt that the compromise was worthless. Atkins vowed there would be no election at all if the BRA left the powers unspecified and crippled the elected committee "like a ship without a rudder." The compromise crushed the opportunity for tenants at long last to have a voice in the programs that would affect their housing opportunities. The ordinance essentially gave the BRA a stranglehold over any elected committee's actions. Over a year's work was threatened with obliteration by one vote.

On the anniversary eve of Dr. King's murder and a year to the month after Tent City, a group from CAUSE went to the headquarters of the BRA in City Hall to protest the BRA's continued lack of action on housing in the South End, and to insist that the BRA assign maximum possible authority to the proposed elected committee. The BRA Director got wind of our intention and promptly cancelled the meeting, but we later confronted him at the headquarters. He offered to talk to any five of us, but we refused to be split up and insisted on being heard as a group. Incredibly, the Director used Dr. King's murder as an excuse saying it was not a day for demonstration because it was the eve of Dr. King's death. We replied that the ceremony planned by the Mayor in honor of Dr. King would be empty fraud if the City did not respond to the legitimate grievances of its citizens. We left at six that evening, but vowed to return.

A week later, at the next scheduled board meeting of the BRA, we reminded the BRA of the front page news story in May, 1968, which stated that construction would begin on 1,286 units of low and moderate income housing in the summer of 1968, and almost a year later nothing had been done, although the BRA had seen fit to destroy habitable housing on the sites. Black businesses and poor tenants had been evicted to make way for non-existent plans. We pointed out, unncessarily, that a people's elected urban renewal committee would never have allowed such a thing to happen.

We faced the question of whether Dr. King's nonviolent tactics were viable, or whether the frustration of black and poor people in Boston would reach the explosion point before white agencies saw any point at all in listening to or responding to our needs.

By late May, the Mayor announced his plans for a special election for a South End Project Area Committee (SEPAC) on July 22, in his words, "to elect representatives who can discuss local projects with the Boston Redevelopment Authority." He considered it "an authentic body with an ability to influence decisions affecting the South End."[1]

Before the elections were actually held, City Councilor Tom Atkins traveled to Washington, D.C. to hear directly from HUD officers what the duties of a project area committee were intended to include. HUD interpreted their directive of the previous June to mean that the community groups were not to be merely advisory, but to be involved in the obtaining of a "mutual agreement" between the local agency and the residents on the projects. The Mayor and the BRA refused to recognize this mandate.

Unable to get the city to specify powers for the elected committee, CAUSE decided on its own course of action. We would simply hold our own election for an elected committee that we considered legitimate. We decided to precede the city election and called for our neighbors to vote between June 28 and July 3. Our criteria were the ground rules established months before at community meetings. The League of Women Voters and the Association of Urban Sisters volunteered to monitor the process.

The People's Elected Urban Renewal Committee (PEURC) succeeded in getting 3,141 votes—over 17% of the total eligible votes in the South End. Forty-two committee members were elected: two-thirds were tenants, 23 were Black, 15 were white, and 4 Spanish speaking. It was a large turnout and we were elated. The new committee's first vote was to boycott the city elections on July 26-28 and letters were sent to all voters to encourage them to withhold participation in the city's sham. The city's election only polled 2,416 voters to elect 35 people: 12 Black, 15 white, and 8 Spanish speaking. More landowners were elected. The city's election cost $50,000 compared to $5,000 for the people's election.[2]

The South End Project Area Committe (SEPAC) and the People's Elected Urban Renewal Committee as it turned out provided a double barrelled pressure on the BRA for action. Although the SEPAC group was more conservative, some of its members were willing to raise important issues. Some of its members were also members of the People's Elected Urban Renewal Committee. At the same time, the People's Elected Urban Renewal Committee served as a prod and saddleburr to the BRA, and the city on issues that SEPAC was unwilling to press.

One of SEPAC's first votes was to suspend all demolition until a survey of buildings could be made to determine which ones simply could not be rehabilitated. Only those would be recommended to the BRA for demolition. This was an important item because it meant more land was actually getting into the control of the people.

SEPAC also complained when the BRA did not inform

members in advance about the Board agenda which SEPAC was to review. SEPAC also insisted on pressing incoming businesses for statements of equal opportunity employment for community residents. The BRA objected to this and said it was going far beyond SEPAC's mandate. With the People's Elected Urban Renewal Committee holding a hard line on one side and SEPAC holding a consistent, but more moderate position on the other, the BRA often gave way on issues it would never have considered before. It took seven years, but in 1973-74, the new SEPAC was made up entirely of a community endorsed slate. The People's Elected Urban Renewal Committee was official at last. The efforts SEPAC had made proved it had enough power to make it effective and to make community residents want to join it.

Chapter 11

STUDENT POWER

"You don't need a necktie to learn"
—*White student*, Boston English High

The original clashes between students and school administrators occurred in the fall of 1968, when a Black student was expelled from Boston English High for breaking the shirt-and-tie dress code. The student was expelled for wearing a dashiki. The more pertinent issue, however, was whether the schools would allow the formation of Black Student Unions. As Toye Brown Lewis, in a New Urban League paper, wrote,

> It's obvious that to school officials, the dashiki represents a change which will placate Black demands but the wearing of African dress is not in itself an issue which demands any radical changes in who controls the education process. The student unions, however, represent an attempt to organize a power group as a bargaining vehicle to deal with other groups which have control in this society. Clearly the Black students have recognized that this is a society of interest groups. In line with their desire to organize their own Black unions, they have become aware that the existing interest groups within the system are not representing their needs or desires. To get their needs on the

system's agenda, they must organize to be heard because the system is sensitized to pressure groups.

The position of the high school officials was that Black students should not be allowed to form a group to look out for their own interests. On the contrary, white student clubs and student government had traditionally operated to the exclusion of Blacks for many years. At the time, Boston English was predominantly white—a fact which dramatized how zoning, school redistricting and other camouflage actions had long served to exclude Blacks from the school entirely. In 1969, 35% of the Boston Public School elementary population was Black; yet only 17% of the high school population was Black with only 10% of those graduating.

Some observers viewed the controversy of the dashiki versus the traditional necktie as a healthy break from the system that promoted conformity and smothered individuality. The uproar indicated that the young people had not been altogether squelched by the school system. But the conflict was to stretch into years, a bitter test of the students' resilience and strength.

Demonstrations led to negotiations over the list of demands and the headmaster agreed to allow African dress and recognize the Black Student Union which would meet once a week with faculty supervision. However, the faculty read an opposing statement over the public address system which suggested that the Union was a racist organization. The Associate Superintendent further undermined the headmaster's position by supporting the teachers.

School administrators were clearly uneasy with the spectre of Black students organizing a group to look after their own internally defined self-interests. Officials understood that a student union might lead to things such as decision-making power for students or greater community control. Tensions increased when school officials insisted on calling police and even requested the National Guard to help "quell" the "disorders." White students joined the Black student strikers demanding that the dress code be changed.

Mayor White and other city officials responded with familiar tactics: stop the trouble and we'll set up a committee to study the issues. Although the Mayor did refuse to call the National Guard as requested by the School Committee, he did little to dispel the loudly voiced opinions of school officials that the disruptions were the work of adult "anarchists" who were influencing the students. The news media failed to point out that the adults really bent on anarchy were the so-called leaders who had failed to uphold the law of the Commonwealth.

The disruptions quickly spread from school to school with students from the King and Timilty Junior High Schools arriving by bus to support the English High strikers. The Dudley transit station in Roxbury, where a multitude of Black students boarded school transportation vehicles, became a hub of protest communications. With a sense of history the Black students even pointed out the similarity between their struggle and that of the Catholics years before in Boston.

To their credit, after some initial hesitation and confusion, Black organizations rallied strongly behind the Black students and the idea of Black Student Unions. The New Urban League, the Black United Front, the NAACP and other organizations and churches offered their resources and support to the students. Black parents organized their own Black Parents Union in support of their children. Though active rebellion began to burn out as students drifted back to school, about a dozen Black student groups across the city banded into the Black Student Federation (BSF) and worked consistently to keep the issues alive and organize increasing numbers of Black students.

Nineteen sixty-nine was a relatively quiet year of hard work. Black Student Unions were organized unofficially in all the Boston high schools and students began to raise funds to support the coordinating activities of the Black Student Federation. The Federation acquired legal help through the Massachusetts Law Reform Institute and began to work on cases of student rights.

Black students were ready to get organized and the Black Student Federation served to reinforce and solidify the consciousness raised by community events, e.g., Marcus Garvey Day and Black Solidarity Day. The BSF became a primary contact for youth, in fact, it was the only active youth group in

Roxbury besides the traditional gangs.

Throughout this time period, it should be remembered, college campuses across the country were in turmoil, frequently their demands centered around Black student organizations. By then the issues were becoming more explosive. Almost all the major universities had Black student unions (many of them started by BSF members who had by then entered college), and the high school students had plenty of models among Boston's multitude of colleges. By Christmas of 1970, new student strikes were in the making at English High.

The children weaned on the protests of the early sixties had come into their own and they had learned well. Their demands brought the educational struggle full circle—they protested the very same issues that had prompted their parents to call the Freedom Stay Outs and the March on Roxbury in 1963. If parents and leaders of the Black community hesitated momentarily to support the student strikes actively, it was because they forgot that they themselves had set the stage and provided the role model for their children to follow. Parents had long ago established confrontation as a tactic, and their children were politicized by experience.

Black students were merely applying new energy and vigor to the issues of the control of (and equal access to) resources, and of the quality of education which the older group had attempted to gain through somewhat different means. The pull of the power system, and the specter of credential requirements sometimes overpowered the parents, who had once led or joined marches themselves. Events took place so quickly that it was easy for some parents and community leaders to lose sight of the alternatives—including special college admissions—for their striking children. But the students persisted, made their points and eventually turned things around to gain a large number of supportive parents.

Parents were proud that their children were taking a stand, and they were impressed with the students' articulate, well-organized expression of the issues. Many parents became directly involved, and those who didn't felt relieved when community agencies began working with the students rather than letting them stand alone. By 1970, when new student strikes were in the making at English High, the students knew that many of their parents were there behind them.

In January, 1970, protest flared again over two students accused of robbery at English High. A demonstration briefly closed the school. Strikers demanded, "More Black teachers, Black Studies courses, and dismissal of charges against the two students." Dorchester High was closed soon afterward following a demonstration against racist comments by a teacher. In early February, three hundred Brighton High students were meeting among themselves about conditions at that school, and on February 4, 600 students staged a walkout and held a rally to dramatize the deplorable conditions at their schools.

Students presented a comprehensive set of demands including improved curricula, more Black faculty and guidance counselors, development of a grievance procedure, more decision power for students, courses in Black history taught by Black teachers, an independent evaluation of the Boston school system by Bridge, Inc., an end to harrassment of Black students and amnesty for strikers. The School Committee Chairman declared the independent evaluation and amnesty to be impossible to consider. Many students continued to stay out of their schools in what was to become the longest strike in Boston's public school history.

The School Committee responded to the demands by calling the police. The Black Student Federation which had been gearing for the confrontation those long months, announced that Black students would not return until police guards were removed. By mid-February, a group of representatives from the Black Student Federation, several Black Student Unions and some parents joined forces to coordinate support for the strikers. Classes in Black History were hosted by the New School for Children, and most students participated in all Liberation School activities.

The community agencies who had been through this before, laid the blame directly on the long-term insensitivity, and the racial imbalance perpetuated by the Boston School Committee. It had been eight long years since 1963 and the original Stay Out for Freedom. Seventeen years had expired since the 1954 Supreme Court decision! The community could not forgive the fact that yet another generation was being forced to cope with issues of racism that should have been settled years before.

Students organized a conference of elected student representatives, faculty and a few invited officials at the end of February. The School Committee Chairman arrived for a new minutes—after being telephoned—to announce an emergency committee meeting two days later. Afterwards, the School Committee Chairman informed students that other members could attend the emergency meeting (the first time that had ever happened). Angry students called for a total strike of Black and white students alike, but some white students held back to wait for the results of the next regularly scheduled committee meeting. White demands were along the lines of carpeting, student smoking areas and telephones—issues of little concern to Black students who had gone to elementary schools that were literally falling down around their heads.

The March 2 School Committee meeting was a disaster reminiscent of the hearings held in 1963 and 1964. The School Committee utilized the tactics they perfected during the debates with the NAACP education committee: they dominated all but a half hour or so of the time, then left the meeting abruptly. As a result many of the grievances were not heard, and feelings flared. At some point a South Boston student stood up with a 1916 English book in his hand (a book still in use in his school), and demanded to know if this was the best the School Committee could do, with a staff of forty, at their Education Planning Center. "Is *this* your curriculum innovation?" he asked pointedly.

In a closed session, the School Committee "approved" the 22 student demands, promising to send Rollins Griffith, the only Black administrator in the system, besides a few principals, to recruit Black teachers and counselors from the South, and to set up a curriculum advisory group. They undermined these apparent concessions by declaring strikers would be prosecuted for truancy or simply dropped from the rolls. In addition, dismissal and possible criminal proceedings were initiated against the ad hoc group of teachers who vocally supported the strikers. The teachers had issued a statement declaring: "Schools are designed to produce citizens who will make do because they don't expect anything better. The children in Boston are being tracked for low paying jobs, the draft, and early pregnancy."[1]

The School Committee continued to insist on the presence of armed police as a "solution" to the "harrassment" born of many years of habitual bigotry; if nothing else, such positions brought students of all persuasions closer together in their rejection of and disgust for such tactics. The school officials lumped all the problems under a heading of "national conspiracies "and "outsiders." It could be truthfully said that the American school system is more of a "national conspiracy" against certain groups of youngsters than were the strikes which were ripping through the nation's school systems.

The situation settled into a grim hold-out contest and the strike continued into April with few substantial results. Though the headmaster of Boston English left and his successor instituted such changes as mini-courses, the most crucial issues were left untouched to fester and worsen.

The School Committee and other school officials had shown absolutely no leadership. The city's basic unwillingness to deal with the problems was all too clear in the Mayor's behavior: when Black students asked him for money to recruit Black teachers, he had none to give; when white parents requested police in the schools, he found a source of money with no trouble.

During the fall of that year, the BSF regrouped as the Black Student Union (BSU) of Boston, because individual unions had been banned over the summer and a federation no longer existed. The BSU maintained a vigilant position on the issues which threatened the students' efforts to gain some autonomy and self-determination.

When Cambridge school officials announced plans to require students to use ID cards, the BSU threatened a lawsuit. The students linked the use of ID cards to the practices in South Africa, Rhodesia and Viet Nam and insisted that, like ties, identification cards have nothing to do with learning. "We feel that the cost to print, develop and distribute identification cards could be going towards curriculum innovation which is desperately needed throughout the city of Boston," said Leon Rock.[2]

The issue went before the Massachusetts State Legislature in the form of a bill against the use of such cards in 1973.

The BSU also did a study on the drug traffic on high school campuses, and organized a massive youth voter registration campaign. The drug study and a student rights handbook, the first of its kind, received national circulation.

By mid-1971, the BSU was seeking alternatives for the students unwilling to return to English High and for those students still in school who were seeking new options. After a series of negotiations with nearby colleges, parochial and private schools, the students helped formulate the Roxbury Education And Development (READ) Program.

With the help of the New Urban League, the program had a year's trial run and then was presented to the Massachusetts Experimental School System, as a model for its previously undesigned high school component The CCED family of schools accepted the model, but there was prolonged conflict with the State Board of Education over control of the school. The Board was not accustomed to dealing with programs which had been "pre-tested" by community people, nor was it quite ready to sponsor a community initiated and controlled school. Short-term funding was allocated at last, and the Model High School, as it became known, completed its third year of testing as a viable alternative to other public schools.

Leon Rock, student leader, once labeled "outside agitator" and "non-student," by the School Committee, the superintendent of schools, and others, witnessed the impact and the results of the student stike. Of major importance in his mind were the organizing skills and increased political awareness that the strike gave a large number of students. The educational conscience of the city was also raised. Within a short time, the State Department of Education echoed the BSU's position, declaring Boston public schools a dual segregation system. The Massachusetts Commission Against Discrimination cited racism in teacher hiring practices. The Department of Health, Education and Welfare then announced it would withhold funds, because the school system was racially imbalanced.

Besides these tangible results, Rock feels it was important for the Black community to see its children moving on the issues, providing role models not only for their younger sisters and brothers, but also for some of the more established leaders as well. Rock pursued a political career running twice unsuccessfully for State Representative.

The efforts of the BSU and others fighting for community control of the schools coincided in the 1971 legislative session with debates around the plausibility of neighborhoods, numbering 150.000 residents or more, forming their own school board, independent of the city school committee.

Ben Scott, who had helped engineer the take-over of the Gibson School in 1968, worked with the Massachusetts Law Reform Institute to push both the neighborhood bill (Senate 448), and a law suit which challenged the at-large school committee elections as being discriminatory against minorities. Senate 448 has been resubmitted each year.

Chapter 12

THE NEW URBAN LEAGUE

The time: High Noon
The place: Statler Hilton Ballroom
The occasion: Annual United Community Services
Board Meeting
Principal characters: Bert Alleyne, Leo Fletcher, Mel
King, Pearl Shelton, Jim Bishop, other board members.

We arrived during the luncheon. Silently we
marched in and, on a given signal, went from table to
table and picked up the leftover scraps.

A large number of cigarettes began to be lit as
guests looked nervously from one to another, and to
us, moving quietly among them gathering their crumbs. The scraps were put into a bag and someone
handed the bag to me.

Up on the podium, still silently, we lined up. Jim
Bishop spoke briefly. I spoke, equally briefly. Then I
tipped over the bag of garbage. "We are not taking
any more of your scraps," I said.

Then we marched out.

Working with the Boston New Urban League for four years during the transitional time between the 1960's and the 1970's, I had an outstanding opportunity to learn about the internal workings of a community agency faced with the challenge of responding to the rapidly changing needs and interests of its constituents. In this case study of the Urban League in Boston, the following chapter provides both a summary of the lessons of the organizing stage in Black community development, and an inside account of how the organizing of the sixties led into the institution building of the seventies. Most of all it was through working at the New Urban League that we developed the philosophy of community development through community control.

When I joined the League in June, 1967, it was located in the downtown business section of Boston and had no full-time professional staff. It concentrated mostly on meeting the employment needs of people through industry placement. By using the On-the-Job Training model, the League was able to promote training and subsequent job placements for Black people at little or no cost to industry. The League also worked to help meet industry's civil rights and public image needs, by supplying minority contacts and workers. Basically the League's work was focused on institutions—schools, health services, interagency councils, the United Community Services. The intention was to get them to change the way they served people, primarily to respond to the needs of Black folks just as they did for other groups.

It was apparent from signs and conditions in the community, however, that a drastic overhaul was necessary to make the League a functional resource for the community. Black people in 1967 were very different from Black people at the time the League was founded in 1910. On one hand people were still interested in opening the opportunity structure within the existing system; but on the other hand and at the same time, people were beginning to feel very strongly about developing their own turf as a viable and independent community. People began to recognize and proclaim that their own neighborhoods, not just white areas, could be healthy, livable sections of the city. It became undeniably clear that Black people did want the opportunity and did have the drive to achieve their goals of community development. There was no longer acceptance of the notion that Black areas are automatically bad and hopeless and beyond repair.

When I was asked to be Director of the League, I agreed because it seemed like a good way to put into practice my ideas about community organizing and, administratively, I was given a free hand in putting the staff together. One of the first changes we made was to move our location from the downtown business area of Boston to the heart of the Black community. With our move we redefined our constituents from industry and business to community people. From there we moved toward community organizing as our major approach to problem solving. We dedicated our organization to community development, basing our work on the belief that people wanted to make our community as good as any. We knew this goal involved wresting control of our own affairs. We called ourselves the *New* Urban League. We tried to make all our moves consistent with these starting points.

Community Development Through Community Control

An overview philosophy is crucial to any organization. For the League this involved defining how we intended to represent the community. We spent a great deal of time on this process of self-definition. One effort took the form of our first Black Paper which laid out the notion that full community development comes only through community control. We were especially concerned with getting a cross-section of opinions from those involved in the experience of community development, including inputs from the National Urban League. In two and a half days we hammered out our overall philosophy and the program areas we intended to move in: educational development, economic development, and youth development. We decided that all our efforts would be related to these areas. We also refined the theme around which we were to operate: Community Development through Community Control. We became involved in situations presenting different aspects of the process of development, convinced that residents must have control of the institutions affecting their community. This meant utilizing the resources of a community for its own development and doing away with the colonialistic relationships which used these resources only for the benefit of the external society.

Operation—Making It Work

> Internal operations became a major priority in line with new thrust goals because of a realization by staff that before we can go into the community and talk about how black people need to gain control of institutions such as schools, small businesses, and other services, that our first task under new thrust is to deal with ways in which the Urban League as an organization, as a system, can begin to work for Black people.

Getting our staff oriented to and operating on our philosophy extended, perhaps prematurely, into making our own agency a model of our professed policy. As a staff we felt we had to believe in community control enough to put our own organization under the control of the community, to experience this process ourselves if we were going to talk about it to others. Over the space of several years, our major problems were related to our quest for unity without uniformity within our organization. Could we tolerate diversity and yet act in support of each other at critical points? Could we allow individual initiative and style, yet maintain our mutually agreed upon philosophy? These are crucial challenges to the viability of an organization. I really don't think that money is, in the end, what makes or breaks a group; I think the hardest job is getting your own people to believe in the organization, in themselves, and in their own abilities; to believe that they can set goals and achieve them. Without this sort of belief, it is impossible to work through the crucial joint decisions that must be carried out to keep an organization functioning.

Our most consistent problem was related to evaluating the staff's behavior and the organization's operation to determine whether our resources were being used to promote and sustain community control. Again there was the difficulty in getting people to be aware of their own power. We were hiring Black staff and working to keep Black money in the Black community; yet the staff continued to spend outside the community. People did not always connect policy and philosophy to their own lives. Nor did they realize in unison their voices could have substantial impact in many situations.

We needed to construct an accountability mechanism or process that could respond to all the diverse ideas and values that occur within a microcosmic representation of the community such as the League became. People had, of course, been conditioned to many sorts of "controls"—the threat of being fired, having their paychecks docked, being ostracized. We struggled with the question of whether to utilize any of these methods as opposed to alternatives such as more awareness sessions to sharpen sensitivity to the issues and problems. We questioned whether to deal with the individual who had difficulties on the job in private, or within a group context. When a breakdown in performance did occur, we tried to probe the possible reasons and then to help the person find other routes to accomplish his or her job.

The key to acting effectively is to integrate job and lifestyle so that all aspects are related and all systems are mutually reinforcing. Our experience yielded endless examples of how difficult it is to achieve this integration. Many times latent issues or problems did not show up until a conflict situation arose. A staff member might organize a group of parents who eventually initiated a school takeover. Suddenly there were new risks for the staff member—perhaps the possibility of arrest, or perhaps a major shift in schedule requiring an appearance with parents at 7:00 a.m.

For a host of reasons, some staff failed to show up for such occasions, either on time, or at all. Something was preventing them from maintaining the connection between their self-interest and their participation in such actions. The school issues were basically all about control, and although people certainly seemed to have an intellectual awareness of the relationship to the philosophy of the League, and to the fate of their own children in their schools, somehow they often failed to internalize this awareness at an action level.

No Profits: No Change

Sometimes after we "solved" a problem, or a particular program came to an end, the staff involved would leave. I think the letdown that caused people to leave came from not seeing the big picture, from people thinking they were producing a shoe instead of a wardrobe. It also came from the lack of a master plan which fostered the crisis orientation, the diffusion of resources and fragmentation of power that were discussed earlier. The paucity of visible evidence that change could result from their efforts also contributed to the exodus.

In Boston, people can't avoid seeing the physical, economic and often the psychological impact of such massive developments as the Prudential Center, Government Center, or the new Christian Science complex. The changes are obvious: people sat down, planned and worked to make Boston different, and they got the attendant payoff—not only financial, but psychological as well. In our work we made many small efforts that resulted in stopping some urban renewal projects, getting rid of some slumlords, getting control of some housing for tenants, and so forth. But in the context of the gigantic changes being wrought elsewhere in the city, our changes seemed pale and insignificant. There always seemed to be more refuse abandonment, and deterioration, to offset every little gain. We seemed never to gather the energy generated from all these efforts and maximize it into a power base.

This consistent lack of payoffs psychologically and functionally binds us to the non-profit myth perpetrated by the institutions that currently dominate our society. In order to get resources for programs we are required to guarantee that there will be NO change. Funding groups give only to non-profit organizations; the system to "support" most social programs, from settlement houses to housing developments, is designed to rule out advantage or gain. Because we have dutifully institutionalized and internalized the idea that we must not benefit personally from community development type work, we are psychologically unwilling to make a profit of any sort.

With "no change" the basic rule, resistance is great to any individual or agency that tries to make an impact; an agency is constantly subjected to criticism and advice about how to run an agency or spend its money. A quick comparison with any large profit making corporation will make it clear how disproportionate this watchdogging of non-profit groups is: when an institution like the United Black Appeal declared that it wanted to share in the profits that come from being in control, the response from funding groups was a flat refusal.

The "profits" of change are manifold: pride, improved self-image, experience, skills, positive reinforcement, cultural strength. On other levels there are benefits in the form of improved education or housing, cleaner streets, a new community facility or some other physical or social improvement. If you work it right, there might be more cash flow, fewer crimes and enough money to do more than maintain the minimum conditions. Change is inseparably linked to profit—a connection that has been excluded from the "non-profit" approach to problem solving—thereby holding us captive in our misguided good intentions.

In 1969 the New Urban League came dramatically face to face with the destructive potential of the established funding sources and practices for programs related to community development and control. The New Urban League had participated in some discussion about how to get the United Fund, a major contributor to the League, to be more responsive to the community's needs. We felt that if the United Fund really intended to contribute to human and community development, it had to be more realistic about allotting enough money to have some real impact on community problems. As it was, the preceding year the Black community received a total of $500,000 (some of which was summer "cool out" money). The Fund's annual intake at the time was $15 million. We suggested that 12-15 percent of the Fund's total collection should be to the Black community programs and agencies, who should have final say on spending.

This controversy was the very foundation of the New Urban League: we were determined to move from being receivers to being self-sufficient providers. We were committed to the struggle necessary to make our own decisions, run our own programs, make our own mistakes and solve our own problems.

We had hopes of encouraging other United Community Service agencies to take a unified stand and simultaneously request increased funding. We found ourselves, however, significantly alone. Money is the baseline of power, the looming threatening source of control over a program's very life; few were willing to challenge its stranglehold. Most would understandably prefer partial life to none at all.

For us, the issue was not just related to our own survival. We felt that the United Fund ought to reassess the amount of money they offered to the community, no matter which agency became the major channel. Above all, the way in which the money was given had to be changed to allow community groups the autonomy necessary to get things done. We felt that money should be given directly to the community for the decision about which programs should receive it and for what purposes. I'm afraid the unwillingness of other agencies to support our demands stemmed from their uneasiness to be held so directly accountable to the people, even though we built in a hedge factor of three years for an agency to meet the criteria for receiving continued funding.

The League's stand provided an untried alternative. Through sheer hard work we manged to get the funds to continue our programming in the mode that supported our objectives and verified our commitment: community development comes through community control. In reality, the League was the only community agency in the position to catalyze such a move to expose the extent to which external funding controls the effectiveness of community programs.

The National Urban League

A most crucial question for any leader faced with the demand for dual allegiance to national and local goals is: just who does a leader serve and how much is he or she willing to risk to deliver that service? At one point I wrote on the issue,

> There is a serious problem within the National Urban League that will continue as long as a) the executives and local leagues do not believe in the notion of community control of the Urban League, and b) as long as

National Urban League continues to operate as if it is a foundation requiring people to submit proposals on the one hand and on the other being in the position to choose which Leagues get special dispensation. It also detracts from the Urban League ever becoming a real movement based on the needs that come from below.

At the Boston New Urban League this question was ever present because of our interpretation of National Urban League policy frequently deviated from national expectations. Our choice of training and community organizing in the primary areas of youth, education and economic development put us much more closely in contact with community people and affairs, a habit the League's policy makers did not necessarily encourage.

Conflicts between national instructions and local urgencies arose from Day One. I assumed directorship of the Boston League on June 1, 1967, but instead of going, as expected, to the national training conference for new executives the week of June 5th, I wound up staying in Boston to respond to the "police riots" which occurred on June 2, 3, and 4. In this case the conflict proved advantageous because the contact with community leadership led to the hiring of our first professional staff person: a technical assistant and consultant on economic and community development. That was our initial step toward hiring professional staff specifically to meet the needs and requests of community groups.

One year later we had the pleasure of a personal visit from Whitney Young, Jr., National Executive Director, who came to discuss the role of the New Urban League in Boston and its relationship to the corporate national structure. Specifically, the national office was distressed by our distribution of "survival literature" after the assassination of Martin Luther King and our participation in demonstrations which led to several arrests.

A Plan—The Map for Leaders

The key to being able to reject or accept alternative solutions to problems, whether in the form of legislation, federal programs, or local action, is having a master plan with both short and long-range components to provide the framework for foresightful decision-making. In spite of all our gains, no picture of what the Black community should look like in ten years had been laid out. Without such a blueprint, community leaders were not able to pool and maximize the internal resources of the community. Without a plan, our assets, inevitably, were spread too thin to be effective.

From time to time pieces of a plan were laid out, but they were generally highly competitive and externally imposed. The Civil Rights movement came closest in recent history to providing a philosophical and moral basis for a plan, but to date neither a viable plan that people can believe in, nor a process that people can see as a way to get what they need, have been developed. If we really believe in the dual function of a leader as both molder and follower of public opinion based on the community's expression of its needs, we must move to respond to the one thing the community has been seeking all along: a comprehensive plan. People expect their leadership to gather all the diverse elements, organize them, and spell out the different roles needed to realize the plan.

The reasons for this leaderless state of affairs are directly related to the scarcity of resources. Local agencies have no control over the allocation of funding by such externally controlled groups as the United Community Services or the Boston Redevelopment Authority. By virtue of their financial power, these external programs or institutions are able to impose their views of what the physical and social environment should be. *They* have a plan, all right.

Without the financing available for long-range, full-scale planning and programming, the Black community is prevented from making a comprehensive effort to solve its problems. The result has been hundreds of short-lived or short-range programs, and correspondingly, hundreds of "leaders." This phenomenon should not be seen as entirely negative. The fact that so many groups sprang up to deal with community problems, in however random a fashion, meant that we now have many people who have gained some transferable problem solving skills. It also expresses the commitment and concern that exist in the community.

Even at the League, in spite of our effort to respond to the expectations of the community, we found ourselves in effect fighting fires. First, we responded to the crisis over the dislocation of families by urban renewal, then to the manpower crisis generated by the Boston Urban Redevelopment Program (BURP), then to the education crisis at the King-Timilty School. Part of the reason we operated in that way was our naive belief that we could solve each of these problems, in isolation, from a plan that covered the entire community context. Part of the reason was that the community looked to us for help in the crisis-by-crisis way they were accustomed to.

We repeatedly emphasized the importance of controlling our own programming, but we failed to talk about how to make it happen. We took the lead in shaping community opinion about the importance of control, but we did not realize that we needed to go beyond that and spell out the process, the ingredients, the plan for getting and using control. As a result, the impact of our efforts to mold and to follow, both as a team and as individuals, was often diffused because one attempt was not visibly linked to the next.

The Leader as Role Model

A leader, consciously or not, is a role model. For his or her constituents, for agencies, for other leaders, sometimes even for kids in the street, a leader provides a pattern of behavior for their consideration and perhaps emulation or imitation. Leadership becomes a lifestyle that integrates community problems directly into the everyday pattern of behavior.

To be truly effective in the leadership role, and a fitting model for community control, a leader needs to be accessible and accountable. At the New Urban League we tried several ways to make this happen. At the annual Board meeting every year, for instance, the Executive Servant (Director) offered his or her resignation so that the Board had the fullest possible license for evaluating his or her performance over the past year. We felt that the best working model of accountability should allow a community organization a way to respond to the ever changing needs and levels of consciousness of its constituents. A board should not have to request a resignation, although it should guarantee a three to four month safeguard period for job hunting.

Another step we took at the League to emphasize the accountability and accessibility of the leader was to change the title from Executive Director to Executive Servant. This change was based on our belief expressed in a statement by a South End resident describing the role that a community agency should play, "If you want to serve me, let me tell you *how* to serve me." As an organization, we tried to respond to what the community was saying. We felt that there was no better way to give an indication of the direction we intended to pursue and the kind of response we intended to offer, than to change this label. We also recognized that a good servant sometimes anticipates his or her master's need, so we intended to keep looking ahead, to see the community as our master.

On the community level, we also tried to take the lead in providing opportunities to develop new role models. We felt one of our main responsibilities was to develop a climate in which those who desired to function in a leadership role could gain experience, grow, and eventually become a new source of leadership in the community. We set out to provide support to people with axes to grind, problems to solve and talents to put to use in the community.

Pitfalls and Peculiarities

With so many demands on a leader, it's not unlikely that some facets of the role model fall short of folks' expectations, enabling some problems to persist. I encountered some unanticipated difficulties, for instance, in the effort to keep accessibility high within the League. The open door policy to the Executive Servant's time led some staff members to feel that their supervisors were talking about them. The paranoia was largely unfounded, but was substantially reinforced on those very few occasions when staff did choose to complain about other staff.

Accountability was another problem: too often all the weight is placed on the leader to make things happen. This tendency needs to be offset by more emphasis on group process in decision-making and responsibility. Personally, I found the administrative and supervisory facets of the leadership role most difficult. I naturally gravitated to what I like to do and know how to do best. I was pretty good at developing ideas, and found lots of ways to utilize that talent; yet I tended to neglect other critical tasks.

I also discovered that I was inclined to hire and support people who had a similar philosophy to myself. We were aiming to organize and build institutions: my instinct to get the developers, and not the organizers became a problem. My value orientation in terms of using time and resources was definitely slanted toward program development instead of implementation. But, as the administrator and role model, I had to lay out a path to get to all our goals, and that meant changing some of my natural inclinations.

My original procedure was to wait until someone came along with a clear interest in the community and an idea of what they wanted to do and then find the resources to put him or her on the staff. By hiring that person I was able to minimize some of the administrative handholding aspects of my job and turn toward the resource role that I enjoyed. It became evident, however, that a staff with so many diverse directions needed more glue. I had to look at the total staff and see who would handle communication and other staff development work.

In large part, my job as leader was to help lay out a procedure to help staff avoid the pitfalls of an agency, such as ours, and to maximize my own effectiveness, by compensating for my particular biases as a leader. Our efforts at staff development became the major way to carry out our function as a leader agency and to complement my role as the agency's leader.

A Pedagogy

We tried to make the total program a learning experience for the staff involved. To a large extent the learning centered on two areas: 1) problem solving in the course of our work in the community, and 2) decision-making about which programs to initiate and what processes to use to achieve our program objective.

Paulo Freire distinguishes between what he calls the "banking" concept of education, the student is the receptacle into which the teacher "deposits" the contents he or she chooses, and "problem-posing" education which "rejects communiques and embodies communication." When leaders confront people with the problems that constrain their lives, a liberating, joint process of dialectical education can occur. Freire writes,

> whereas banking education anesthetizes and inhibits creative power, problem-posing education involves a constant unveiling of reality. The former attempts to maintain *submersion* of consciousness; the latter strives for the *emergence* of consciousness and *critical intervention* in reality.[1]

We felt there was no better way for our staff to gain skill at community development than to be involved with the problems that impinged on their own lives. Struggling to solve a problem was in our eyes the most effective form of educational experience. We then had to determine the process which would help the staff develop a consciousness about what they had been learning and how to utilize it for "critical intervention." Our "training" was really an effort to show people how to survive in a problem-filled environment.

We especially tried to institute democratic participation as the functional process of the agency—a process which proved extraordinarily difficult. We encountered major problems simply getting people to believe that they could play a role in decision-making; much less that self-control could lead to agency control, and ultimately could lead to community control.

We tried a number of ways to encourage democratic participation, beginning with a stratified arrangement in which program leaders met with their own sections alone. We soon discovered that too frequently there was no way to guarantee that things would really get done, so we moved toward taking care of business in full staff meetings. The main drawback of this system was the need for long, often boring meetings (with endless reports to cover all departments of the program) and the unsatisfactory level of attendance—usually 75 to 80 percent.

Even though staff meetings were held only twice a month, some staff actually made other appointments to avoid them. Nevertheless, we pursued the full staff meeting approach in an effort to build a "we-ism," a positive group self-image and identity that would help people relate to what the agency was all about and understand how they could play a role in the agency's operation even at the most fundamental levels.

The major stumbling blocks to our whole effort to make ours a participatory agency were the following:

1) Difficulty to get people to believe that what they actually said made a difference in policy and action in the agency. 2) Some staff found it easier to be told what to do, to be led. 3) Lack of practice in decision-making, especially with such a cross-section of people. It became clearly evident that democracy is a very slow, sometimes frustrating and painful process, especially to those who consider themselves to be action-oriented. 4) Non-participation no matter how we tried to draw them in. I think that had to do in large part with people having trouble differentiating between fact and feeling. We were faced with the problem of getting people to back up their feelings with facts. There was great debate about the importance of supporting Black owned business like Freedom Industries, for instance, but the arguments pro and con often centered, I suspect, around some very deep-seated feelings about whether Blacks could successfully operate a business.

Still seeking to allow our diverse group to move with some semblance of unity, we finally found that a combination approach was most effective: breaking into small groups facilitated the process of making decisions as a full group. Each small group, deliberately composed of people from different areas of the agency which gave people a chance to challenge their colleagues, was to define the problems we were working on as they saw them, develop the issues that were expected to arise, and look at the steps they felt would be useful to solve the problems.

Groups learned to look at both positive and negative factors, to prioritize, and to determine ways to convince the other groups that their chosen strategy was workable. Such groups helped to break down some of the supervisory relationships usually taken for granted, and encouraged all staff to participate in the early stages of formulating approaches to problems. For a large staff, this technique can help build cross-program relationships which provide a good base for long-term program development.

A Way of Life

The point of departure of the movement lie in men themselves. But since men do not exist apart from the world, apart from reality, the movement must begin with the men-world relationship. Accordingly, the point of departure must always be with men in the "here and now," which constitutes the situation within which they are submerged, from which they emerge, and in which they intervene. Only by starting from this situation—which determines their perception of it—can they begin to move. To do this authentically they must perceive their state not as fated and unalterable, but as merely limiting—and therefore challenging.

—*Paolo Freire*, Pedagogy of the Oppressed[2]

An agency cannot work effectively if its participants are not doing the work for themselves. If the staff doing organizing (for a housing coop, school parents' group, etc.) does not see their efforts as a way to improve their own situation then they are really in the same bag as whites who come into the community to "fix things" in a missionary model. We were attempting to create within our own agency a process that people were part of and in so doing, to develop a new lifestyle and set of values. The League program was designed to help people achieve developmental goals, and in achieving them to define themselves and a new life pattern.

In a number of ways, however, we sometimes made it difficult for our staff to live the sort of integrated existence we sought, because of both internal and external pressures. The program policy of spin-off had some drawbacks. Staff members were often sent out into the world on their own, before they were ready and the attendant pressures from the community or within their own staff made it tough for them to reach beyond basic survival needs. Because we often spun off programs in isolation, people didn't see themselves as an extension of the parent League, which was itself (or could have been) part of a larger plan or design for community development.

In effect, our attempt to use our resources as wisely as possible by generating rather than simply supporting programs, created a situation in which we were eroding our own base. By pushing people out on their own, we unwittingly prevented the ongoing, cohesive development of the League itself. We set out to build an organization, then effectively worked to keep it from functioning as an ongoing entity.

Some of our staff retreats and intensive group sessions proved to be the best ways to get people operating on the basis of self-interest. They provided an intense and close environment in which people worked together to understand the implications of community control on their own lives. Staff members could often have been more effective on their projects if they had been less afraid of getting the League in trouble with some of our so-called friends in power positions. If the staff had seen the need to challenge some of the archaic and detrimental structures and relationships in the community in terms of their own needs and those of their neighbors, they might have been more willing to undertake a confrontation. Their actions, even on a small project, could aid or hinder the process of gaining community control.

Some very major decisions were made by the entire staff on retreats. At one retreat, during our second year, discussion yielded a suggestion that League personnel prepare ourselves for personal survival by means of a community survival fund to be financed by a donation of 5 percent of each staff member's salary. When the question of pay differential within our organization came up (especially since 5 percent of some of the lower salaries was a fairly substantial sacrifice) the most impressive decision of the retreat was made: to establish a minimum wage toward which some of the survival fund would go. In fact, this suggestion gave us the impetus to work out the minimum wage without the use of the survival fund money.

We settled on a minimum pay for all employees of $100 a week; we also agreed not to make any training referrals for less than our own minimum. We were careful to double check with the Boston Welfare Rights Organization to be sure that our minimum was consistent with their standards. We wanted to demonstrate our belief that every agency would be better off hiring fewer people with more realistic wages.

The survival fund also had implications for our relationship with other community funding agencies and mechanisms. With the creation of the survival fund, people began to see more clearly their relationship to the white community or white supported funding sources. Eventually this recognition led to our controversy and confrontation with United Community Services.

Being In Control

Efforts to get some control over neighborhood affairs hinged in part on our ability to handle control when we got it, so that a major task in the development of our staff was helping people deal with the psychological, social, economic, cultural and political ramifications of being in control. One approach we took both within the agency and in the community was a reconsideration of the definition of a holiday.

We had a number of discussions to determine which days, which past heroes, what events of significance to honor. We considered the days already legitimized by the Board of Directors and then took up the various suggestions that we make changes to honor W. E. B. DuBois, Malcolm X, Marcus Garvey, and Martin Luther King. At that time none of these individuals were celebrated in the schools, although now some of these Black heroes receive recognition. This meant that the staff was considering adjustments in personal habits, family and school vacations, and work holidays. We had to figure out how to respond to holidays instituted in the schools but not at work. The issue was really one of reordering our lives around our beliefs.

The most important elements of this reorientation was a commitment to Black awareness sessions. The staff agreed to gather on the morning of this holiday and discuss the meaning of the honored person's life, his or her impact on Black community development, survival, Black thought and culture. All of our staff were included and eventually we broadened the meetings to include the staff from other community organizations. These talks gave us a chance to work through some of the Black values and problems in community control and the relationship we were concerned about.

These meetings, significantly, provided a time to break bread. People would bring different foods, eat, talk, and then feel free to go on their way. I think those times were really important to what went on in the agency and contributed to the growth of the organization, staff, and all the people who became involved. We were attempting to deal with why a particular person or ideal was important to us; it became a time for re-affirmation of, rededication to, and reflection on what we were all about. These days were not seen as time off, but as a pause: time to think about why we were doing our jobs. We were attempting to institutionalize the values of that person and his or her work in the community. By honoring particular types of behavior, we provided a role model for our children. These honor days gave us a chance to get close, to communicate and comprehend what people were about on a personal level, all of which led to better working relationships across the program areas.

Service or Repair?

Our most constant challenge as staff was to keep questioning our own style and purpose. Were we a service organization or were we going to move wholeheartedly into community organizing and community development which might have more permanent impact on community problems?

There were continual discussions about how to take what we were doing, at times service oriented by habit or tradition, and make it a basis for organizing. When we asked ourselves questions about education, for instance, we realized that even to begin to organize folks in the schools, we would have to take into account problems related to health, clothing, nutrition, housing and employment. In fact some of the people we were trying to get involved couldn't relate to our organizing efforts until these other items were taken care of. If we were about solving problems, we couldn't be involved in narrow, one dimensional services. It was necessary for the entire staff to reorient their own perceptions and approaches toward the view that every problem was part of a whole system or network of factors. Staff had to plan their work with a broader view of the impact and ramifications it could have.

All of our experiences reinforced our belief that the service approach is in fact not the answer. Rather we must look to the more basic issues around the level of income, which is what frees people to deal with the interpersonal problems that cause more conflict and confusion in our society than anything else. Freed from the frictions which are unavoidable when people are anxious about their next meal or their child's health, people can begin to work through the problems which otherwise seem insurmountable and obstruct chances to move ahead.

We finally came to the point of questioning the need for a large staff of people with highly specialized skills. It began to seem much more purposeful to train people in a more general-ized action process that could be utilized to solve problems. By moving away from the belief that only "professionals" could have certain organizing and problem solving skills, we could equip more people with the basic skills underlying the special-ties. We could increase the probability that each of them would precipitate and follow through problem solving, rather than being bound solely to one narrow portion of the problem.

Evaluation

Before going on, we need to evaluate the years spent at the League. The success of the New Urban League depends, of course, on the criteria used for evaluation. With hindsight, it is fairly easy to perceive the points at which we did *not* achieve our goals, although some of these "failures" were due to a lack of understanding about the underlying needs for some of our program plans.

As mentioned earlier, there were some contradictions built into our programming and methodology. Effective develop-ment must be an inclusive venture, not one in which the welfare of some groups of individuals is disregarded or overlooked. It is easy, however, to get distracted by the variety of perspectives from which one must work depending on political and social factors. At times we didn't work consciously enough against the psychology of status, i.e., workers vs. management, "ins" vs. "outs," which interferes so readily with moving as a group.

Additionally, the spin-off model counteracted our interest in fostering a "community" within our agency, by drawing away some of our best talent. In spite of our goals, we were basically operating on a capitalistic model like most other land or program development agencies: come in, set up, and then keep on stepping. This model harbors some dangerous potential for exploitation because the people with talent or power have the option of leaving without accountability. This approach also worked to some extent against our laying long-term plans.

Nevertheless, we did make some successful efforts. If the evaluation criteria are related to developing an institution to meet the immediate needs of the community, we were successful to a large extent in the short run. We also managed to develop several methods or processes for solving a problem.

In terms of improving the awareness of the general public, reaching a larger number of people, even politicizing people and getting them to play new kinds of roles in the educational process, we made great strides.

Most importantly, we helped generate and support a number of institutions which have contributed greatly to the political and economic interests of the community. The United Black Appeal has increasing potential to serve the community as a collection, allocation, and evaluation agency for community funded projects. The United Community Construction Workers(UCCW) has led the way for important strides in Black construction work, even with the opposition of some state agencies to the quotas they demand. Child's World Day Care Centers, the Big Brother Alliance, and the state Model High School program are all examples of programs developed based on community needs.

In terms of our original design and commitment—community organizing for problem solving, energizing efforts, creating institutions where necessary, providing support, spinning off independent groups, and gathering resources for community use—we made a good beginning.

PART III.

THE INSTITUTION BUILDING STAGE: Black Skill Development

There was significant change in the self-image of the Black community during the organizing experiences of the sixties. We started out with minimal confidence; we organized; we verbalized issues; and we made some things happen through the marches, boycotts, and negotiations. The confidence and experience gained through the organizing process prompted us to begin thinking differently about what we wanted to gain. Just as a person grows up and realizes that no one else can provide what you want as well as you can, because you really are the only person who can *know* what you want, Black people began to realize that just getting access to the existing institutions was not the best way to meet our needs. Our enlightened consciousness about the failure of existing social and economic institutions to meet the needs of the community of color, moved the community to develop two distinctive approaches to getting our needs met more appropriately. Our plan of action was focused on getting existing institutions and the society as a whole to change in ways that will fulfill its promises to us all. The other major approach was to create alternatives within the Black community to meet our collective needs without depending on the general society for progressive solutions.

In the first case, the community worked to "institutionalize" solutions, particularly through court cases. The suits brought on the issue of segregated public schools resulted in court-ordered desegregation in 1974. A case brought to challenge the at-large elections of both city council and school committee members in Boston, however, was unsuccessful.

In the second approach, parents organized new schools, Black workers organized a new union, and Black businesspeople began to consider new ways to promote community economic development using methods which were bypassed by conventional financing and business development institutions. What all these efforts had in common was that the community took the initiative to get the services it wanted, or to provide those services for itself.

The results of these two types of institution building included the Massachusetts Experimental School System, a state funded alternative primary, middle and high school; and the Metropolitan Council for Educational Opportunity (METCO) a parent initiated program to place Black students in white suburban schools. We saw the development of a successful community-based housing industry. Black businesspeople in Boston started successful, Black oriented businesses like Freedom Industries and Circle, Inc. Black workers organized United Community Construction Workers (UCCW), while others took the approach of institutionalizing equal employment opportunity through existing union and training programs. Then UCCW moved out of its organizational phase to taking action and initiative as an institution in its own right.

These developments in Boston reflected trends nationally. The dual approach to getting our needs met—through developing new institutions and through insisting that existing systems do what they should do in the first place for people of color— dramatized the larger tensions between national leaders: Malcolm X pressed for Black community control, Black-owned business, "doing for self" through the Muslim community; while Martin Luther King pressed the society as a whole to live up to the standards of equity and justice which are promised in the Constitution and laws of the nation.

The two approaches reflected the conflict the Black community felt as it became fully aware of the gap between white society and Black needs. Part of us felt that we should make society do what it was supposed to do; while the other part of us warned that we shouldn't waste the energy trying to force white people to change their behavior—we should just go ahead and do for ourselves. We were faced with the uncomfortable question of whether "integration" meant assimilation. In terms of our definition of "integration" (a place in the seats of power and decision-making), the most "integrated" groups were those that were "separated" and had taken power and responsibility for themselves.

Other national factors were also felt in Boston. When the systematic elimination of our leaders did not stop the development of institutions which provided for greater community control of resources, other steps were taken to slow our developments such as the almost total severance of housing funds during the Nixon administration. As the nation's leaders tried to slow the inflation lit by the Viet Nam War, cutting the funds supporting community based housing development was an easy step to take. The Office of Economic Opportunity (OEO), which was a major source of funding for community based ventures which led to institution building, was dismantled. These attempts to stifle the creative (and threatening) alternatives being developed in the Black community had severe effects for a number of Boston projects. But it also may have had another effect. In their need for support, community programs began turning to one another, establishing links which would lead us into a new level of community development.

Through the institution building stage, the Black community was developing skills of all sorts that would enable us to build a new community. The acquisition of skills came along with the steady improvement of our self-image on the scale of negative to positive, with the acquisition of increased power through political successes (the election of five Black members of the Legislature in 1971 and the triumphant election of John O'Bryant to the School Committee in 1977), and through the personal successes of Black community leaders who moved into influential positions in a wide variety of government and private institutions.

In the process of assembling these skills, even though many of the efforts were rather isolated from each other, the community gathered strength and know-how which can be the basis for more expansive and interconnected development of community institutions which could alter the way this city is run. As Byron Rushing once told me: "If all the white people disappeared from Boston tomorrow, we could run this city fine."

Chapter 13

COURT ORDERED DESEGREGATION

It is important to understand the connection between the story of the Boston public schools in the 1960's and the eventual implementation of the court order to desegregate in 1974— almost ten years after the Racial Imbalance Law was passed in the State Legislature The issue of "forced busing" is often discussed by parents, officials and Black and white students as a totally arbitrary and disconnected action of the Court. "Busing" is not viewed as a method of transportation but as a symbol for federal intervention, violation of private rights, and a veritable invasion of segregated neighborhood turf. The term "desegregation" seems to have disappeared from the language—the news media's presistent use of "busing" has helped divert attention from the constitutional basis of the issue.

In fact, history shows that "busing" was not forced but invited. It was demanded by the consistent and deliberate actions of the Boston School Committee and, it should be pointed out, by the voters who repeatedly elected the people who violated the constitutional rights of Black children. On the one hand, the eventual total restructuring of the Boston schools which took place under the court order was the product of blatant racism practiced by the School Committee and the Boston electorate for twenty years. On the other hand, restructuring was a result of the efforts of Black parents and community leaders to organize an effective demand that the school system be more responsive to the needs of Black students and the Black community.

Throughout the time that Black students were striking for greater control in their schools during the late sixties, the Boston school system was in court as a result of the overt racist policies of the School Committee. The U.S Department of Health, Education and Welfare (HEW) had repeatedly threatened to cut federal funds to the school system on the basis of evidence that the Committee was maintaining a dual enrollment system. By 1972 it had filed a court suit and in March of 1973 decided to withhold HEW monies from the schools. Over the same period, since the mid 1960's, the State Department of Education under Commissioner Gregory Anrig had been trying to force the Boston schools to comply with the Racial Imbalance Law to no avail. The State had used various tactics to encourage compliance with the Law, including providing 65% of new construction funds for schools which would improve racial balance. But while the Boston system took state funds designated to reduce racial imbalance, the number of imbalanced schools increased and Boston remained the last major city in the Commonwealth to comply with the Law. The State had been embroiled in court proceedings since the mid 1960's when the Boston School Committee sued the State Board for withholding state funds. A group of Black parents filed a class action suit requesting desegregation of the public schools system in 1972.

Political support for the concept of balanced schools had steadily declined since the mid sixties, particularly as suburban systems became increasingly worried that they, too, might have to comply with stricter interpretations of the law. The passage of Chapter 636 of the General Laws, legislation which provided thousands of dollars to school systems for programs to decrease racial isolation, was evidence of this increased opposition.

Annually, bills to repeal the Racial Imbalance Law itself were filed and on several occasions passed, but Governor Sargent repeatedly vetoed the bills and enough votes were mustered to uphold his veto. The State Department of Education was also attempting to develop new carrots to increase voluntary desegregation, including the magnet school concept which was to become a prominent part of the court order, and the State's experimental school system, which in many ways became a momentarily bright model of community controlled education before funds were terminated.

With a campaign for re-election on the horizon in 1974, Governor Sargent began looking for ways to maintain his traditional liberal posture on racial balance without alienating the increasingly resistant suburban groups which were beginning to organize opposition to the law. Recent metropolitan busing solutions ordered by courts in other cities (Charlotte-Mecklenberg) did not help their fears. Suburban state representatives were pressured by friends and relatives from city districts as well as their own constituents. The Chapter 636 legislation was something of a hedge as Sargent, sensing the erosion of support for racial balance, tried to offer a more palatable incentive system on the one hand, and a buffer if the Racial Imbalance Law should actually be repealed on the other.

During the 1974 legislative session, one of the first major issues confronting the newly elected Black Caucus was desegregation. At that time, all the Caucus members were from the city of Boston, and we were the only elected officials of color for our constituents. Many of us had been involved in the struggle for decent education in Boston's schools for many years so it was natural to try to work on the issue through the legislature.

The Joint Legislative Education Committee called a meeting of all the Boston representatives and senators just before Judge A. Garrity handed down his decision, in the hopes that we might develop an alternative solution which would avoid the necessity of a court order. Using the Racial Imbalance Act as a basis for our discussion, we proposed an approach which had been used by the Atlanta schools, essentially a community control approach which opted for a different sort of political solution. The crux of the Atlanta plan was that the balance of power was changed; schools in Black neighborhoods would move to Black control of hiring, jobs, curriculum development. We recognized that white people might resist such a plan if they believed that they would lose some jobs.

Our proposal tried to take this complication into account by working to increase the number of teachers of color to a level consistent with the student population. We proposed that the State assume the cost of salaries for the first year, and over a four or five year period the cost of salaries would be assumed by city government. We were pushing to increase the total number of teachers, not to push white teachers out of jobs.

Rep. Michael Daley facilitated that meeting. We went through several hours of negotiations. The issues were exemplified by exchanges with South Boston Senator Billy Bulger who was confused by the idea that we wanted a consistent policy across the city. At a hearing on community control he asked, "You mean South Boston would control its schools and you would get the Black schools?" He couldn't conceive of the idea that we wanted to increase control in our own schools and not necessarily take over schools in places like Southie. Finally, the meeting broke up with real possibilities for a plan in the air. We agreed to meet at ten o'clock the next morning to proceed, but by that time some of the white legislators had talked to officials from the Boston Teachers' Union (BTU) and had been told, "No way." Suddenly the issue was not busing kids from school to school; the issue was economic control. The teachers union was not about to lose control of even one faculty position, even though we were not talking about setting up a competing situation.

It was clear from this experience that, contrary to all the public proclamations from white leaders, the children were not their central concern. The chance to develop an alternative proposal, which could forestall a court order, was stopped by their determination to retain full white control of a school system which is increasingly Black. There was no willingness to share the power and decision-making even when it would mean no displacement of white teachers or administrators.

Judge Garrity was faced with overwhelming evidence. The School Committee had kept excellent records of its policies and plans to keep the schools segregated; and the long history of Black parent protest, court cases, and attempts to have the existence of de facto segregation publicly recognized provided a cumulative record of the resistance to voluntary desegregation. In effect, the Judge had no choice but to respond to history. His findings make the link between the 1960's and the necessity of a court order explicit.

He found that the Boston School Committee and the State Board of Education had "by deliberate action, failed to provide Black children with the equal eduational opportunities guaranteed by the 14th Amendment."[1] The Judge found that members of the School Committee " took many actions in their official capacities with the purpose and intent to segregate the Boston public schools...such actions caused current conditions of segregation in the Boston public schools." The specific actions he cited included changing districts, feeder school patterns, deliberate incorporation of residential segregation into the school system, segregation of teachers and administrative personnel, discriminatory recruitment, and construction of new buildings in ways designed to "intentionally segregate schools at all levels." The members of the School Committee, the Judge declared, have "knowingly carried out a systematic program of segregation affecting all of the city's students, teachers and school facilities and have intentionally brought about and maintained a dual school system. Therefore, the entire school system of Boston is unconstitutionally segregated."[2]

Our approach to community controlled schools was based on the recognition that our young were not getting the kind of education we knew they needed in white controlled schools. Our approach for community control of schools was that hiring, firing, planning curriculum development, programming would be based on needs as we assessed them. We believed that we should get a proportional share of education money and would operate in our communities in a way that was inclusive of and open to parents and student control in the process.

White people and white representatives had to step to a different drummer, one which wanted to keep Black youngsters and Black folks out of their neighborhoods (schools and housing). But white people wanted to maintain control over the cash registers (jobs and contracts). Their approach to busing was to prevent access and involvement by Black people, while maintaining control over the resources necessary for education. We were willing to compromise to the extent we would get control. The middle ground for us was around the teachers—hiring 1,500 additional teachers to achieve racial balance on school staffs. The idea was not to cost people jobs, but to add to the number of people doing the job. We thought we could develop a win/win situation by getting the State to pay for the interim period. White leaders, however, saw this proposal as a win or lose struggle.

The Phase I Plan for the desegregation ordered by Judge Garrity was essentially the State Plan which the State Board of Education had been attempting to implement for some years. It was a basic population balancing scheme which had to resort to busing to remedy the deeply entrenched patterns of segregation in schools and residences. The plan was based on the magnet school concept which had been tested in the Trotter School, Boston Latin and Technical High School. It assured that if particular desirable skills are offered at particular schools, white students can be attracted back into the system. The plan also used a geo-code system. The geo-code system numbered the streets and blocks in the districts of the city as a way of locating students and then, based on the population characteristics of the students, determined which schools they were to attend. This facilitated computerized busing assignments. In addition, school districts were paired to simplify the reassignments of students. The ironic pairing of Roxbury High with the adamantly all white South Boston High was the result of a law which had been passed some years earlier stating that no student should be transported more than a set number of miles from their homes. Geographically, South Boston High was the only other high school which was within legal distance.

The violent resistance to the court order by white neighborhoods—notably South Boston—is now history. Buses were stoned, students were attacked, white parents hurled racial epithets, fights broke out in school hallways, classrooms and playgrounds. Black students were unable to participate in after school activities safely. The resemblance to Little Rock almost twenty years earlier was disheartening, but the Black students and the Black community as a whole met the situation with dignity and determination.

It should have come as no surprise that the white community would react to desegregation with violent resistance. South Boston High had for generations been a closed school. When I ran for School Committee in the early sixties, I remember being told by a City Counselor that there was an unwritten code that no Black wouldever graduate from "Southie." And for many years there had been threats and violence against the few Black people who dared to move into public housing units in South Boston. Media reporting of the incidents did not help; South Boston was repeatedly portrayed as a "close-knit" community as though that were a sacred American value which justified violent reaction to anything which might disrupt the familiar patterns.

The intensity of the opposition to desegregation was heightened by the fact that the resisters received support from many elected officials, including Gerald Ford, President of the United States, who was actually quoted as saying that he disagreed with the Judge. In effect, he announced that he supported people opposed to providing and protecting constitutional rights. And several of Boston's City Councilors, including Mrs. Hicks, hung huge red letters in their office windows at City Hall, so that the name of South Boston's anti-busing organizationROAR —(Restore Our Alienated Rights)—was spelled out across the building. Mayor White was also quoted as saying that he did not believe that busing would improve education for anyone—a flat denial of the constitutional issue involved in the court ruling.

The sad legacy of the Boston Irish political history was portrayed again in the organized resistance of groups like ROAR, the South Boston Information Center and the South Boston Marshalls who advocated violent "protection" of their neighborhood from "invasion." These groups have, by the way, ,made effective use of of the tools developed during the Civil Rights Movement.

For all the years that the Irish have been in power in Boston, their leaders have continued to treat them as though they were a persecuted minority. The defensive, hostile mentalitty which evolved was the result of being constantly reminded of the historical discrimination against the Irish. This attitude has made them prey to the demogogic leaders who continually use the specter of anti-Irish sentiments to keep their constituents voting for one of their own. The major irony is that not since the days of Mayor James Michael Curley (whose extremely effective personal patronage machine was ousted with the support of the old Brahmin power structure in 1949) have these leaders delivered any of the benefits of power directly to their own constituents.

Some of Boston's Irish leaders have encouraged attacks on Black people, yet they do not challenge the banks, corporations, universities and all the other power groups whose boards of directors still read like a list of Yankee Who's Who. The poor white communities like much of South Boston do not get much in the way of basic services from their leaders. The entire Boston school system suffered during the years the School Committee adamantly resisted improvements that might also promote desegregation. South Boston High was no better a school than many of the Black schools which had been so neglected. In fact, the parochial schools were the only alternative for white Irish families who sought a sound education for their children.

In the context of this violent resistance to desegregation in Boston, Black parents and students took an approach that contrasted dramatically to the behavior of white disruption. Led by Mrs. Ellen Jackson, who had started Operation Exodus many years earlier, the venerable Roxbury institution Freedom House (begun in 1949 by Otto and Muriel Snowdon, long-time leaders in Roxbury) opened an Institute of Schools and Education which played a major role in preparing the Black community for the desegregation experience.

Organizing a coalition of Black community agencies such as the Roxbury Multi-Service Center and the Lena Park Development Corporation, and hundreds of volunteers, Freedom House established an information service, rumor control center, and emergency assistance with transportation. "The principal concern," of everyone involved, said Mrs Jackson, "is the safety of every child and the right of every child to quality education." Volunteers were posted as monitors at bus stops in Roxbury, and provided before and after school care for students whose parents needed such assistance.

"We stand united at this critical time to provide leadership and resources to the parents and children who will be attending our schools," stated Mrs. Jackson. "We call on other sections of the city to assume the same responsibility." [3]

The Freedom House coalition enlisted dozens of community leaders to meet with students and their parents, to plan a unified community response in anticipation of white reaction, and to calm fears, answer questions and encourage calm. Chuck Turner, longtime advocate of Black economic development; Elma Lewis, once a member of the NAACP Education Committee and director of a nationally known center for Black artists; Leon Rock, leader of the Black Student Union and participant in the student strikes during the late sixties; Paul Parks, member of the early NAACP committee and then director of Model Cities (eventually to be State Secretary of Education); Tom Atkins, leader of the sit-in demonstration at the School Committee in 1965 and officer of the NAACP, as well as City Councilor and one-time candidate for Mayor; Ruth Batson, also a early NAACP committee member; and members of the Legislative Black Caucus—all of us joined together to meet with parents and students. We assisted the efforts to keep calm in the Black community, and to prepare our children for the harsh realities that awaited them in formerly all white schools.

As the violence continued and we all became increasingly worried for the safety of the students (and increasingly convinced that the city officials were not prepared to take steps necessary to control the violence), it was hard not to wonder if we were doing the right thing. There were times when students had something to teach us. I will never forget a conversation I had with a 15-year old student assigned to South Boston High. "We have to go," she declared with passion. "If they run us out of that school, they can run us out of the city. They will be able to stop access wherever they want." The adults of the Black community had no choice but to offer support to young people as brave and clear about the issues as that young woman. It was clear to many of our students, certainly for that young woman, that the court order was not just a matter of education; it was an intensely political experience from which she and hundreds of others were getting an entirely different sort of education.

Her statement, unfortunately, was prophetic and over the next year or so the Black community was to witness the beating of a Black man on Boston City Hall Plaza by a group of young whites just leaving a meeting of an anti-busing group invited to City Hall by a city counselor. They assaulted Ted Landsmark with an American flag on a pole in full view of the offices of the city government and dozens of spectators.

There were Black/white confrontations at a public beach in South Boston within walking distance of a predominantly Black housing project. A group of students from Philadelphia were assaulted by a gang of whites in Charlestown as they visited a national monument—Bunker Hill, ironically a symbol of the American Revolution. There was also violence in the Black community and one white man was fatally beaten.

The increasingly hot climate of hate in the city prompted a coalition of Black agencies including Freedom House, the Black Ministerial Alliance and the NAACP to request aid from the federal government to secure the safety of Black youth. As early as October of 1974, the coalition sent a letter to the Congressional Black Caucus and the Attorney General requesting that federal marshalls be sent to Boston immediately. The letter stated: "We urgently need your support in resolving Boston's most pressing urban issue, the inability and unwillingness of the city's elected officials to fulfill their obligation to protect and support our Black community's pursuit of public education for our youth." The coalition went so far as to urge Black students not to attend school in South Boston, Roslindale and Hyde Park because of the number of violent incidents in those schools.

Representative Royal Bolling, Sr., of the Boston Legislative Black Caucus, had issued a similar demand for federal troops just before the Coalition's letter was announced, called Boston "the Little Rock of the North" and cited the "complete breakdown of law enforcement in several Boston communities in which our children are being bused."[4] Apparently he was not exaggerating, for at the start of the next school year, when federal marshalls were indeed utilized in force in Boston, Stanley J. Pottinger, head of the Civil Rights Division of the U.S.

Justice Department, stated that "with the possible exception of Little Rock, Arkansas, in 1959, when Federal troops were deployed, no other desegregation effort in the country's history has used as much manpower and resources."[5]

Phase II of the court order went into effect for the 1975-76 school year, but not until after the Black community, again led by Freedom House staff, had critiqued the original plan which included a "metropolitanization" approach and "freedom-of-choice" method which many members of the community found too reminiscent of Southern plans. Ultimately Phase II was modified to include greater emphasis on the magnet school approach, increased participation by universities and institutions and businesses, and a more detailed participation plan for parents both in local school districts and city-wide.

There were a number of issues inherent in the court orders which deserve careful consideration. Personally, I feel that the magnet school concept is questionable, since it is developing a two tier system of attractive magnet schools and "ordinary" schools. The assumption is that all schools cannot be "magnets" for students, with the inevitable result that some schools will remain undesirable and inferior. In addition, the assumptions implicit in the magnet concept are that white students have to be "attracted" to attend school with Black children. It also implies that there is nothing inherently attractive or unique about a community school which is designed to meet the specific needs of its surrounding area. I feel that these assumptions harbor racist values and that the basic issue of control of resources by the users of schools is still avoided.

The question remains whether a school system controlled by people who practice the "politics of scarcity"—always pitting groups against each other for "scarce resources"—and who believe that some children are more deserving than others, can or will ever provide adequate resources for those who are not in control. The intransigence of the opposition to the court order makes it nearly impossible to make desegregation a positive approach to improving the quality of education in the Boston schools.

Because the political climate of the city is so poor, many potentially valuable alternative efforts are thwarted or do not even get discussed. The City Wide Parents Advisory Council is an important step in the right direction, and many dedicated parents of all colors have been working creatively and energetically to improve both the climate and the quality of the schools. The court order and subsequent rulings have also enforced the hiring of Black teachers and administrators, and although the percentages are still below the optimum point, the hiring process has been opened up to people from outside the system and to parent involvement. All these are important steps in the direction of equity and quality.

The story of court ordered desegregation continues. Violence still mars the small steps of progress and power struggles still continue within the system for control of decisions. Attempts are being made to dilute existing parent involvement. But there have been some clear lessons from the experience of desegregation which the Black community should heed.

First, we have learned that we must stand firm in demanding our constitutional rights. We will not allow the denial of any right, or we will be denied access to every right and all resources. At every point where we see people attempting to deny constitutional rights, whether it is the harrassment of public housing tenants, or the denial of financial resources to people who want to remain in their urban home places, or assaults on visitors from out of town who do not know the "boundaries" between Black and white territories, we must stand firm and insist that constitutional rights are protected. For every incident we allow to go unchallenged, we will find ourselves fighting dozens more. Struggle, as our young people are now finding out, is the highest form of education; and we must continue the struggle to protect our lawful rights or face control by the ignorance of those who would deny them.

Second, our experience with desegregation should make sure that we do not have another generation which has any illusions about where whites in this city stand on civil and human rights. In the fifties people opposed to our activism would say, "This is Boston, not Birmingham." Yet, in fact, this city is to be compared in every way to the most entrenched opposition to civil rights in the South or anywhere else. We cannot afford illusions any longer.

Third, we should use this experience to understand *why* we have gone through the struggle for desegregation. What is the purpose of the education that we have been fighting for? So many of our young people do not know why they are going to school. We have had to concentrate so much energy on explaining why and how the schools are bad that we have never had the time to specify exactly what we mean by a "good" education and what it should be used for. We need to extend our struggle for our youngsters to secure other opportunities and jobs to give the educational experience a point and purpose. We can no longer afford to use the crutch of claiming "This is a racist society" so everything is hard; we *know* that now beyond all doubt. We should learn from this experience that we have to be about political and communtiy development to deal with reality.

Fourth, we should have learned that although the court order provides some of the critical elements of community control of the schools, particularly the Citywide Parents Advisory Council, and participation in hiring decisions, the written plan does not guarantee actual accountability or control. The order has in effect created a new school system with new people, a new school committee, new curricula and programs. But it is like a new suit of clothes or a new car. The real question is who is wearing it or driving it? We *should* have learned that *we* can be the driver; if we do not step into control, we have failed to seize the times. The tools are right there in front of us, but all the court orders in the world will not guarantee that we actually use these tools to take control of the system and make it work for all the children instead of just some.

In some ways we have allowed ourselves to be used: We worked relentlessly for our kids, but it was the Boston police who got the overtime pay. Bus companies made a profit off of the order; computer technicians and consultants got work; transitional aides were hired; tremendous sums have poured into the school system, all because of what we were doing for our children, because it was right. But we must realize that all of what has been accomplished is just a beginning: We have built a new institution, and it is ours to claim. But we may give it away before we realize it if we are not alert.

Finally, we have learned the hard way that there are dozens

of methods of subverting the intention of the order even with the hard work of groups like Freedom House and the many other community agencies active in desegregation implementation. At least three approaches are now being used to resegregate the schools from within, as happened so often in Southern schools. Tracking is allowing classes to remain 70% and more white in schools which are at least 50% Black. Special education classes are also being used to separate children by race, and suspensions continue to be a way to remove a disproportionate number of Black children from the schools.

Chapter 14

JOBS NOT PROMISES

RACISM IN THE UNIONS:
The New Boston Plan

The struggle to enforce the implementation of the Racial Imbalance Law in the public schools in the 1970's was paralleled by the struggle to assure that workers of color were given a proportion of the public funded construction jobs, ultimately through the enactment of the "New Boston Plan."

This chapter describes how Black workers united with Black students to force contractors to hire Black workers, and how this organizing became institutionalized through the legislative passage of hiring quotas for workers of color. In Chapter 15, we will see how workers of color, Black, Hispanic, Asian and Native American came together, through the Third World Jobs Clearing House, to allocate jobs among themselves; and finally how workers of color are uniting with white workers to demand Boston Jobs for Boston People.

As we saw in Chapter 8, Black organizing in the construction trades led to the formation of the United Community Construction Workers (UCCW). UCCW was founded on the belief that Black workers must organize to defend their own interests. The necessity for Black workers to organize themselves became dramatically apparent shortly after Martin

Luther King's assassination. On April 5, 1968, at the regularly scheduled meeting of the advisory committee to the Bureau of Apprenticeship, those present were discussing what they could "do" in light of the murder. The head of the Plumbers Union (later the head of the Massachusetts AFL-CIO) said that his union didn't have to do any more because "we let one in last year." Martin Gopen, a white member of the New Urban League's staff, who attended the meeting, was so incensed that he walked out and asked all others in attendance of good will to the Black community to do the same. He went to the League office and began to map out a strategy to increase the pressure on the construction industries. A major portion of the strategy was to involve the Black students on Boston's many college campuses, first to raise the level of consciousness about how their universities were failing to comply with federal guidelines to hire minorities to work on campus construction, and second to enlist them as watchdogs to insure that compliance was maintained. Over the next four years students at almost a dozen Boston area campuses were enlisted in this phase of the resistance against the unions and contractors.

One of the first federally funded projects that was selected as a target was the giant Government Center complex where only 12 Black workers were employed out of 200. The $22 million project included, of all things, the new Department of Employment Security Building funded in part by the Department of Labor. The Vappi Company was told to hire 30 more Black workers or the project would be picketed indefinitely. In this case the federal compliance officer backed the League's charges and ordered that Vappi hire the workers and institute a more effective compliance program for itself and its subcontractors. Vappi was also a target on the construction of Harvard's Law School where only one of the 35 workers was Black.

Members of the Black Law Students' Association confronted Dean-elect Derek Bok and John Dunlop, who was a consultant to the United States Department of Labor on equal opportunity and the unions, with a report citing, the noncompliance, and forced Vappi again to hire more Black workers within two weeks. There was some particular justice in getting Vappi to comply since the same company had been the chief contractor on the Prudential Center seven years earlier, one site of the STOP protests.[1]

By July of 1968 it was evident that the Black community was in for a long fight. Getting compliance from a few local contractors was one thing, but getting cooperation on the federal level to enforce minority hiring across the board was quite another. On July 16, the AFL-CIO News blared headlines claiming that a national conference of building trades presidents had adopted guidelines for the employment and training of model cities residents for the model cities building programs across the country.

There was great fanfare about the unions taking "initiative" to see that the needs of the residents were met, but once again there was no mention of, or provision for, community participation in the design of these plans. The group decided to contract the Workers' Defense League of New York to do "training. "The facts and figures of past tradition spoke of the amount of commitment trade unions would have to recruit and train minority workers: in the building trades in Massachusetts in the summer of 1968 there were 3,134 apprentices, 58 of them Black. Of the 661 electrician apprentices, 8 were Black; of 137 structural iron apprentices, none were Black; of 300 plumber apprentices, 7 were Black; of 353 sheet-metal apprentices, none were Black; of 265 steamfitter apprentices, 1 was Black. That came to less than 2% Black apprentices registered in the Massachusetts building trades.[2]

In a Boston Globe Magazine article at the time, Ian Foreman wrote:

> ...The labor unions which control most of the jobs, especially since 1933, have generally with few exceptions, denied Black people in numbers the opportunity to be trained for, receive and move up the ladder in jobs that are satisfying and well paid...The sheer power of the labor unions politically and economically since the New Deal...places them on a very hot spot in this racial crisis.[3]

The head of the Boston Building Trades Council was also president of the Ironworker's Union which had no Black apprentices. This same person was also responsible for implementing the "affirmative action" program to bring model cities residents into the building trades for training and membership.

After the passage of the 1964 Civil Rights Act, unions actually used it to tighten the entrance requirements by insisting that a high school diploma or "its equivalent" be held by each applicant. This wording allowed the rule to be bent for whites and more easily tightened for Black workers. Such a requirement is all the more ludicrous when you know how many union leaders do not have diplomas themselves. Unions also instituted longer training periods for apprentices at low pay. This procedure delayed Black workers from becoming journeyman or advanced trainees. New age limits also served to keep older, somewhat experienced Blacks from entering the training programs. Many unions also adopted a dubious clause requiring "good moral character."

However, UCCW and the New Urban League went after a federally funded construction project for an elderly housing tower in Egleston Square. This time the delegation attempted to "use the existing system" starting with the HUD compliance officer. After being unavailable for two weeks, he finally arranged a meeting at which he admitted that there appeared to be a violation of the existing law in terms of the number of minority workers on the project (zero), but he passed the responsibility for compliance on to the Boston Housing Authority. After all, HUD only funded the project.

The BHA likewise said that it had no control over compliance and sent the group to the BRA—Boston's urban renewal agency. The BRA said yes, the project was probably operating illegally, but the final responsibility lay with the Department of Commerce who administered this HUD grant. They, of course, pointed the finger back at HUD.

IT TOOK SIX WEEKS TO MAKE THE ROUNDS AND THE GROUP WOUND UP EXACTLY WHERE IT STARTED. Nothing radicalized the men of UCCW more than such an attempt to do things through the existing system. It was clear that more direct action was called for, so 30 men went down early in the morning and stopped the job by closing and locking the gate. Three busloads of riot police appeared as did the head of the building trades council and other officials, but no negotiations took place.

On the second day, the group demanded an audience with Perini, the head of the construction company in charge of the contract. Eventually, the group's demands were met when Perini agreed to employ minority workers in 50% of the skilled and 100% of the unskilled labor positions. The building was finished ahead of schedule at no extra cost with a total of 60% minority labor. It is still standing today which is more than can be said for some other buildings constructed at the same time with far fewer minority workers on the job. But a price was paid: union officials pressed tresspass charges and UCCW leaders did 30 days at Dear Island Jail.

Not long after, UCCW began to look outside the Black community for target construction projects. They took on the Aberthaw Construction Company, chief contractor for the new NASA center being built in Cambridge. The NASA site was chosen not only because it was federally funded, but also because it promised well paying jobs of five years duration, steady jobs which were scarce for the Black workers who were usually sent to the boondocks for short assignments causing them to lose their place on the union placement waiting list.

The first round of negotiations was again attempted on a nonconfrontation basis, but Aberthaw and the unions refused to consider UCCW's request for the immediate placement of more Black workers on the job. Aberthaw's reaction indicated that the confrontation route would continue to be the most effective way to break down specific instances of discrimination in the construction unions. The stage was set for a steady series of direct action challenges to construction sites across the city of Boston for the next three years.

The Philadelphia Plan

What has happened in Boston is typical of the racist trade unions which have assumed complete control of the programs to the detriment of the Black community. All hometown solutions are a monumental hoax and are no substitute for vigorous enforcement of civil rights laws. The only workable solution for getting minority persons into the construction industry is to

set quotas for the hiring of a specific number of persons within a definite time schedule.
                —*Senator Edward Kennedy*, November 9, 1971

1968 had been a year when the fear of retaliation for King's
death coupled with the liberalism born of a booming war economy prompted an astounding number of experiments, gifts, and
new levels of cooperative effort from white business. But Black
leaders were not satisfied with this small beginning, and pushed
for a greater committment from the white community to provide the resources and power for Black people to build their own
community.

Pressure was increased against the construction industry.
The Massachusetts Advisory Committee to the United States
Commission on Civil Rights, headed by Father Robert Drinan,
laid bare the total lack of improvement regarding compliance on
federal construction projects, and demonstrations took place on
half a dozen Boston campuses over minority hiring issues. At
the same time the tug of war for control of the "affirmative
action" training programs in Boston was leading up to the
eventual intercession of the federal government to create the
"Boston Plan" as a counterforce to the "Philadelphia Plan"
which was working too well to force compliance in the construction trades. By the end of 1969 white resistance would be so
strong that it almost counterbalanced the apparent gains of the
previous year.

It is worth examining the Philadelphia Plan because it
became the touchstone for Boston community efforts to obtain
compliance, and the target of unions and contractors who
wanted to maintain their ironclad control over the hiring of
workers. The Boston Plan was touted as the answer to the
problem of minority hiring and a substitute for the imposed
numerical requirements of the Philadelphia Plan.

At the hearings, members of community groups in Philadelphia spoke to the effectiveness of the plan which, although
called "imposed" by federal officials, was the result of voluntary
cooperative effort among the various federal agencies in Philadelphia and the Area Coordinator for the Office of Federal

Contract Compliance in the U.S. Department of Labor. The plan was an effort to comply with Executive Order 11246 and the 1964 Civil Rights Act.

The key architect of the "Philadelphia Plan" was a Black lawyer, working for the Labor Department who developed the concept of tables specifying the number of person hours to be filled by minority workers throughout the construction of projects assisted by federal funds exceeding $500,000. The Plan required that contractors include such a table in their bids. No longer were bids to be selected on the basis of cost alone, but on the potential for alleviating discrimination. These tables served as a device to measure compliance in terms of a "contractual committment" to employ "a specific minimum of Black workers in each craft at every stage of construction."[4]

The manning table was one way to stop the misleading reports by contractors about the number of minority workers they placed. To many companies, one day's work by one minority person equaled one placement, a definition which completely ignores the plight of the worker who was on the job perhaps ten days (not necessarily consecutively) over a six month period, winds up without a union card, but still gets counted as ten minority "placements" by the contractor.

The Philadelphia tables called for 20% of the person hours, per craft or trade, to be positioned by minority workers on the jobs covered by the Plan. By enforcing a minimum number, the Plan had broader potential for hiring minority workers than the old unofficial quota systems. It provided a way to counteract the insidious institutionalization of tokenism in the construction industry. The plan also made a point of putting workers in all levels of trades, not just as laborers, as was the tradition.

The only problem with the Philadelphia Plan was that it worked too well. The plan exerted such pressure on the contractors to comply that they began lobbying full force against its use. By the time of the Drinan Hearings, the Philadelphia Plan had come under attack from the U.S. Controller General who insisted that bidders were not specifically informed of the manning table requirement prior to the opening of bidding. The controller's stated quarrel appeared to be minor; he merely insisted that "any" administratively prescribed standards or requirements to be imposed upon bidders as condition of the contract or award, must be sent out in the invitation for bids.[5] But his objection was sufficient to deter, or provide an excuse for avoiding, further use of the plan for several months.

Members of the Coalition to Save the Philadelphia Plan spoke at the Drinan Hearings about their efforts to be sure that the "New" Philadelphia Plan, due to be issued the day after the hearings, was no less effective than the first one. White workers were becoming angry at the delay over the plan because they, too, were laid off while it was being rewritten. They were saying, "I don't care who I work next to, just so long as I work."[6] Resistance to the plan by unions was manifested by new, lengthy apprenticeship programs, new high school diploma requirements, and examinations to be passed.

The answer to the problem was known as the "Hometown" plan or the Boston Plan, which basically allowed "every good faith effort" to hire minorities to substitute for actual hiring according to numerical goals as in the Philadelphia Plan. Emphasis on this phase essentially gutted the contractual manning tables of the Philadelphia Plan and allowed contractors to consider an ad in the paper, or, in the most blatant cases, simply signing their "agreement" with the Hometown Plan, to be compliant. The Hometown Plan leaves no degrees of compliance but merely assumes that "participation" equals full compliance. Before long, the Hometown solution was to be proposed as the official arrangement for obtaining compliance in Boston. It is little wonder that Bok took a hard line with the Black law students over the construction at the Harvard Law School, setting the precedent for the way demonstrators would be handled later in 1969, at Harvard and elsewhere. Nor is it surprising that the Department of Labor continued to pursue the Hometown solution in Boston, and eventually across the country, instead of instituting the Philadelphia Plan in other cities.

In the meantime, the community was continuing to plan ways to pressure the industry directly since there was no satisfaction forthcoming from the Drinan hearings or other such channels. At a New Urban League planning session, a ten year projection of construction on Boston college campuses was the basis for deciding to make a strong push to involve Black students in the effort to equalize hiring on campus sites. Harvard was planning $170 million worth of construction, MIT over $100 million, and U. Mass Boston $800 million over ten years. By November, 1969, the New Urban League was deeply involved in carrying out that plan.

It was no accident, however, that in September of 1969 the New Urban League experienced a financial crisis that nearly proved fatal. The issue arose around the funding available to the League from conventional sources such as United Community Services (UCS), the allocating arm of the United Fund. During the summer, a Black member of the UCS Board called the League to say that a white member of the Board was upset because of the League's activities in challenging the unions and was recommending that the League not be funded by United Community Services. He also tried to get support for barring the League from UCS, at a meeting of the Greater Boston Labor Council.

As a result, the New Urban League was informed that their budget request of $175,000 was denied. Its actual funding was cut from the $66,000 of 1968 to $61,500 for 1969. In response, the League announced its withdrawal from the UCS altogether. The League went directly to the Massachusetts Bay United Fund with an appeal to fund the League directly without going through the unresponsive allocation agency, but that request, too, was rejected.

The New Urban League was up against the "service" mentality which had dominated the social and economic programs in the inner city. In an article for the Urban League magazine *Survival*, Alan Clark, director of Bridge, Inc., laid the problem out,

> ...Any effort that addresses itself to symptoms while disregarding and ignoring causes cannot bring about any real change in these conditions...which are rooted in institutional racism and in the structure of society itself.
> ...Attempting to ease the symptoms of poverty has long been the emphasis of many social service agencies.

The net result of this emphasis has been that the poor
and the denied have been made a little more comfortable, but nothing has been done to change the conditions under which they live.

...In short, a pillow has been propped up behind the
patient's head. He has been made a little more comfortable but the disease has been allowed to continue to
eat away.[7]

The New Urban League was being penalized for its insistence
on activism and its dedication to the theme of community development through community control. But we were not stopped.
A huge amount of energy went into obtaining funds to keep our
staff on board, and we proceeded with our plans to dramatize
the injustices in the construction industry and our program to
keep building our community.

Black workers and students began by organizing students
on the Tufts University, Medford campus, against the Volpe
Company, formerly owned by Ex-Governor John Volpe, who
was Secretary of Transportation under the Nixon Administration. In June, the Volpe Company had received complaints from
the Mass. Commission Against Discrimination, filed by the
League, about the lack of minority workers on the Tufts/Jack-
son dorm project. Complaints were also issued to Volpe about
their work force on the student union building at Brandeis
University, and also to the Aberthaw Company for the chemis-
try building at MIT. By October 23, 1969 there were 82 white
workers and only one Black worker on the Tufts site.[8]

On November 5, students dramatically shut down the construction site, some even chaining themselves to the fencing
around the project. On November 7, students voted to stage a 2
day strike, and the Tufts Afro-American Society requested that
Tufts initiate a coalition among other key schools in the area to
take action on minority employment. Faculty showed strong
support for the students at first, recommending that the University withhold payment from Volpe until 20% of the work
force was made up of Black workers (or 21 workers). On
November 8, some one-third of the students stayed out of class
and staged a symbolic march to the construction site which was

ringed by 150 riot equipped police hired by the university.[9] Father Drinan scheduled hearings on campus and recommended that there be a moratorium on further demonstrations, that Volpe make a public list of all job openings expected on the job up until Christmas, and that federal or state mediators be brought in.

Paul Parks, director of the Boston Model Cities program and member of the Mass. Advisory Committee, went a step further to suggest that a specific percentage of Black or minority workers be specified now for any new work that the university might undertake. By Tuesday, November 11, the U.S. Department of Labor announced that it was sending two "fact-finders" to determine whether a government plan aimed at equal opportunity in federally assisted construction should be implemented.[10] On the same day the Boston *Record American* reported that the Department of Labor said it would establish a Boston Plan to solve the issue. The article noted "the Labor Department's campaign to put more Blacks and other minority workers on jobs is taking different forms in different municipalities." The Boston Plan certainly was destined to be different from the Philadelphia Plan.

A few days later, Harvard's Organization for Black Unity (OBU) issued a series of seven demands related to the status and pay of workers in Harvard's "affirmative action" plan. Getting no satisfaction on their demands, the Black students took over the Dean's office and University Hall early in December. The university's negotiator was Archibald Cox who worked out a tentative agreement with the students while they were still in the Hall. When Harvard obtained an injunction against the students remaining in the Hall, the students left without incident.

On December 12, Harvard announced disciplinary action: all seventy-five students involved were suspended from the university, a move foreshadowed by Derek Bok's strong stand against the Black law students the previous year. At the same time the University announced that it would hire "in proportion to the relevant population area" and award a similar proportion of the work to Black contractors.[11]

On December 15, a huge rally was held on the steps of the

church in Harvard Yard. One thousand Black people came to hear Floyd McKisick of the Congress on Racial Equality (CORE), and a number of local leaders speak. During the rally it was suggested that any Black contractors tapped for work by Harvard refuse until the suspended students were reinstated, an idea which did not take root with the contractors who stood to gain some $1 million dollars worth of work. Ultimately, agreements resembling manning tables were arranged for any contractors and subcontractors utilized by Harvard for its training and building.

As 1969 turned into 1970, demonstrations based on the inequitable hiring practices were held at Boston University, Brandeis, Wentworth Institute, and MIT. During the winter of 1970 meetings were held with the Governor's staff to work out an employment plan for the huge amount of construction scheduled for the new University of Massachusetts campus to be built on Columbia Point, a predominantly Black neighborhood in Boston. The proposed plan required that any contractor bidding for the project had to undertake enforceable affirmative action including the immediate employment of local journeymen with training with pay for other unskilled workers. Residents of Columbia Point were to get first preference in job hiring, and Black contractors first preference in acquiring subcontracts. These efforts were duplicated at Southeastern Massachusetts University by a coalition of Black folks in New Bedford.

The Boston Plan

By working together, Black students and workers had forced the racist construction companies to dramatically increase the number of Black workers being hired. However, in 1970, the "Boston Plan" was finally implemented. But, the Boston Plan was thoroughly rejected by the Black community. Herbert Hill wrote,

> ...one would be hard pressed to find something substantive to enforce. There are no duties or responsibilities for unions or contractors, as there are no stated

goals to determine whether the parties involved are living up to the agreement.

There is an overall goal of moving 2000 men into the trades over a five-year period, but there is nothing in the contract requiring the unions to do this until at least 1975. The 2000 figure would cover 24 towns within the Route 128 area and would represent the involvement of 26 different trades. The unions will experience over 2000 retirees in the next five years and the overall net gain would be negligible.[12]

The goals would provide only one person per trade in each city per year. Hill also pointed out that the phrase "every effort" was much too close to the words "all deliberate speed" which had turned out to be "another farce of major proportions." On June 18, 1970, the day the Boston Plan was signed, the New Urban League joined the NAACP in outspoken criticism and rejection of the Plan.

The industry, clearly in the strong position, simply brushed aside the criticisms saying that the important parties had been involved in the drafting of the plan. The Boston Plan received its official funding of $608,000 on July 16, but it showed no further signs of life for almost three months. Apparently feeling they could rest easy with the Plan simply being signed, industry made no moves to facilitate the hiring of a director or staff for the administration of the program.

By September, angered by the inaction and stalling, the community coalition moved on the construction at Boston City Hospital located on the edge of the Black and Puerto Rican communities but with a work force that was ninety-five per cent white. The three days of demonstrations, in which more than one hundred twenty workers participated, resulted in seventeen arrests, including some Workers Defense League (WDL) staff, which dismayed the upper echelons sufficiently to press for some action. At long last a director was hired for the program and WDL was contracted for the training components of the Plan. In mid October the Construction Jobs Program of Boston, Inc., a nonprofit corporation, was finally established to administer the Plan. There was, however, no full time compliance officer in Boston until the summer of 1971, and then the one man assigned to Boston was responsible for a six state area.

By January of 1971 the criticism of the Boston Plan was surfacing more strongly than ever. Only 100 of the 350 worker goal had been achieved. The Boston *Herald Traveler* reported that the Plan was moving at a "snail's pace."[13] On Jan. 15, UCCW withdrew its participation in the Plan. Leo Fletcher issued the "UCCW Manifesto," a document clearly stating that Black workers intended to work in and build their own community without the interference and control of the white unions or their contractors. The Manifesto staked out the turf that UCCW considered to belong solely to the Black community and specified the number of Black or minority workers expected on jobs within that territory. By August of 1971 it was obvious that the Plan had been a failure, and it was not refunded.

The Boston Plan was in turn replaced by the "New Boston Plan" in the winter of 1972. The "New Boston Plan" required that job-by-job minority requirements were to be written into any state contract within Boston communities with substantial concentrations of minority residents. The minority requirements were to be stated in terms of person hours, trade by trade, a substantial difference from the Boston Plan which, the state explained made no provision for collecting data on minority person days or for cooperating with the Mass. Commission Against Discrimination. Furthermore, the federal office of Contract Compliance in the U.S. Department of Labor had just been dissolved with no assurances for a replacement agency. The state felt, therefore, that it had to establish enforcement procedures of its own.

Accordingly, on October 13, 1972, the state placed an ad in Boston papers for bids on a library for Boston State College. The "bid conditions," numerical goals, in terms of minority person days, were written into the contract. The state Secretary of Transportation and Construction, Alan Altshuler, held several meetings with the Massachusetts Association of General Contractors (MAGC), who wanted the bid conditions struck from state contracts. The Massachusetts Association of General Contractors, which included our old friends Vappi and Volpe construction companies (who were doing a combined total of

$155,000,000 worth of public building contracts) filed suit against Altshuler and the Massachusetts Department of Transportation in November. MAGC claimed that the bid conditions were illegal bacause they "conflicted" with the "Boston Plan," and violated the due process and equal protection clauses of the Fourteenth Amendment. They also objected to the power vested in the Massachusetts Commission Against Discrimination (MCAD) by the state and the insistence on numerical "quotas."

United Community Construction Workers (UCCW) was allowed to intervene as defendants with Altshuler and the State, and the Judge undertook the case for judgement by February, 1973. An opinion was rendered on May 31, 1973, almost exactly one year after Altshuler issued his position paper on the state compliance plan. In his decision, Judge Frank Freedman noted the dreadful record of minority hiring in Massachusetts unions—3-4% among twelve unions in 1968, 7% among 21 unions in 1972. He found that the purpose of Altshuler's plan was not inconsistent with the Executive Order 11246 and that the federal government had not assumed "exclusive control over matters of employment discrimination on projects which are partially funded by the federal government." Judge Freedman found no conflict with federal policy or standards and no problem with a state policy being stricter as long as all federal requirements are met.

Perhaps the most significant and far reaching aspect of the decision was in relation to the plaintiffs' objection to a numerical "quota." "Unfortunately," stated the Judge's decision,

> Our country's history is replete with examples of racial classification and "quotas." They seem to have been effectively used in the past to promote and maintain policies of racial, religious, and other forms of discrimination, all diabolically insidious to the American dream of equal opportunity. Inequality of citizenship has been the result. It was a long time before there was any official awareness expressed over the drastic effects of unconstitutional discriminatory practices.[14]

The 1954 Brown Supreme Court decision recognized the harmful effects of segregated schools and initiated a number of court decisions which recognized "that the Constitution could not tolerate discrimination of any kind, whether it be intentional or otherwise. Proscribing discriminatory conduct is not enough, however," stated Judge Freedman. "The more difficult task is to correct the effects of what has been done in the past and see that it does not occur again."

In arguing that numerical quotas are not illegal, Freedman drew on a prior case which stated that "while quotas merely to attain racial balance are forbidden, quotas to correct past discriminatory practices are not. The Judge also cited a case against the "racial quotas" of the Philadelphia Plan in which it was ruled,

> The Philadelphia Plan is a valid Executive action designed to remedy the perceived evil that minority tradesmen have not been included in the labor pool available for the performance of construction projects in which the federal government has a cast and performance interest.[15]

Chapter 15

BOSTON JOBS
FOR BOSTON PEOPLE

The recession that began in 1973 resulted in a decline in Boston's construction industry, thus diminishing the number of jobs available to workers of color.* What this meant was that workers of color, Black, Hispanic and Asian, particularly those in construction, were being increasingly confronted by white workers who were saying "Hey, you know, wait your turn. How can you expect to have jobs?" That is, that attitude became very traditional. Very American. "Get in line. we're first; we're going to take our share. And when we get through with our share, then you can get your share."

The other thing that was beginning to happen that made things difficult for community activists in Boston trying to deal with the construction industry, was that the pie was not growing. Yet the number of people wanting a piece of the pie within the community itself was increasing.

The Hispanic community was relatively small in the 1960's when United Community Construction Workers was getting

*This chapter is based on a speech made by Chuck Turner to the Community Fellows Program at MIT on April 15, 1980.

started as an organization. They did not become actively involved in housing development until later in the 1970's. Until that time, Black workers and Black organizations provided the major thrust. As a result, talk about minorities was focused around the question of Black workers. In particular, minority became synonymous with Black as related to the construction industry. However, by 1972 and 1973, we began to realize that the Hispanic community had been doing work around housing within their own community for a number of years. They had projects that were designed by the Hispanic community and which were going to be developed and built by Hispanic workers.

For the first time, the Black community began to have to struggle with the question of territorial rights and prerogative. What is your share and what is my share? The same was true of the Chinese community to a lesser degree because they were not in the same trade. The issue with the Chinese community came up because projects were being built in Chinatown and organizaitons like UCCW were trying to get a share.

In 1975, UCCW began looking at the situation that faced them: a slowdown of jobs, and increasing tension with some of the other ethnic groups. In particular tension with Hispanic groups in the South End, magnified the question of who was going to get what. The Black workers said to themselves, it's time for us to expand the pace, that is, it was time for us to link our efforts with the efforts of other ethnic groups, and begin to form one vehicle that would serve us all. Representatives of UCCW went down to talk to the folks at Iniquilinos Boricuas en Accion (IBA) since it had the main development projects going, and it was obviously a key source of jobs. Then they went to the Chinese American Civic Association, and to another organization that was just forming, the Chinese Economic Development Corporation. In all those places, we said essentially the same thing, "It's time for us to get together."

As this was happening, the training plan that the unions and the contractors had been running jointly without community participation was challenged by the Mayor of Boston. Mayor White said that he wouldn't fund the plan unless there was a joint plan drawn up by the contractors, unions, and the com-

munity. When negotiations broke down, this group of Third
World organizations suddenly found themselves in a position
where they had a clear shot at the $200,000 that the unions had
been using to run the program before. They did what was
natural. They went to the city and said we have formed the
Third World Jobs Clearinghouse and would like to be funded to
run this program.

When it became clear that we were going to get the money,
a number of issues surfaced. The Hispanic community began to
say, "What is going to protect our interests from yours?"
Because as they looked at it, they had not been satisfied with the
Black community. In the case of the Boston Plan, though it was
controlled by the unions and the contractors, it still had Black
people running it. The Hispanic community looked at that program as a Black community program, even though it wasn't in
reality, and used that as one indication of what they thought
was discrimination by Blacks in construction against Hispanics.
They said that we don't feel comfortable with getting involved
with you unless there's some kind of protection.

This was not an easy thing for the Black organizations
sitting around the table to deal with. In some cases they saw
themselves as the more progressive organizations in the community, so that they were not used to being in a situation where
they were being challenged in terms of their own sense of
justice and cooperation and sharing. There were a lot of tight
feelings. It was something that was not easily accepted by the
Black community, because if you shut your eyes and listened to
the conversation going on, it sounded as if the responses of the
Black people to the Hispanics were very similar to what white
people had been saying to Black people. What eventually happened was that Black organizations realized that it was more
important to unify with the other ethnic organizations than to
protect our own organizational egos, or to protect American
principles of democracy.

The Hispanic position was that they didn't believe in one
person one vote. Looking at the board, there were six or seven
Black organizations represented that could qualify as board
members in terms of the criteria: they must be involved with
construction or with housing development, or with something

that leads to the creation of jobs. But there were only two, perhaps three, Hispanic organizations, one or two Asian organization, and one Native American organization. (The Native American community hasn't been mentioned because they had not been active in construction fields in Boston, as a community, and had not come to the initial meetings.)

The issue that the Hispanic community raised for the Black representatives at the table was that they wanted a voting system that would protect their interests. They wanted to have one vote per ethnic group. They wanted the board structure to have caucuses of the different ethnic groups and each caucus would then elect two representatives that would serve on a board of eight. The voting power would be split between the Black community, the Hispanic community, the Asian community, and the Native American community, on an equal basis.

The Black organizations were split with one group of people saying that we can't afford, even within this situation, to give away power; and another group saying to let the power of the collective protect the interests of each group, rather than try to protect our own interests within that by having a numerical majority. Narrowly, the principal of one vote per ethnic group was accepted by the Black representatives, and eventually, it was accepted by the other ethnic groups.

The unions and the contractors opposed the Clearing House. Their opposition was unsuccessful and in September of 1975, Third World Jobs Clearing House was funded for $200,000 to place 360 construction workers during the coming year. At that point, another interesting thing happened from the standpoint of community politics. Representatives from the Chinese Economic Development Corp. came down to the Clearing House and said, "How many jobs are in it for us? We don't want to be a tokenistic appendage to the body of the Clearing House. Where's our share?" That led to a series of negotiations in terms of what share of the staff positions the Asian community would have.

It is important to understand that at the Clearing House there were many discussions about intracollective actions. All the ethnic groups have similar feelings of having been slighted by one another, of not wanting to lose face. No one wanted to put him or herself in a relationship to another person or group where it can be seen by the members of its own group as having been taken advantage of. The Clearing House forced a certain kind of awareness about our role as Black people and our behaviors and practices in relationship to other ethnic groups of color, as well as other white ethnic groups. The main thing that happened during the first three or four months of the Clearing House was that it hit the Clearing House staff that they were in charge of something that was very dangerous.

They had money to be a vehicle for jobs to go to construction workers of color. But, if there were no contracts and if there existed an affirmative action plan in Boston and in the state of Massachusetts that was not being implemented, where were the jobs going to come from for the community of color? If there was no flow of jobs, we were going to be sitting there looking like we were the source of the problem. When it became clear that there were serious problems in terms of jobs, we held meetings to inform the workers of that fact.

In all honesty we had to say to them that if they in fact wanted to have a good flow of jobs, we were not going to be the source of them. Nor was the city's Affirmative Action Program going to be the source of jobs. It was not being enforced properly, and it had not, in five months of our existence, provided one job for any worker. No contractor who was working on a city contract had come to our door.

We found out that the Department of Public Works in the city of Boston did not even have the Affirmative Action language in their contracts that were going out. When we asked the assistant director of the Public Works Department why not, he said that he didn't realize that there was any language that was missing. When the workers were told of this and other experiences, they decided to go back to the streets. From February of 1976 until May of 1976, there were perhaps 10 to 15 demonstrations at different sites throughout the community of color. The effect of the demonstrations was to dramatically increase the flow of jobs into the Third World Jobs Clearing House. By the time the workers got through demonstrating, the percentage of workers of color in construction jobs throughout the community had hit in general a 40% mark, about six or seven jobs per site.

On May 2, 1976 during negotiations at a pumping plant station near the Southeast Expressway, some Black workers went to the site and closed the job down. White workers from South Boston, and a racist group called the South Boston Marshalls heard about it. They said the plant was in open territory, and they were not going to allow anything to happen to white workers on that site; they were going to see to it that it was not closed down. The next morning there were negotiations between the contractor at the site, representatives of the Clearing House and representatives of the workers' association. While those negotiations were going on in the contractor's trailer, word came down that a group of white workers had formed a ring around the site, and that the Marshalls had come along with them. When the Marshalls and the workers found out that Barletta, the contractor, was down in the trailer, they came 'down to the trailer and a scuffle started with the Black workers. The police came and things wound down.

However, at noon that day, workers from construction sites throughout the city of Boston coverged on City Hall, two to three thousand strong. They presented their demands to the City Council members that the Clearing House should not be funded, that armed police should be put around all major sites, and that the City Council should protect the interests of white workers. The incident got a lot of publicity because the construction workers were very violent. They broke windows, brandished some firearms, and made everybody there feel that if the white workers' interests were not met, they were ready to do violence to get them met.

The city councilors had been psychologically intimidated. The unions had achieved what they wanted to achieve. It was clear that the council was not going to give anything to the community of color. As a result of this intimidation, the Clearing House was investigated because it was alleged that they were spending money on the demonstrations, that people on our staff were involved in demonstrations and therefore, we were violating the law and should not be eligible to receive federal funding. Though the investigation wasn't followed through, police guards were stationed around the construction sites.

At the same time, the number of workers of color who were involved in the demonstrations decreased in numbers. The workers were saying, "We've been out in the streets a long time. We're in our thirties, it's too much." Many of them wound up getting jobs in other industries, in other trades. The ones who were firmer in their purpose began to develop various strategies to keep jobs, but the core of workers who were engaged in the struggle began to drift away.

The Clearing House, for the next year, was essentially defunded. The City Council voted 9 to 0 to cut our funding. However, there was a technicality which put the Dept. of Labor in a situation where they said essentially that the Third World Jobs Clearing House had done nothing illegal, and if the city did not fund this program, all Title I money in Boston would be rescinded. City officials, for a while, did not believe it. Mayor White kept the Clearing House going with month to month funding. Eventually, the lawyers for the city of Boston said, essentially, "You're right. We've acted illegally. We're ready to fund you." We were funded for the rest of that year.

However, the month to month funding left the Clearing House in a position where we could not very effectively do much, except maintain our program. We were politically hamstrung. The staff was demoralized. And at that same time, the workers had begun to move in different directions. We were in a very difficult situation. The City Council had voted 9 to 0 against us. The Mayor obviously wasn't supportive. And our workers didn't have the strength right now to go back out into the streets again. The question was: "Could we maintain a political thrust, and at the same time not jeopardize our funding?"

Boston Jobs for Boston People

We began to counter this problem by forming an alliance with white organizations in the city of Boston around the concept that in Boston, there should be a share of the jobs for Boston workers as well as a share for workers of color. We felt that politically, unless we could create an alliance with whites in the city and begin to translate our struggle into terms which they could understand, that we would never have a fair share of the construction industry in Boston, peacefully, and probably not at all.

In June 1977, we got John Carroll of the Department of Public Works (DPW) to take a survey of how many Boston workers were employed on DPW construction sites. At the East Boston site there were only 19% Boston workers, at the Highton Rd. site there were 35%, and at the South End expressway site were 45% Boston workers, though 35% of the workers were Black workers. In the white neighborhoods, there were very few Boston workers, whereas in the Black neighborhoods, there were more Boston workers. On one site, of the 66 operating engineers, only 6 were from Boston, and half of those were people of color. White workers from Boston were not getting the jobs, nor were the workers of color, especially among the higher trades.

Based on these surveys, it became clear that Black workers and white workers had a common interest in making sure that Boston jobs went to Boston workers. However, we felt that it would be futile to organize individual construction workers. Therefore, we decided to go to the neighborhoods, to talk with the neighborhood organizations to see if they would be interested in working together to demand more jobs.

Starting in Jamaica Plain and Roxbury, we got the support of three or four organizations, and eventually we formed the Boston Jobs Coalition, a coalition of about 40 organizations from all over the city, including Charlestown and South Boston. Using this alliance as evidence of widespread support, we began negotiating with city officials in June, 1978. We demanded the hiring of more Boston workers on city construction sites.

Although the negotiations continued to drag into the next year, the Boston Jobs Coalition adopted the following principles:

1) that a minimum of 50% of the total workforce, craft-by-craft, on all publicly funded or subsidized development projects in Boston to be comprised of Boston residents;
2) that a minimum of 25% of the total workforce, craft-by-craft, on all such projects be comprised of minority workers;
3) that a minimum of 10% of the total workforce, craft-by-craft, on all such projects be comprised of women workers.

In addition, the Coalition required that job training and

apprentice programs be filled according to the same percentages; that the Boston Jobs Coalition, and the Third World Clearing House be officially recognized organizations for the recruitment of Boston workers; and that contractors be forced to publish detailed information about their hiring practices and the composition of their labor force.

Negotiations continued to bog down until the Mayoral primary in September 1979, when I pressed for Boston jobs for Boston people as part of my platform for Mayor. As we will see in Chapter 18, to the surprise of the pollsters and the Mayor, I came in third in the primary with 15% of the vote. In the run off between White and Timilty, White tried to coopt the support of my constituency by issuing an executive order that committed the city to adopting the quotas that the Boston Jobs Coalition was pushing for. In addition, two weeks before the final election, the Mayor made these quotas binding on all construction jobs in the city which received a tax abatement (121A). This was a major success for the Coalition, and demonstrated the importance of pressing for our issues through the electoral process.

Since White's re-election in 1979, the city has established an Oversight Committee to monitor the compliance to the program by the unions, the contractors, and the City government, in conjunction with the affirmative action Jobs Monitoring Program. As might be expected, the contractors do not want to pay for the added cost of training residents, while the unions resist the undercutting of their control over job placement. If the unions cannot supply the workers, the contractor can hire outside the union hiring hall.

The struggle came to a boil over the construction of Copley Place which will create thousands of jobs, as well as hundreds of thousands of dollars of tax cuts. In face of contractor and union opposition, the Mayor seemed to be backing down on his commitment to Boston jobs for Boston people. However, the final Copley Place plans included the Boston resident plan with the 50, 25 and 10% formulas, although enforcement is still not clear. The Boston Jobs Coalition is an important example of how workers of color can ally with white workers to block the attempts of contractors, unions, and city officials to pit them against one another.

Chuck Turner, who was one of the key figures in the formation of the Boston Jobs Coalition and the Third World Jobs Clearing House, concludes that, "Affirmative action has made it possible for white Boston workers to become the first white construction workers in the country to have their rights to a job affirmed by city officials, and implemented through the structure of affirmative action."

Chapter 16

FREEDOM INDUSTRIES

Frustrated by the difficulty of getting jobs within the white controlled businesses and unions, the Black community moved in a natural progression to the institution building stage during which there were concerted efforts to develop Black owned and controlled businesses.

In the immediate aftermath of the killing of Martin Luther King, during the tense hours when Boston—and the nation—had visions of its inner cities going up in flames, the Dudley Terminal Merchants' Association, an almost all-white group in Black Roxbury, issued an unsolicited letter explaining that they understood the colonial nature of their relationship with the Black community and that they were willing to work toward the transfer of businesses in the Dudley Street area to Black management and ownership. By May 1, 1969, a Small Business Development Center (SBDC) opened with its first order of business being the transfer of Roxbury businesses from white to Black control.

The SBDC was designed to provide a "wide range of financial and technical assistance for Black persons wishing to get into small or medium sized businesses." Besides the Dudley

Terminal Merchants, the SBDC formed a working relationship with the Grove Hall Community Development Corporation which was running seminars on small business in conjunction with the New Urban League and the Black United Front. As a result of these efforts, a number of businesses were turned over to Black businesspeople, though a large proportion of the white owned businesses simply opened up one job for a personnel manager here, one sales person there and on occasion a vice-president's position. This response by the white power structure to the murder of Dr. King was really a form of "institutionalized tokenism."

The communication industry is a particularly good example of the trend: a number of visible jobs became available for reporters and receptionists and the like; but there were no jobs on the technical and production ends of the media industry. The Urban League Skills Bank and the Minority Media Committee got a dialogue started, but the unions, especially the electrical workers, still had a stranglehold on the industry. Like the sudden surge in the amount of money available for other types of Black development, the wave of job openings did not prove to be lasting. There was no significant change in employment practices.

Of more lasting importance to the Black community was the formation of Freedom Industries by Attorney Archie Williams who had been active in the NECDC plans, CIRCLE, and the Black United Front. Freedom Industries was designed to recirculate the money it made through the Black community. It was conceived as a series of interlocking businesses including an electronics assemply plant, a graphics and advertising company, and a chain of supermarkets. Also part of the plan was Freedom Foundation which would be used to channel profits back into the Black community for new business development and other community projects. Williams saw Freedom Industries as a tool to generate and operate new business, make fiscal and technical resources available to people establishing new businesses, provide venture and grant capital, and develop new ideas for other community controlled, profit making business.

When asked his motivation for starting Freedom Industries, Archie had this to say:

Every organization I worked for was a begging organization. They spent a lot of time looking for, begging for funds. The poverty program was entirely designed around granted funds. I always felt that the guy who was knocking on the door begging would never be able to influence the structure of the house. He may be given a crumb, but that would be all. I had difficulty in understanding why people who had so much talent had to spend so much time away from their avowed purpose just chasing money.

He also found his politics, or the politics of his associates, could be used against him financially:

For instance, Virgil Woods picketed the Supreme Market on Columbia Road in an attempt to get them out of the community and transfer the property to the Black community. The idea was the duplication of the Algerian nationalization formula. The first year 20%, the second year 40%, etc...When the financial community downtown heard this new direction they panicked and seriously considered bringing criminal charges of extortion against Virgil. Well, in a round about way, Permanent Charities, which wasn't related to anything but was funding NECDC for administrative costs at about $15,000 a year, got the word back to us that our involvement with Virgil seriously jeopardized Permanent Charities' continued funding. We didn't withdraw with our involvement with Virgil at all, and we didn't lose the funding until later on; but that is an example of the kind of thing that grew the germ in me that Black folk would always be on their knees unless we could influence the community or have economic self-reliance in some significant way.

Archie spent a year preparing for his new venture by talking to people at the Harvard Business School, at banks and insurance companies. "I'd go down and talk to them and ask them questions and never ask for money," he says. "I'd go down and tell them what else I was doing; I'd show them the financial planning that I had." The preparation paid off, because by the time he had found ways to launch the various parts of Freedom Industries, Archie had some valuable contacts for obtaining the necessary loans. The first segment to get off the ground was the electronics component which was designed to do subcontracting work for the then booming electronics business along Route 128. "I went out to Digital Equipment Corporation," recalls Archie, "and it was just a stroke of luck—because at the same time Digital was looking for some Black people to get involved with it. They had approached CIRCLE and Dr. Willard Johnson didn't indicate any interest, so we pursued it and got a contract." With the financial backing of Ed Fredkin, a white businessman who had just made some shrewd business moves and had money to invest, Freedom Electronics opened an office and began production in August of 1968.

At the same time Archie began negotiating with the Stop & Shop corporation to buy two supermarkets in the Black community. Stop & Shop made it clear that even if they sold the stores they would not sell Freedom Industries the goods to go with it. This meant we had to find an independent distributor. Through his many business contacts, Achie was advised to contact the Purity Supreme corporation which had just bought out a chain of stores including two in the Black community which had uncertain futures. "So," recalls Archie, "we went to see them; Leo Kahn was the president of Purity Supreme. I still don't know to this day whether he made out or whether we made out, but in any case if I were asked straight out whether he made a commitment beyond the average I would say that he did." Archie Williams recalls,

> ...He said he would sell the two stores to us for $400,000; that included the land, building, furniture, fixtures. This store needed a little work; the other store needed a great deal of work. So we went to John Hancock for the mortgage; they took a first mortgage on furniture and fixtures, gave us $500,000 for which we used a hundred thousand to renovate the stores most of which is in the Talbot Ave. store. Purity Supreme further agreed—and this is the key, because we hadn't been able to raise the additional funds—to

sell goods to us at the same price that they sell to their own stores. They also agreed to provide supervision by department experts as they do in their own stores. They further agreed to take our managers into their organizations and train them initially, and to allow the people that they had on their staff to remain with us for a period of six months and guaranteed them a job in their other organization if they wanted to leave us. So we got that money; we needed another $200,000 for operating expenses and inventory. We went to the Episcopal Church on a national level in New York and borrowed $200,000, fifty of which was supposed to be for inventory of this store, fifty for the inventory of the other store, with fity thousand operating capital. It turns out that when we did finally buy the inventory it was $75,000, so we started out in the hole. We started out owing almost a million dollars.

With the opening of Freedom Foods (the first store opened in November of 1968, the second in February of 1969), Archie found out just how difficult it was to run a Black business in the Black community. Morale dropped among the employees who were uncertain about the fate of the stores; the stores became the target of skepticism, extremely high standards, theft and great expectations. Says Archie, "We were viewed...as saviors, we were viewed as traitors, we were viewed as super rich and we were struggling like hell."

It was a constant struggle for almost five years before the grocery stores had to be closed. "We were losing money while learning the business," says Archie now. "Unfortunately there was not money to underwrite that lesson." Ironically, he feels that "by the time we went out of business we were perhaps—in terms of just straight operating a supermarket—one of the best operators around. But we just had no more money."

Looking back he sees several clear mistakes. One was trying to maintain a large central staff for Freedom Industries, the parent company; the staff "was not necessary," he now feels, and "ate a lot of the money up." Second, the company trusted a large investment house, Kittery-Peabody, to underwrite the

Freedom complex. But after months of stalling, the agreement was terminated by Kittery-Peabody even though they had put a large sum of money into interim operating costs. Says Archie, "I wasn't attuned to the change in attitude downtown." It became extremely difficult for the business to raise money or obtain financial support of any kind. Freedom Foods was closed and became Freedom Stores in the hope of receiving some investment through the new Model Cities Community Development Corporation, but that too failed to materialize and the food store portion of Freedom Industries was closed.

Freedom Foods made some tremendous accomplishments before it closed, however, the two stores achieved a 21.5% margin, sales averaged 27% higher than before Freedom operated the stores. "We trained a lot of people for positions in supermarkets," assesses Archie Williams,

> and they are working in much higher positions than they would have before. We had a tremendous impact on ethnic food availability in the Black community. When we started out they were damn near giving us the chittlins—it was great—and pigs' feet. And we started selling so many of them that the other stores started stocking them and so now they are still stocking them. Collard greens: it was almost unheard of for Stop & Shop or First National and other stores to stock them and now they are stocking them regularly both frozen and fresh.

Archie feels that many employees, including some of the ex-convicts that the store made a policy to hire without discrimination, came to have a more than ordinary positive involvement with their jobs and the stores. Although Freedom Foods has closed, the parent corporation, Freedom Industries remains alive and has kept its original promise to pour money back into the community with contributions from Freedom Foundation.

Unity Bank

Just about the time Freedom Industries was getting started, Unity Bank—the first Black bank in Boston—finally came into being. George Morrison says that the opening of Unity Bank started a level of competition for Black financial business that had never existed before;

> ...in fact before Unity opened I think probably the most positive thing happened. First of all most of the banks in the Dudley Street area didn't hire any Black folk, we couldn't get basic loans. They would run you through all kinds of games...When it became clear that Unity was going to open, Shawmut Bank had a loan officer on the street. That guy made a loan on the street—he made one in my office, he came in, rapped on about what's going on, I ran the thing down to him, told him about the problems I had with the bank, he sat in that office and me out a loan right there on the spot. That was the fear, the threat of Unity's opening.

The idea for Unity Bank came from John Hayden, a Black graduate student. He brought together a core group of people in April of 1966 to work towards establishing a Black owned and controlled bank to serve the Black community. The original core group included Don Snead, Marvin Gilmore and John Byrne. After considerable effort, Unity Bank opened in June 1968 with assets over $1.2 million dollars—70% of which was raised by subscription in the community. Don Sneed became the first president, and the bank within two years had assets worth $19 milllion. However, as we saw earlier, the bank went into receivership in August 1971.

Community Development Finance Corporation

Another step forward in our efforts to institutionalize our community economic development strategies was to create the Community Development Finance Corporation (CDFC). As we saw in the sixties, the Black community faced a perennial problem of finding either private or state funds to finance community businesses. NECDC, CIRCLE, and FUND of the United Front were each attempts to provide a mechanism for accessing the capital necessary to back our community development efforts. But in each case we were not able to arrange for a continual flow of funding.

The problem of lack of capital arose once again in the early seventies, with the renewal of the discussions for developing the South West Corridor transportation system, and the resulting changes in residential and commerical developments. The South West Corridor Coalition wanted to find a way to attract capital so that the communities surrounding the corridor would be able to control the changes in commercial and residential patterns resulting from the change in transportation routes in and out of Boston.

In response to this need, CDFC was conceived of and developed by the Wednesday Morning Breakfast Group, a group of professionals and students concerned with developing legislative solutions to community development problems, who met Wednesday mornings at MIT for breakfast. Over a two year period, led by David Smith, Elbert Bishop and Brad Yoneoka, the Breakfast group developed the landmark legislation establishing CDFC as the first state agency in the country responsible for financing community development by providing equity and loans.

With a $10 million dollar initial capital fund, CDFC has provided significant amounts of capital to local Community Development Corporations. The funds are being used to undertake projects of benefit to their communities by establishing community oriented businesses.

Another legislative achievement of the Wednesday Morning Breakfast Group was the passing of legislation which established the Community Economic Development Assistance Corporation (CEDAC) to assist community development corporations and nonprofit community groups, particularly those planning to apply for funding from CDFC. CDFC and CEDAC provide clear examples of how to use the legislative process to set up institutions which can provide ongoing assistance for community development through community control.

Chapter 17

GENTRIFICATION:
Creating the Bantustan

> Such poverty as we have today in all our great cities
> degrades the poor and infects with its degradation the
> whole neighborhood in which they live. And whatever
> can degrade the neighborhood can degrade a country
> and a continent and finally the whole civilized world.
> —*George Bernard Shaw*

As we saw in earlier chapters, South End residents learned from
the disastrous fate of the West End that urban renewal was
"urban removal" for low income, indigenous residents of downtown neighborhoods. In defense of their neighborhood, South
End residents advanced from service activities, to organizing, to
institution building characterized by Black community development in all areas. First came the service programs, assisting
residents with relocation, necessitated by urban **renewal** plans;
then came the questions about those plans and the subsequent
organizing that occurred as various groups gained the technical
know-how to challenge the plans. Out of the challenge came
CAUSE which emphasized the rights of tenants, and insisted
that residents be provided political power in the renewal process. CAUSE and the other tenant groups like ETC, CATA, and
SETC led to a set of institutions which became involved in the

management of property, housing development and the broader issues related to improving living conditions. As a result of
the Tent City demonstrations, and the work of CAUSE and
PEURC, SEPAC was formed which gave residents influence
over the urban renewal process.

In the 1970's, the battle over housing was fought between
the realtors and the Boston Redevelopment Authority on one
side, the agents who have sought to "gentrify" the South End,
to make it suitable for the gentry, the middle and upper class
white professionals; and, on the other side, indigenous communities, mostly low-income, unemployed or working class
whites and people of color who have fought against being displaced from the South End by developing their own community
controlled housing.

Community Controlled Housing

The seventies were a time when housing did get built in the
community of color. There should be no question that in the
past ten years with a wide variety of groups involved, using both
public and private resources, both community initiative and
private development approaches, hundreds of units of housing
have been constructed for people of color, by people of color.
Models that are being emulated across the country started right
here in Boston. People from the community have attained the
skills necessary to plan, design, finance, develop and manage
housing.

Of all the many successful developers of housing in city
neighborhoods, several stand out as examples of a new dimension of community building that goes far beyond the physical
construction of residences. The Lower Roxbury Community
Corporation (LRCC) has developed hundreds of units in midrise
and townhouse form in the Madison Park area. From the early
fight with the development officials who wanted to confiscate
most of the land area for a huge high school complex back in
1965, the LRCC has managed to organize millions of dollars
and other resources necessary to develop the housing to replace
at least some of what was demolished to make way for the
school. The school's athletic facilities have been designed to

serve as an accessible asset to the community. The LRCC model is of a planned area that relates the community and city infrastructures in a way that ties into the overall development of the community. This model reinforces the value of community people being in control of the planning process. Using LRCC's method, planning becomes a coordination process connecting the community's needs to other planned city facilities or developments.

Inquilinos Boricuas en Accion (IBA), Puerto Rican Tenants in Action, grew out of the housing activities of the Emergency Tenants Council. As we saw earlier, ETC forced the BRA to give it permission to develop Parcel 19. This project turned out to be the first housing construction program in the nation to be developed and controlled by a community group on such a large scale. IBA is responsible for a thirty acre area in the South End. Over the past twelve years, IBA has developed 815 housing units, the centerpiece of which is the Plaza Betances, a Puerto Rican style community plaza named after the famous Puerto Rican doctor Roman Emerterio Betances, who bought slaves so that he could free them. In addition to housing, IBA is involved in daycare, healthcare, after school programs, social services for the elderly and disabled, as well as in assisting the commercial development of the Puerto Rican community. IBA is solely controlled by the residents.

In much the same way that IBA developed out of ETC, the Tenants Development Corporation (TDC) developed out of the South End Tenants Council (SETC). SETC developed nearly 400 units of housing. Unlike IBA or LRCC, however, SETC chose a scatter site approach to housing development. Rather than concentrating housing in one geographical area, they chose to develop housing all over the South End. Low Cost Housing Corporation was another group that operated in the South End on a scatter site basis. (This approach, by the way, should have pleased the gentry by diffusing the presence of low-income families in any one area. Objections are still made, however, because it is not the actual concentration of low-income people that is the issue, but the race and class differences that count.) Because of the scattered locations of this housing, the approach of developing a comprehensive community was not as easily used.

The Roxbury Action Program (RAP), on the other hand, is a group that began with some scattered sites in one neighborhood, but went far beyond the basic plan to develop more housing units affordable to community residents and created a vision of a total community—a "model Black community." RAP's philosophy is that Black people must do for themselves, control their own land and decide for themselves the future of their communities.

Located in the Highland Park area of Roxbury, RAP has developed housing and commercial space, a food store and a laundromat. RAP operates the Marcus Garvey Community Center, a continuing education, drop-in center for teenagers in the community, as well as an urban internship program to help young Black people learn about community development.

IBA, LRCC and RAP take a broad view of community planning. Each of their approaches reflects their philosophical bases. RAP focuses on the views of Marcus Garvey; IBA centers on its Puerto Rican heritage; and LRCC did not go into the past, but built around the present by naming buildings in the complex after people living in the community. The Madison High School playing field was named after Jack Crump, a man who spent years with the youth of the area developing sports teams. In each case it is not just housing that got built, but a sense of community.

Another important phase of the housing story is management. The community has been able to develop the capacity to plan, package, finance and construct housing. Ironically, we ran into problems in management and maintenance. What did not get built into the developments was enough funding to provide good management and protective maintenance. If community developers or contractors ran into difficulty with quality of work, there were no extra funds to fall back on. (This is one of the pitfalls of "nonprofit" work.) This created more problems all around and led to tenants reorganizing, and even though the housing was relatively better than what people had had access to previously, tenants came into conflict with owners of the community housing.

With the added burden of energy costs and continually increasing costs of maintenance, a number of projects were brought to the brink of foreclosure. Fortunately, in some instances, the issue was dealt with by tenants who organized, went to HUD and hammered out a new policy to deal with such situations by supporting tenant managed ventures. Instead of selling to the highest bidder, HUD agreed to negotiate a tenant owned and managed building.

Gentrification and Displacement

One of the major issues propelling change in many city neighborhoods is "displacement." The history of the South End is a preview of what is happening to neighborhoods across the city and country. The "displacement" of people of color has resulted from racism and government policy. During the desegregation process, people of color were steadily pushed out of South Boston, Charlestown, and East Boston, particularly out of public housing units, as racist violence escalated. A petition was filed in court asking for an injunction against the city government receiving Community Development Block Grant funds from Washington for neighborhoods in which people of color could not safely live. The lawsuit accomplished very little in terms of demands put to the court, but it did put some pressure on the city to work on getting people in some areas of the city to be more receptive to housing people of color.

"Displacement" was further compounded by the failure of the Boston Housing Authority to provide secure places for people of color who want to live in neighbrhoods like East Boston or South Boston. The pressure for people of color to leave these neighborhoods came at a time when the Authority had hundreds of uninhabited units on its hands—the result of vandalism and the failure to use protective maintenance.

While racism and the lack of government protection pushed people of color out of white working class communities, government planning is pushing people of color out of the South End to make way for the "gentry." Mayor White through the BRA and through encouragement of local realtors has sought to "balance" the South End by making it a more desirable place for white professionals. What has consistently happened is that government programs wind up helping people who already have access to resources, to the detriment of the people for whom the government programs were supposedly designed. While these programs may not start out on that track, it seems to be an inevitable outcome. Even when there is some payoff for the people the program is supposed to help, very often it is usually more beneficial to people who already have resources.

We watched, for example, federal housing money go to people with low-income tenants to bring the units up to code. But more often that money went to newcomers and owners of more than one building and with incomes over $18,000. Perhaps those people just knew more about how to take advantage of such a government program, but in fact the Boston Redevelopment Authority was acting out part of the Mayor's overall scheme to increase the number of upper income people in the city. The BRA made a conscious effort to direct funds to such owners. I know of at least one person who did a good job of getting that money out to the elderly and low-income residents and was moved out of his job by the BRA.

Subsidies are give-aways, welfare for the rich in disguise, an unfair use of the taxpayers' dollars. Some "subsidy" programs are used by large landlords or homeowners who do not actually fit the guidelines but who can apply because of the income level of their tenants. Another kind of subsidizing has taken place in the South End as well, where millions have been invested in roads, sewers, new brick sidewalks, street lamps, and the like. These improvements were not put in for the people who have been living in the South End for many years; they were made to increase the desirability of the area for newcomers with higher incomes. The investment increased property values and added one more method of pushing out the low-income home owners and tenants who could not afford all these subsidized improvements as their rents and taxes soared. These subsidies have resulted in a dramatic turn over in ownership on many blocks. It is obvious by looking at the city census that in a five to seven year period the income and occupations of the people living in parts of the South End has changed radically.

As the high income folks move in, rents go up and the

low-income folks are forced out. One of the forms this process takes is the conversion of low rent apartments into high priced condominiums. The majority of condo dwellers are coming to the city neighborhoods for convenience, not to stay and participate. It is the proximity to downtown, the physical characteristics of the buildings which are attractive; people do not come for greater involvement in neighborhood issues and business.

The harsh truth is that the BRA planned to reduce the population in the South End and similar desirable areas of the city. The BRA intended that 12,000 people should be displaced in order to reduce the undesirable "density" and to attract new residents who could pay more taxes into the city. While the area was not attractive to people outside the city, the people inside the neighborhoods were struggling to make them liveable communities. They developled the capacity to build their own housing at affordable prices. However, this didn't sit well with the city fathers and the city planners.

The truth is that the subsidy issue is merely a cover for the racism which is part of the basis for redevelopment schemes in the first place. Although the people who return to the city are often an unconscious part of this process, they nevertheless help to recreate the sterile and homogenous communities they supposedly left behind in the suburbs. They are aided by the government officials who see them as more valuable and less trouble than the people already living there and who are in need. We need to be clear that the resistance to subsidized housing is but another manifestation of northern style racism, compounded by the rising cost of commuting and the fashionaable trend toward city living. As we watch the pressures of "displacement "spread to the white working class areas of the city such as Charlestown, South Boston and the North End, we will see ethnic and class prejudice in their full force.

But if subsidies and government planning are not enough, there are some residents of the South End who are willing to take matters into their own hands. The Committee to Balance the South End claims that the construction of more low-income housing will have a negative "environmental impact" on the neighborhood. It apparently escapes them that ethnically, the South End is one of the most diverse areas in the city. Even

economically, the range is more varied than most neighborhoods, and the further influx of upper middle class white folks is
actually threaten 'g the unusual balance that has long existed.
Consistent with their perversion of the Environmental Protection Act, this group wants to establish quotas for low-income
residents.

They have been particularly involved in trying to block the
growth of the Puerto Rican community in the South End. When
their court suit failed to stop IBA's plan to make a community
center out of an abandoned church on Tremont Street, using
the argument that the church is an historical monument, the
church was destroyed by arsonists. The suspicion is that the
Committee for a Balanced South End was responsible. They
wanted to control the South End, to make it profitable for
themselves, and they would do anything, including arson, to get
control of the land.

A similar policy has been incorporated into the system of
apartheid in South Africa. The South African government has
systematically forced Black families to relocate away from the
major urban centers to Bantustans located in the desolate,
remote countryside. The Black workers who work in the mines
and factories can only see their families a few times a year.
By isolating the Black majority in the countryside, the white
minority regime hopes to fragment and destroy the ability of the
Black people to take control of their country. The displacing of
the Black population out of the center of Boston to the edges of
the city, Mattapan and Hyde Park at present, is similarly an attempt to fragment and disperse the Black community away
from the racist heart of Boston.

During this same time, however, there have been signs of
some new forms of community housing development. The
Black Housing Task Force was formed to deal with the resurgence of racism in housing. The Task Force was motivated by a
number of issues, and Black developers have become involved
because they have realized that they could lose considerable
investments if they do not help turn the situation around. They
also realized that they are still deeply involved in the community
years after white developers tried to take advantage of the
subsidy situation during the sixties and eventually pulled out to

leave Black developers with the responsibility. Finally, Task Force members wanted to deal with the threat posed by racism. They realized that if Black people were going to have housing, they have to assure it.

The Task Force is a hopeful model because it is a conscious assessment of the capacity of Black developers and other members of the community that have built housing in the spirit of IBA or RAP with quality and expertise to equal any others. It is through the linkages of people with the many and varied skills it takes to build housing (and communities) that we may be able to counteract the concerted effort to "close out" urban renewal and with it the community's vision of its own future.

Chapter 18

POWER TO THE PEOPLE:
"Whose City is This?"

A reporter recently asked me, "When did you get into politics?" Pausing for a moment, I responded, "When I was born." A baby cries out to get her or his needs met. We raise our voices together to get our needs met. Politics as we are defining it is the process of getting one's needs met, either individually or collectively. Everybody has to see themselves as a politician, not politicians who wield power to satisfy individual greed, but politicians of the people, politicians who realize the interdependence and equality of all people, who realize that the satisfaction of everyone's needs requires everyone's empowerment, not the aggrandizement of the few, and patronage crumbs for the rest. In the middle of the word politic is the letter "i." I like to think of that "i" as standing for "I," me, for personal responsibility, for your and my responsibility to raise our voices, to press for the satisfaction of the needs of all peoples.

The Black Caucus

Beginning in 1971, there were a series of attempts to bring community and electoral organizing together, to hold Black candidates accountable to the Black community through an

212

on—going Black political organization. The first attempt was the calling of the "Bostown" Political Convention in August, 1971.

> For the first time in the history of Massachusetts polit-
> ics, the Black community of "Boston" will come
> together to select its own candidates for public office.
> Through the mechanism of an independent Black pol-
> itical convention we are seeking to unify the Black
> community around the issues which the community
> deems most relevant. The nomination of candidates by
> Black community residents will be an unprecedented
> event in Boston Politics.   —*Press Release*

The convention endorsed several candidates (including Tom Atkins for mayor), adopted a platform, and began a voter regis-tration campaign.

The following spring, thirty-seven Massachusetts dele-gates attended the first national Black political convention in Gary, Indiana. The delegates ratified a Black agenda, dealing with the use of busing to gain quality education, the role of Israel in the Middle East, and the inauguration of a "National Assembly. " As a result of this convention, the Massachusetts delegates set up a Massachusetts Black Political Assembly agenda, agreed upon in Gary, and took an oath to fight for resolution of these issues if elected to office.

On April 15, 1972 there was an "Action Caucus 72," a political convention of people of color, to endorse a candidate for U.S. Representative to run against Louise Day Hicks. The community endorsed Hubie Jones. Though Jones did not win, Hicks was defeated by John Moakley, a democrat, who ran as an independent. One of the problems behind the Jones candidacy was that despite the community endorsement for him, Mel Miller, owner of the Bay State Banner, a community based weekly newspaper, ran against Jones. The resulting competition between the two turned into a bitter fight based on personali-ties. This led us to abandon the development of a process by which we could seriously look at the options and make some decisions based on the importance of developing leadership to provide a cooperative approach to what Hubie Jones focused on (i.e. issues of concern to the community). Mel Miller spent his time trying to discredit Jones, rather than running a campaign to expose issues and propose solutions. Hubie Jones won the community aspect of the election, because people understood that Miller wasn't a serious candidate who was ready to deal with the real needs of the Black community.

These three attempts to establish accountability from Black elected officials came to fruition in 1972, with the establishment of the Massachusetts Black Caucus. As a result of redistricting in 1971, five Black representatives were elected to the House in 1972—Doris Bunte, Bill Owens, Royal Bolling, Sr., Royal Bolling, Jr., and myself. After the election, members of the caucus met with David Bartley, the Speaker of the House, who agreed to provide us with a staff person. The five of us realized that we had to combine our resources in an effort to meet the needs of the Black community. We agreed that the purpose of the Caucus was:

> ...to work toward Black empowerment across the State of Massachusetts...and the Caucus also understands that part of the reason for the Black Community's long-standing disempowerment is the ethnocentricity which exists in the system. It does not plan to perpetuate that behavior but rather to end it by seeking to build bridges with all people who believe that the system ought to operate in a pluralistic fashion to relate to them.

The Black Caucus was the real beginning of institution building in the electoral process. It was the first Black political organization which sought to connect community and electoral organizing on an on-going basis. On New Years Day 1972, hosted by the Elma Lewis School, the five Black State Representatives held their first joint inaugural. It was phenomenal. The five of us took the following pledge:

> As a member of the Massachusetts Black Caucus, I pledge that I will conduct the daily affairs and decision making of my activity, and/or office, so as to reflect the actual, explicit desires and concerns of the Black Community beyond question. In this manner I will con-

stantly act out of my accountability to the manifest
interests of the Black Community.

This was the culmination and the beginning of all that we had
been striving for since Ruth Batson's attempt to get elected to
the School Committee in 1959. Black elected officials were
united together with the community to raise a unified voice for
the need for Black community development through community control.

One of the first major efforts of the Caucus was to focus on
police/community relations. Each of the representatives held
meetings in their districts to discuss both police violence and
police protection. After that we brought all the districts
together. Fifteen hundred people came. The results: the Caucus
was given a community mandate to go to the city with a series of
proposals dealing with crime analysis, police training, police
monitoring, and community security patrols. However, when
we met with Police Commissioner Robert DiGrazia, we ran into
a stone wall. We got nothing out of DiGrazia. As a result, police/
community relations have continued to deteriorate.

However, the major accomplishment of the Caucus in the
first two years was legislating a Black senatorial seat through
redistricting. In Boston, the major Black wards were grouped
with strong Irish and Jewish wards. As a result, there had never
been a Black senator in Massachusetts. In response to this lack
of representation, there was a court order, in 1973, to redistrict
the senatorial districts. The first two redistricting plans proposed by the senate would not have significantly affected the
chance of electing a Black senator, and were blocked by the Black
Caucus. A third plan, which the Caucus helped to draft included
a Black district. Staff members Kay Gibbs and Dianne Renfro
researched and organized the effort.

In 1973 the third redistricting plan was ratified. There was
one unexpected vote by John Loring (R) Acton, Mass. Rep.
Loring was contacted by a constituent, who asked that he not
vote for a redistricting plan, unless provisions were made for a
Black senator. This contact helped to shape his decision, prior to
that time he had not made up his mind (voters *can* impact the

decision-making process of their elected officials).

The new senate seat, however, led to new problems in the Black community. The election for the new seat led to a bitter contest between Bill Owens and Royal Bolling, Sr. Bill Owens, on the one hand, represented the younger generation of Black politicians. He was in the National Black Political Assembly, and other Black elected official organizations. Royal Bolling, Sr., on the other hand, was the senior member of the Black Caucus, and had fought hard for redistricting. He was an independent who had built his political career with his own hands over the years.

Bill Owens won the seat in the November election, and on New Years of 1975, he held his own separate inaugural before other incumbent Representatives held their celebration at the Elma Lewis School. The conflict between Owens and Bolling not only split the community, but seriously weakened the Caucus as well. As in the Jones and Miller contest in 1972, the campaigns were not fought on the basis of the issues, but deteriorated into personal politics taking precedence over the needs of the community.

This conflict between building personal power, as opposed to empowering the community, served to weaken the Caucus, and to weaken its relationship with the community. This was manifested by the break-down in the attempts to work on police issues. Some Black elected officials thought that the demands being made by the community would have a negative effect on their electability—that the demands of the community would be too radical. These officials felt that the more radical demands of the Black community would jeopardize their support by the more conservative Black middle class. But how could any Black official be "too radical" given the oppression confronting the great majority of Black people in Boston? Finally the result of this split was to retard our attempts to form and independent political organization.

Charter Reform

In Boston, the School Committee is made up of five members, and the City Council is made up of nine city councilors. Both elections are at-large elections where people from all over the city vote for all candidates, and those candidates receiving the five, or nine, highest number of votes get elected. This type of an election favors those groups which have the largest voting block(s), and in this case whites, particularly the Irish from South Boston and West Roxbury. Also, in this type of election the number of seats available determines who gets represented. The fewer seats, say in the case of the School Committee, makes it even more difficult for smaller neighborhoods, or for people of color in Boston, to be represented. This is gerrymandering by numbers, not by political boundaries. In addition, at-large elections favor candidates who have more money to spend on city-wide campaigns for advertising, campaign workers, etc. This makes it possible for the Brahmins in Boston and the organized public worker groups to put their support behind those candidates which are most supportive of their interests. An at-large elections allows those with the largest demographic block or those with the most money to centralize control over the city. As a result, the Black community has continually failed to gain representation on the City Council and the School Committee. The same is true for Allston/Brighton, Mission Hill, Jamaica Plain, and many of Boston's smaller ethnic neighborhoods.

In the November 1974 election, there was referendum question #7 (Charter Reform #1), which called for the abolition of the School Committee, and the appointment of the school superintendent by the mayor. This proposal was Mayor White's attempt to co-opt the movement to gain greater representation on the School Committee by the Black community and other ethnic groups without representation within the city.

Appropriately enough, the main opponents of Question #7 were the anti-busing organizations, ROAR, the South Boston Information Center and the East Boston Information Center who saw the referendum as a threat to their control over the School Committee, and their ability to prevent busing and to dole out patronage. The referendum was defeated.

In August of 1975, the Black community led by Attorney Margaret Burnham went to the United States District Court claiming that, "the at-large system effectively cancels out, dilutes and minimizes the voting strength of the Boston Black community in School Committee elections."[1] The Court ruled against the claim that the at-large system was unconstitutional, attributing the lack of Black representation primarily to low Black voter registration and participation. Similarly, the judge's position was that Italians and other minorities had succeeded in getting representation and therefore if Black folks would get out and vote they too could have representation. Once again, the problem was projected as Black people, not an exclusionary system which had repeatedly defeated Black efforts to change it.

After Mayor White was reelected in November 1975, he established a Committee for Boston which held a series of meetings, inviting community residents to discuss issues confronting them and possible solutions. A recommendation made by the committee was that the escalating violence in Boston could be alleviated by decentralizing power through Charter Reform based on district elections. However, Mayor White instead filed legislation to make the School Committee a department of city government under the control of the City Council. The State Representatives from Boston were able to defeat the measure in the legislative committee of Local Affairs.

Two years later in the 1977 election the issue of neighborhood representation resurfaced in a referendum known as the "Galvin Plan." The Galvin Plan called for reorganization of both the School Committee and the City Council. Both would have nine district and four at-large representatives. Significantly, Mayor White did not support the plan, and it was opposed by the folks from South Boston and Charlestown. Despite the racism of those who are opposed to representation of people of color, to democratic participation of Boston neighborhoods, the Galvin Plan only lost by 3800 votes. The near approval of the Galvin Plan was the closest yet we have come to ending city imperialism—where people from one community decide what goes on in other communities, and take resources from those communities for their own development. That kind of imperialism is not any different from those policies pursued and determined by the United States government to exploit the resources of people of color in Africa, Asia, and South America.

However, Black attempts to be represented on the School

Committee finally met with success. Back in the November 1975 elections, John O'Bryant ran for School Committee. An anti-busing newspaper distributed in South Boston prior to the election read:

> Well, wake up Southie. Do you realize you gave 834 votes to John O'Bryant (in the primary) who is a pro-buser...I was in the Army with O'Bryant and believe me, he's not IRISH. He is a Black Man from Roxbury, and believes in forced integration and Forced Busing.[2]

O'Bryant lost. This was not the first time. John O'Bryant had been campaign manager for my unsuccessful attempts in 1961, 1963 and 1965, and had lost in his bid to be State Representative in 1964, 1966 and 1968. O'Bryant had been a teacher and a guidance counselor in the school system for fifteen years.

But in 1977, John O'Bryant won, after almost two decades of trying to change the school system. He was the first Black person to be elected to the School Committee in more than seventy-five years. All those years finally paid off, as O'Bryant had the solid backing of the Black community, the white, liberal middle class, and a fair number of working class whites who knew John because of his work in the school system. Given his years of experience, John was able to pull together an effective organization that was able to bring out the votes from these constituencies.

The Black Political Task Force

Although the Massachusetts Black Caucus continued to provide a framework to unify Black legislative efforts, particularly around the desegregation plans between 1975 and 1978, it was not cohesive enough to become a major force in organizing people of color in Boston. During this period, I was re-elected in 1974, 1976 and 1978, and was able to push through major legislation on community economic development as we saw in Chapter 14. But the next link in the institution building stage of Black political development was the formation in 1978 of the Black Political Task Force.

John O'Bryant, given his widespread support in the community, was a major force in the establishment of the Task

Force. The purpose of the Task Force was to increase the political power of people of color,

> ...The Task Force will strive to establish a unified voting constituency among peoples of color...In addition to that, the Black Political Task Force will screen, endorse and work for those candidates committed to the following: 1) The Empowerment of Peoples of Color, 2.) The Redistribution of Goods and Services, 3) An Elevated Standard of Life for Peoples of Color and, 4) Full Employment.
> —*Press Release*, March 25, 1979

For the first time the Task Force brought together community people from over 27 different organizations and agencies. It has a much broader organizational base than any other previous Black community organization, and it is not tied to any one person or group. The Task Force won't just endorse candidates because they are Black, and it would also consider endorsing white candidates. Also, the Task Force pressured people to follow through on their committment to people of color if they are elected. It was the first organization which could really organize the community, and hold elected officials accountable.

1979 Mayoral Election

> We are here to announce a process which we have initiated...to campaign for mayor of this city. We are stressin ; a process because we believe we must move away from the practice of politics by personality...We must turn to a process which builds ongoing decentralization and participation in which we can all take responsibility for managing the affairs of the city in each community. For us the central question is: Whose city is this and who should benefit from its wealth? We are reaching out to people who can answer the question in ways that show their willingness for running the city themselves. Why do I make this announcement? Because I care about this city and I believe in empowerment. Why in the South End at a curbstone? I do this on the street because I worked on the city streets and ultimatetly I believe it will be these people,

here on the streets, who will make the city work for all
of us. I make this announcement on this day because
Martin Luther King is a symbol of what is best in the
United States.[2]   —*Press Release*, Jan. 15, 1979

Thus began my bid to be mayor of Boston. Over the next eight
months, we built support for the campaign by gathering peti-
tions to bring up the Galvin Plan again for a referendum, holding a series of educational forums on who this city belonged to,
and seeking financial support from the widest possible group of
supporters. From August 3 through August 5, a Black Political
Summit was held, with more than sixty people from Boston's
Black community to review the political position of Black Bostonians in the 1970's and 1980's. The three day talks ignited a new
level of solidarity, and agreement not to succumb to those forces
which seek to divide the Black vote. The Summit agreed to
support my candidacy, and the candidacy of all Black aspirants
who are willing to be held accountable to the community of
color.

In this campaign, the "process" was what we were about.
That process included the development of a coalition, and the
development of a network of people from different communities
willing to take responsibility for creating an organization in
their community that would continue independently after my
candidacy. The point was to build a structure that would have an
impact on other decisions to be made in the community, particularly around the electoral process.

We approached the campaign from the position of having a
ward and precinct organization that could have real political
power, and from the standpoint of the issues that the various
groups from across the city were involved in. Our assessment
was that there were many groups attempting to get access, that
each group was going after its goals on a one-by-one basis, and
they were being played off against each other. Ultimately, what
has happened is that these groups have to recognize that, and
come together and say, "This is the bottom line" by which I
mean the point upon which each group stands, and which all
groups have to support and recognize.

The issues were clear—the problems of racial and sexual

violence, the problems of access for a variety of groups, rent control and displacement, employment, energy, the distribution of the wealth of the city, taxes and representation. The central issue of representation and power in the communities was the one around which the neighborhood organizations developed. The issues in their communities were reflected in the positions of the campaign.

Interest groups were also able to develop positions for the campaign, including groups like the Alliance for Rent Control, the Gay Caucus, women's groups, the Third World Jobs Clearing House, the Boston Jobs Coalition, and the elderly. Working with them, we dealt with particular problems, and we developed a set of position papers reflecting proposed solutions.

This was the process. What we said, in effect, was that if people were serious about decentralization, then the campaign process had to be decentralized. If people were serious about community control, then they had to be responsible for taking control. I wanted people to understand where I was coming from in relation to the issues that concerned them. I wanted to talk about my vision of the city, but just as importantly, I wanted to put people on notice that we were going to deal with the issues. Furthermore, we had to get people to realize that it was up to them to make their issue an important one in the campaign. With the rent control issues, and with the Boston Jobs Coalition, things happened on both those issues because I was able to change the nature of the debate during the campaign. I was able to do that because I had the kind of organized support that made it possible.

Looking back over our primary campaign, I think we made the following mistakes. First, if people had really believed in their own power we would have won. The press and many people in the community thought that a Black candidate could not win because of the racism in Boston. True, the racial climate in this city did have a very real impact on the campaign. However, I also believe that the issues were most important. The difference was in increased voter registration. People who had not registered came out to register. That's an indication that people were identifying with each other around the issues. A survey after the election determined that more than half of the people who voted for me did so because they identified with the issues. It is clear to me that the candidate who can best frame voter issues in their proper context, and simultaneously possess an organization which goes after the votes successfully can win—and I don't care whether the person is Black, white, male, female, short, tall, or one-legged.

Secondly, people did not support their own issues. The 60,000 tenants who were going to be affected by rent decontrol did not vote for me (I supported rent control). Issue oriented groups have not realized the importance of using the electoral process to address their needs. I won 53 precincts—which was more than anybody else won, other than the Mayor—but we didn't turn out the volume in those precincts. We were just not geared up in a way that would maximize the turnout in each of the areas. The election came down to a question of organization. White beat Timilty because he had the better organization— that's the only real difference between the two of them. We beat Finnegan because we had the better organization (and we confronted issues). In terms of per capita vote costs, we had the best organization by far. We brought our people at one-third the cost of the Finnegan campaign, and one-sixth the cost of the White and Timilty campaigns.

Thirdly, our candidacy failed to help the voters analyze and assess the performance of the incumbent Mayor. With respect to the Black vote, although we were able to articulate how people were being taken in by Mayor White, they were more afraid of the opposition that Timilty posed. At a meeting at the Trotter school, Doris Bunte confronted the Mayor and his supporters in the Black community with the fact that in Charlestown and West Roxbury (predominantly white areas) folks were only being taxed at twenty-five percent of the property value, whereas in Roxbury and North Dorchester, we were being taxed at seventy and eighty percent.

In 1975, the Mayor said that if he got the Black vote and was re-elected he would change the tax inequality. Four years later there had been no changes. But still the Black ministers, who can influence sixty-five percent of the vote in the Black community, supported White in the final election, again without getting any firm committment from him. The Black vote was taken for granted, while excessive taxation without representation continued.

On the positive side, the "process" worked. People understood each other better. People from different wards or interest groups were able to speak effectively for the concerns of other areas or groups. We had some remarkable examples of this during the campaign. One night when several meetings were scheduled simultaneously, and I couldn't make one in Jamaica Plain, one of the people from Jamaica Plain got up at the meeting and spoke about the campaign and the issues. I was at the Forest Hills Station the next morning, and a woman walked up and said, "We didn't miss you last night," which I took to be a sarcastic comment. But she went on to explain that the guy who had spoken in my place had presented a very clear picture about what the campaign was, and what the issues were. She decided to work for the campaign.

For me, that was a clear indication of the ability of the whole group to begin to erase some of those lines that were between them. People began to speak to the total needs of the group. People began to realize that working together was more effective than working separately. The whole is greater than the sum of its parts. The bottom line is that it's all of us or none of us, and that there's plenty to go around. There is plenty. I know that that flies in the face of energy issues and the like, but the only energy shortage that we're facing today is the energy for goodwill. If we mine that energy, we can produce unlimited amounts of the other kinds of energy.

"The process" left behind a city-wide, neighborhood-based, multi-issue, political organization, The Boston Peoples Organization.

The Boston Peoples Organization is committed to gaining control of our neighborhoods, jobs and government. Through community, labor, and electoral organizing, we strive to overcome racism, sexism, economic exploitation and all forms of oppression. Furthermore, we are united around a vision of Boston as a community of diverse people who can respect each other, who can work together collectively to solve our common problems, and who will help each other to fulfill our potentials to the fullest extent possible. The Boston Peoples Organization is for power to the people of Boston. It is time to come together, to move out of our isolation, to eliminate the oppressive conditions that surround us, to create a humane society.

The Boston Peoples Organization was formed in late 1979 and early 1980 by folks who had been involved in the campaign, working in the neighborhoods and on issues. They realized that if we were going to turn Boston around in the 1980's we needed to build a city-wide organization which could truly lead to the empowerment of Boston's communities and oppressed peoples.

On December 9, 1979, the anti-racist violence committee of the Boston Peoples Organization held a city-wide planning and informational meeting to begin developing strategies to combat racist violence in Boston. Over 200 people from all over the city, from the communities, churches, and anti-racist organizations came together to plan how to expose the work of the Ku Klux Klan and the Boston Marshalls, and to develop anti-racist training programs in the schools.

The Boston Peoples Organization marks a new stage in the development of a progressive political movement in Boston. Through the Boston Peoples Organization, the Black community can unite with other communities and groups fighting for empowerment.

Struggle

It's a struggle
Developing Solidarity.
It's a Struggle
Being Positive.
It's a Struggle
Making Common Unity.
It's a Struggle
Shaping Reality.
It's a Struggle
LIVING.
It's a Struggle
Because it's slow
But if we Struggle
At developing Solidarity,
Being Positive,
Shaping Reality,
Making Common Unity,
We will all Grow.

Because to struggle
Is to work for Change,
and Change is the focus of Education,
and Education is the Basis of Knowledge,
and Knowledge is the Basis for Growth
and Growth is the Basis for
Being Positive and Being Positive
is the Basis for Building Solidarity.
Building Solidarity is a way to shape
Reality and Shaping Reality is Living
                and Living is Loving,
                        So Struggle.

                                    —*Mel King*

PART IV

COMMUNITY DEVELOPMENT

We have come a very long way from the days of the Service Stage. We can see dramatic changes in our self-image, identity, experience and skills, both as individuals and as a community. There is, as we have seen, a history of effort and many successes with every imaginable type of business, organization and venture in the community of color.

In the realm of education we learned first of all to stand up for our own worth. We have moved from the days of providing tutoring programs for our children on the assumption that it was somehow our own fault that our children did not do well in the public schools, to understanding (with the verification of the Massachusetts Courts) that the Boston school system was indeed deliberately segregated. We have demanded that the public school system be more responsive to our children through court action and consistent organizing within our own community as well as city wide. When necessary we went outside the city (with the METCO suburban school program) or bused out children outside our own neighborhoods (with Operation Exodus). We moved to challenge the existing system by taking to the streets when we had no other recourse as during the School Stay Outs, and by developing our own alternative schools, including the State Experimental System. We at last managed to elect a Black member to the School Committee and have taken a major role in the court ordered city-wide Parents Advisory Councils. We watched our youngsters follow our lead and act on their own demands during the student strikes of the late sixties and early seventies. Black parents are continuing to work for multi-cultural curricula, bilingual education and adequate programs for children with special needs. Through this process of struggle we have learned, we have taught others, and we are continuing to develop the skills and programs which will bring equitable, quality education to the public school system.

In the area of housing, we have moved from the era of simply trying to obtain more assistance for Black families being moved out of desirable downtown neighborhoods, to organizing to resist being removed, and then to actually redeveloping our communities as the Lower Roxbury Community Corporation has done to renew the desolation left by the Southwest Corridor, as IBA has done in the South End for the Spanish Community, or as RAP has done in Highland Park.

We have learned how to design, package and finance our own development process based on human need and a concept of community missing from strictly commercial developments. We have expanded the concept of "shelter" to contribute more directly to community, or the socio-cultural context of family life. In spite of numerous attempts to block the successful completion of some of these new community developments, the community of color has made housing one of the most productive of its battlegrounds. IBA has just won the latest round of deliberately obstructionist court proceedings and is beginning the last phase of construction. Although there remains a tremendous housing shortage and the conversion of housing for higher income residents is creating a crisis in many central city neighborhoods, this is an area where we have built expertise as well as hundreds of new units for low and moderate income families.

As far as jobs, we have "earned" an understanding of how non-profit relationships between the community of color and the existing economic power structure keep us at an economic disadvantage. We organized boycotts and selective buying campaigns to secure jobs. We have also confronted the racist practices of unions, government agencies and local contractors, winning some important battles in court and in negotiations with the groups who control the jobs in Boston. We struggled to sway national policy away from the toothless "Boston Plan" for minority hiring, and we have developed our own job creation, training and placement programs, including United Community Construction Workers and the Third World Jobs Clearing House. We have even begun developing some of our own financing mechanisms, such as Unity Bank, the Black United Fund, and the Community Development Finance Corporation to help support community ventures. And most recently there has been the establishment of a city-wide Boston Jobs Coalition which is effectively pushing policies to protect jobs for Boston residents.

In politics, we have moved away from the old patronage days under the Taylors to the explicit commitment of the Black Caucus and the Black Political Task Force to the community of color through political action. We placed John O'Bryant in office, and the vote in the 1979 Mayor's race showed the substantial interest in alternative politics based on what we have learned during our struggles and on the issues still affecting our community.

The entire process of learning and action described above throughout the three stages is, to my mind, community development. It is through this process that we can begin to put our visions for a better city into action. Some community groups have already made significant strides toward developing full-fledged communities—combining culture, housing, social programs and a physical turf in their plans and programs.

In addition, the later part of the Institution Building stage has been a time when groups began to interact more with each other—providing the basis for a more comprehensive approach to community development across the city. As community groups move through the process of these stages, they gain the self-confidence, the experience and the skills to move into the more complex and effective approaches to community development. Just as a person is better able to relate to other people in a healthy way once she or he has settled issues of identity and gotten on base internally, the community groups which have been through the process are more comfortable working with other groups to build something better for both of them. Groups still needing to settle their identity cannot trustfully relate to others. During the latter years of the 1970's coalitions —serious, on-going institutions designed to work on issues over the long haul have been formed on jobs (Boston Jobs Coalition), politics (Black Political Task Force), housing (All City Housing Organization) and schools (City-wide Parents Advisory Council). The learning we've acquired over the past three decades has provided a stronger basis for making rational decisions about how to get community needs met without competition or duplication by existing groups.

The final chapters of this book outline a vision for the way that we can take control of our communities and our future— what sort of city and political structure we should be working toward and a strategy for getting there. The key to both vision and strategy is trust among ourselves. We need to develop the skills that will allow us to follow through on decentralization of power in ways that maximize both personal involvement and cooperation for common goals. With trust we can build the confidence to criticize for improvement and strength, and the ability to decide clearly and without opportunism how to distribute the work that needs to be done in our community. The pieces are all here: confidence, ability, vision. Now it's time to pull it all together.

Chapter 19

A VISION
FOR OUR CITY

Where there are
no limits to growth
visions of plenty abound;
where visions of plenty abound
growth is unlimited;
mind set is critical
the 8 straight up sets limits,
lazy ∞ on its side
is infinite.
See.

—*Mel King*

Where are we all going? Unless we have a vision of where we would like to be, based on the values we consider to be essential and indisputable, we cannot map out a plan for getting there, or for changing what needs to be changed to build the city we want to live in. We cannot move ahead without an overall philosphy or direction. Coming together around a particular crisis or a single issue like the Viet Nam War, nuclear power or housing is not enough. Our work for this new decade is to bring people together to define the basic values that must underlie each effort we undertake.

We must develop a full-scale vision of where we want to be so that every individual, every group, can clearly see how their work fits into the whole and contributes to the full resolution of the issues which are shaping our times. Otherwise we will continue to work in fragmented cells, unable to draw sustenance from each other, and unable to see the ultimate goals. To

231

prepare ourselves for the inevitable struggle within our communities around values, definitions, criteria and purposes for our continuing efforts, we need to determine the principles of unity which can help to facilitate the debate which will come.

Principles of Unity

My own vision, of the city we can build together, is based on a belief that people can and want to struggle through to a better place. I also believe that people are not content simply to survive the rough times coming. People are seeking a higher level of community consciousness, in the process of figuring out how to survive and grow. My beliefs are based on several assumptions.

First, that people neither want to oppress nor to be oppressed.
Second, that people want change that allows them to express their creativity.
Third, that people are curious about self and others, and seek new discoveries.
Fourth, that people want positive and humane individual and community experiences, based on love and respect.
Fifth, that people want to be in harmony with their environment, using the environment and technologies to provide opportunities for needs to be met, not for greed to be fed.

And, finally, that people want to keep a clear perspective; to understand why we are here; and to understand our relationship to the universe.

I assume that we are not there yet and know that people are very often scared to do what is necessary to get us closer to the vision. For me, the people who are working at making all this come true for themselves and others are expressing the highest form of human development, which comes from a sense of neighborly love. We, as individuals and as community, need to be about getting people to deal with fears which immobilize us and bar us from our basic instincts toward growth, change and harmony.

Our fears often are fed by the pressure of problems which appear to be becoming more intense: scarce jobs, lack of affordable housing, food shortages, depletion of energy and other natural resources. Fighting against these problems can be the basis of alliances, but fears can only be alleviated if we also come together on the basis of common commitment to internal democracy and citizen involvement. We must advocate resistance to the deeper issues of racism, sexism, classism and exploitation. At the same time we must not be afraid to confront difficult issues on which alliance members have differing feelings. The alliance will fall apart if people are unwilling to struggle through the issues which divide as well as come together over those items which naturally unite us.

My vision is based on the belief that people are willing to go through the difficulties of confrontation because we know, from experience, that being honest supports learning, growth, and liberation based on humane values. The main purpose, the main value behind so much of our struggle, past, future and present is to create "community." By that we mean the human context in which people can live and feel nutured, sustained, involved and stimulated. Community is the continual process of getting to know people, caring and sharing responsibility for the physical and spiritual condition of the living space.

Why then is "community" so important? It is a matter of humanity. Creating and maintaining community is the best way to meet people's needs. People relate better, more completely in a community. Working with their neighbors people can accomplish an amazing amount of good which simply will not happen under an impersonal government program. We need to make use of the person next door and not depend on people outside the community to solve our problems and satisfy our needs. People flourish in a more personal environment, their strengths can be cultivated, their weaknesses can be improved upon, with the support of neighbors who possess complementary skills and strengths. "Community" counteracts the frustration, depersonalization and fragmentation which our current society forces on people.

"Community" is important for establishing a common bondedness, for creating a sense of identity, for maintaining and creating cultural continuity, for giving social expression to oneself as a part of a larger whole. "Community" promotes self-development beyond the immediate family, toward involvement in ever-widening breadths of community, city, state, nation, world, and universe. "Community" is the base from which people can begin to understand what else is going on in the world.

The impact of foreign policy is felt in heating oil prices and gasoline costs; land values change on the basis of city and national policy. Food prices shift with the truckers' strike over fuel prices. All of these forces make more sense if a person is involved in a "community" where there is some possibility of reacting with unity and creativity as such problems threaten the stability of the whole "community."

The smaller size and potential familiarity of the neighborhood makes it more possible for people to take interest in what is going on, whether it is a neighborhood band, sports teams, the repair of sidewalks or streets, or the budget for major community projects. The neighborhood is a base and stepping stone to broadening involvement.

If it is these human aspects of community which are most crucial, the definition of *community development* immediately takes on dimensions quite different from the traditional urban renewal or bringing in new industry. *Community development* must lean heavily on *human development* —the most natural ingredient for developing the best possible resources in a community are the people themselves. It is not the physical structures, or the dollar signs that count in the end, but the way people feel about themselves, each other and the place they live.

Using a people-oriented definition of development, a community becomes more developed as it becomes more diverse, incorporating more cultural and ethnic traditions, and developing the skills and confidence to solve their own problems.

Long ago, in the first New Urban League Black Paper written in the summer of 1967, we sketched out our definition of community and development,

> We envision a community in which technology, materialism, the profit motive and notions of "progress" take a back seat to humanism and human dignity.
> We envision a community in which there evolves a new morality based on the richness of human possibili-

ties and the depth of human communication and self-respect.

"Community control," a vision for the Boston Black community since the decade of the Sixties, is not a simple idea. It means, in my mind, people taking responsibility for making decisions in their communities. On the one hand, this involves a collective approach to all community problems and issues: working together. On the other hand, from a personal perspective, taking responsibility entails understanding that you have not got it made until you can help others to get where you are or beyond. Otherwise you will always be defending what you've got, and you cannot work with other people under those circumstances. As people work together and look out for each other, those most in need will be able to rise up, pushing all of society in an upward, forward movement. In this sense responsibility means looking out for yourself through looking out for others.

Ideally, a community approach to problem solving involves the greatest number of people possible. The more people involved, the more creative the solutions will be and the greater likelihood of people participating directly in shaping their communities and themselves. In reality, however, it is difficult to organize many people and to set up systems which encourage so much involvement. If we want to develop such a community problem solving process, we have to learn more about group dynamics.

These definitions say a lot about how we want our city to look even with the politics of scarcity pressuring us. In my mind, the community we envision, pieces of which we have been building for years, will be constructed around these values:

Sharing: people freely offering to each other what they have, knowing that they will be able to do more, in the end, and to have more for everyone, if resources and skills are pooled. Decisions about distributing and utilizing our resources are the most difficult we will face in the 1980's. We must have a sense of interdependence, abandoning the idea that every person can make it on his or her own. It has never been true, despite our American mythology; even the Pilgrims desperately needed the

Native Americans to survive. It has been that way right from the beginning. Only when we admit that we are all in this together will resources be distributed equitably.

Compassion: people empathizing with each other, knowing that so long as one person is hungry or enslaved or oppressed, we are all diminished. The situation in South Africa is compelling because we know that if it is possible there, it could happen to us here, too. Active opposition to that oppression is the only effective and meaningful expression of compassion.

Creativity: people using their skills and talents fully, to solve problems rather than to make money or to beat someone else out. We are clever enough to solve problems in ways that will benefit us all by creating jobs or products we need. An intensive energy and water conservation campaign could provide a significant number of jobs, while making it possible to save a noticeable proportion of the amount of energy and water now consumed. Composting organic wastes can produce topsoil for city greening and food production (trees and shrubs also reduce energy consumption and improve air quality). Composting would help solve the increasing problem of urban waste disposal. Incineration of other wastes can produce heat which can generate electricity, or, used directly, heat buildings or provide steam for industrial purposes. Co-generation is a technical term for maximizing the energy from one function (such as incineration) by using otherwise wasted heat to generate electricity or steam for other purposes. The term should be applied to many other efforts that we should undertake to coordinate and cooperate in problem solving creatively.

Respect: people recognizing the value of other people and our other natural resources. It is vital to our survival that we return to respecting the earth and the incredibly delicate and complex natural systems which we continue to abuse (although they have shown remarkable resilience, they do not have infinite endurance for abuse). We breathe this air, too, and people of color need to be a part of anti-nuclear battles and all other efforts to safeguard the condition of our environment. Our technology is only as good as we make it; the ultimate responsibility for its consequences falls on each of us, whether inventor, operator, or bystander. We must respect each other: each person has to be seen as a potential component of our whole community. But we must also demand respect for each other. We cannot tolerate abuse of others from greed, sickness, or addiction. We must stand together and challenge any lack of respect for people that appears in our community whether it is rape, robbery, murder, manipulation, bullying or indifference. After all, we cannot respect others unless we respect ourselves.

Without unity among ourselves around these values, we will not be able to develop comprehensive solutions to the immensely complicated problems obstructing the growth of our comunity community as we envision it. It is clear that we cannot fix things in the ways we were taught. Those in power keep trying patchwork and half-hearted solutions. We need to conduct a searching assessment of our goals and our methods. The problems that can be labeled "housing" or "energy" or "food" are all connected, and interconnected still further to the very structure of our economy as it stands. Piecemeal programs will not do the job; isolated efforts will be engulfed by the scale of the broader problems.

A community built around people's needs, a city which functions to meet people's needs, will become a reality only if we share, cooperate, redistribute resources and tax our creativity to the utmost. This process of growth will entail some very uncomfortable experiences as we root out our prejudices and confront our fears. One of the first steps in this process is to define the problems we intend to confront. Racism, sexism, exploitation all demand this attention. There is considerable confusion about some of these terms, confusion which will only make the learning process more difficult.

Racism for Black people is the denial of their humanity by white people. Racism is a matter of power: racism is dehumanizing, devaluing, and focused on the controlling and exploiting of one race of people by another.

There are those who throw stones, and there are those who sit by and do nothing about those throwing the stones. Both are racists. Silence is assent. Many white folks may not consider themselves to be racists, but they help maintain the institutions of racism by not doing anything, by simply accepting the status quo. As Malcolm said, "You're either a part of the solution, or you're part of the problem. "

Recently white people have been trying to redefine racism in a way that includes Black people. Many white people, including police and city officials, are using the word "racist" to apply to all types of violence whether initiated by Black or white. They call Black people who attack whites "racist" as if the conditions under which they operate are the same as those of whites. It simply isn't true. A Black person who does violence to a white person may be a reactionary, but cannot be called a racist. Reverse racism is not possible, because the power relationship is the key and people of color in this society do not have that kind of power over white people. Violence is not to be condoned. But we have to be very, very clear about what is motivating people: and we have to put a halt to white people justifying racist behavior on their part by pointing to violent Black reactions to a racist society.

When I asked the commissioner of the Boston Metropolitan District Commission why Black folks were being denied access to the public islands and beaches under MDC jurisdiction, he responded, "Well, I can't go to Roxbury." White folks are using Black people's resentment of the denial of their humanity to further deny their humanity.

Whether in the home, the job, or the media, women are supposed to serve the psychological needs of men, while having no real power to determine their own lives. Sexism is the denial of the humanity of women by men.

The Women's Movement is overcoming male dominance not by dominating men, but by embodying values which support and extend our common humanity. Women are identifying themselves as women. They are not mirroring macho behavior, but creating new ways of relating which go beyond degrading sex stereotypes.

Concerned men need to come together as men to deal with the situation they have benefited from. Men have to learn to support one another, to let go of their male privilege, to overcome the self-hatred that keeps them from changing their sexist behavior.

There is an important difference between racism and sexism that trips us up. If a white woman wants to, she can join with white men in racist and exploitative relationships over people of color. Any white woman can benefit to some extent from her membership in white society in a way that no Black man can no matter how macho his behavior. Any attempt at behaving in a sexist way with white women has generally resulted in death for a Black man. (Just check the statistics on sentencing for Black-white rape compared to Black-Black rape.)

Black women, on the other hand, are at a double disadvantage. Their humanity is denied by both white racism and by male dominance. Black women have to overcome the racism and sexism that permeate our society at large, and the oppression that they personally confront at the hands of Black men. In the struggle against racism, we cannot have a house divided against itself. In order to eliminate racism, Black women and men are going to have to overcome the sexism that divides us.

Sexism also extends to the oppression of women and men because of their sexual preferences. The assumption that only heterosexual relationships are acceptable and fulfilling is another example of prejudice that is often used to set people with common concerns against each other. Much of the recent violence in Boston is an attack on people who are asserting their rights: people of color, women, gay men and lesbians. All of these groups are seriously disturbing the white, male, "straight" foundations of our society. If we understand each other we will be able to put aside all the negative "isms" and turn toward our common concerns.

Economic exploitation is another problem which needs definition so that we can be clear about how to deal with our own behavior and how to get on with business.

Of the 150 realtors on the Greater Boston Real Estate Board only 5% of them are registered to vote in Boston. This means that most of the land and buildings in Boston are owned and controlled by folks who live outside of town. While Boston is described as "a city of neighborhoods" made up of diverse ethnic groups, the more fundamental reality is that the city is torn by racism and elitism which are perpetuated by those who have controlled the wealth in Boston from the very beginning.

Ownership and control of the land, housing, and factories

has given a very few people tremendous economic power and status. They use this power to extract greater profits from the workers in the factories, and from the tenants in the neighborhoods.

Alongside of those who control the ruling heights, there has arisen a considerable number of young professionals who have higher incomes and status than the working folks who have lived in the neighborhoods of the city for the past decade or more. Due to the increasing cost of commuting, and the appeal of the cultural diversity of the inner city, these young professionals are being lured into condominiums being built by the realtors and banks. Working people, Blacks and Puerto Ricans are forced out of their homes and neighborhoods where they have tried to build a community.

The escalating war between young professionals and the residents in the neighborhoods that they are displacing is one more chapter in the history of the attempts of those in power to maintain a segmented city so as to be able to enrich themselves further at the expense of others.

Oppression, whether as people of color or as women, as lesbians or as gay men, as workers or as tenants, as elderly or as youth, as handicapped or as undocumented workers, is possible only as long as we buy into it. We will remain oppressed as long as we continue to fear those who put us down, inflicted upon us by those in control.

We should make no mistake about the fact that this culture is on its way out. A culture which spends billions on bombs and can't keep people fed and housed has got to be on its way out. Jessie Della Cruz, a migrant farm worker who tells the inspiring story of managing to buy one of the farms where she and her family had been exploited for years, has some wise words about how to spend our energy: "Fight the people who bring out the meanness in you." She knows that it is too easy to be baited into fighting the people closest to you rather than the exploiters who corrupt us. Confronting our own behavior patterns is part of what I call the struggle for the mind. This internal struggle centers around the way we see ourselves, and what we think our potential is: do we believe in our own power? Jessie has won the struggle. She understands her own value in spite of the culture she lives in. And she is clear about what forces we are fighting against.

The first step toward freedom is to stop identifying with those who oppress us—to reject their values, their way of thinking, their way of living. By taking pride in ourselves, we can root out the self- and community-destructiveness that has crippled our efforts in the past. By overcoming racism, sexism, and elitism within us, we will have the strength, confidence and understanding to eliminate the institutional bases of oppression.

The institutions, and the behavior of the individual in those institutions, which support racism, sexism and economic exploitation are the "enemies." On the other hand, in the same way that Black women and men need to understand that they are not each other's enemy, the different groups that are coming together to overcome their particular forms of oppression must have a committment to overcoming all forms of oppression. If a person, whether white or Black, male or female, straight or gay, worker or professional, does not directly confront racist, sexist or elitist behavior, and the institutions they are part of, the problem will continue to exist. People demonstrate by their actions that they are genuinely striving to liberate themselves and others. We envision a city where men will seek the opportunity to deal with male-female issues; where Black and white, Black and Hispanic and other groups will work actively on rooting out the troublesome places in our relationships. We envision a community in which people will not fear correction because they care enough about basic humanity to give something of themselves, in order to get even more back.

We envision a city in which many of us are willing to make those changes as individuals, family members and as community participants. We will build a city based on our values. An impossible picture? Not at all. A strategy for moving toward this vision, and a community structure providing the security within which to struggle, follows.

Chapter 20

A STRATEGY FOR THE 1980's

Black Leadership

The Black community is in a unique position to take the lead in formulating and implementing a strategy to move all of us toward the vision we have for our city, and for our future. The Black community has a special responsibility. No other modern people has had to deal with the oppression of slavery, racism and—in the words of W.E.B. DuBois—"the experience of being both Black and American." We are legally Americans; but the denial of access perpetuated by racism has given us insight into the potential and the perversion intrinsic to the American system. We know both sides: the intense hope and the intense frustration when hope is betrayed.

We know, from this experience, that we cannot leave our future to chance and we certainly cannot surrender it to the custodians, historical and contemporary, of American society. We have won some court orders which insure hiring of Black people and whites on a one to one basis; however, we should also know from experience that such orders do not change the attitudes and behavior of the old timers in the system. Getting some jobs, and buying into the familiar politics of scarcity which encourage us to get a share and keep quiet, will never build the changes Black folks need to see. At times we have been the most outspoken critics of this society and its values. Our duty is to make a positive structure—necessary for the development of a truly humane city, community, society—operational.

Our experience has given us a unique perspective from which to lead. But the responsibility of leadership requires that we confront the racism that makes us desire to keep our distance from the system, even when we get jobs within it. We must continue to raise some very basic questions, of society, and of ourselves. Why do we often choose not to engage other people—particularly white people—when there is no way that we can exist on this earth without some rapport and some contact? We must constantly ask ourselves whether we have fallen victim to the politics of scarcity which keep us from challenging. Will we be like the Irish of Boston? Irish people and their political representatives hold a tremendous amount of power in this society, yet they continue to imagine themselves a persecuted minority, having little or no capacity to lead or to share. Sometimes being the "worst off" or the "most oppressed" or "persecuted," can become a crutch, blinding people to their participation in oppressing others. Are we still at the point where the pain of dealing with others is so great that we stay out of involvements and keep our distance? If so, we cannot take a leadership role.

In fact, recognizing and building on our strengths facilitates repair. The other role requires that we build models of our vision in our own commmunity. We will find as we build models of humanity and caring, that we will be providing leadership to get similar models instituted throughout the city—in other communities. We will find that our external leadership role and our internal community role are knit closely together. To play these roles Black people must develop new relationships in two critical areas—the community and the family.

Family Relationships

An important place to start changing community relationships is within our own families. We call ourselves "brothers and sisters." Traditionally we have used a lot of affectionate familial terms for describing the Black family. Actual family structures were originally shaped by the African Diaspora—with kin scattered in the Caribbean, in the central and southern United States and New England. Our families were scattered and sometimes untraceable (with all due respect to the research work of Alex Haley). Our mobility, population growth and economic trends caused us to migrate from the rural South to northern urban centers. As a result traditional family structures were forfeited. In bygone years, the phrase "we take care of our own" described the way the community used its resources to support those who needed assistance. However, public welfare programs have modified that reality. Fifty years ago no Black child would have been put up for adoption; children who needed homes found one within the kinship community. Our history is one of familial support. Today oftentimes single parent families are isolated from support systems and kinfolk. We should take a look at whether or not our move into the prevailing system is in our best interest. We could stand to lose most of our strong Black family heritage. The new reality in American family life may make our families and our community more susceptible to outside control if we let our values be swept away by trends.

The development and organization of our community depends upon relationships that generate the understanding that *we* are not the enemy. Black women and Black men should take the old adage "United we stand, divided we fall" to heart. If we are not together as family, it is unlikely that we will be able to get beyond the current foot-in-the-door tokenism we have been offered. Institutional racism and oppression is so great that it requires maximum effort from the community to obtain any concessions.

We call each other "brother" and "sister," but I am reminded of a meeting where a Black woman turned to a Black man who had called her "sister" and said, "I'm not your sister and I don't want you to treat me like a sister because it means you don't see me as a person to build a relationship with. And I don't believe in incest!" It is possible that terms of affection and familial identification can be used to keep us at a distance from each other, keeping us away from the more "dangerous" areas of personal encounter and development. There are other forces in the community which make it difficult to relate to each other. Violence against women is supported tacitly—pimps are not ostracized and we don't deal with their presence in our community; we stand by and watch fights "in the family" even when the odds are terribly imbalanced.

Racism has made it difficult for the "model" American family to develop in the Black community (even if we wanted it, which is not clear). Its force is felt nevertheless, especially by the men who are constantly told that the way to indicate their superiority and to assume the "model" male role is through violence, mastery and control of women and family members. What we need to do is question and discuss behavior patterns, and develop a family structure of our own that is based on the importance of equality.

One of the origins of tension between Black men and women is the old myth about who has access to the few resources available to us in this society: who gets the jobs? who should get them? Sometimes men are less than supportive of Black women who begin to get jobs worth having. History tells us that the jobs which Black women were able to get in the past (domestic household work) which Black men were excluded from, were hardly worth having in the first place. The American economic system has been so closed to our race that we cannot get hung up on who gets the scraps thrown to us. This issue is rarely addressed so as to dispel myths and to envision each other as partners in new work.

We see rape and murder as the ultimate violence against women, but in a way these are just the tip of the iceberg. There are so many other forms of violence, more psychological in form, that contribute to the erosion of our family relations. All this is compounded by lack of communication. We have to get out of the trap where Black men see themselves as the sole breadwinners, judging themselves by a white model; a model to which they have no access to begin with. The more we subscribe to these images of ourselves, the more vulnerable we become to self-fulfilling prophesies about the alleged weakness of the Black family. A person who has not gone through a positive group experience in a family or similar setting cannot, later, relate to people in groups successfully. If Black people are not able to see themselves in a positive, deserving manner, we cannot interact with others in a positive way. We cannot build a family, a community, or a coalition on negative memories.

Until we confront the day to day brutality which we force on each other, we will not be able to counteract the way individual hatreds get played out between groups, and ultimately nations. Imagine how great it would feel to throw off the false images of what others think we should be like—to be our natural selves! It's a lot easier running the 100 yard dash without an extra fifty pounds of baggage. The excess energy that would be released could be channeled to deal with the enemies we face, not against our family and our community, the very people we love. Shedding the weight of inappropriate roles and expectations will free capacities—restricted and repressed. Now think of how much we can get done.

If we succeed in revising our innermost relationships within the family, and then within the groups which form our community, we will set off an everwidening chain reaction of change. People who relate differently within their families will start relating in new ways on their street; on their block, and in their community. The potential will spread to new relations within the city, and across the state, and eventually, nationally. People will view the world and international relationships in new ways; even our place in the universe will appear different. Like nesting boxes that fit one within the other, each aspect of our relationships , from family to inter-galactical, contain other relationships, and are contained by broader relationships. We will be able to understand the intricate interconnections of our lives with our work. It will be clearer how each part, however small, fits into the system as a whole, playing its part and insuring the healthy functioning of the entire system. And we will be able to see more clearly how we can build this system in ways that support our vision, and ensure our development as a people and as a community. Then we will be able to share our vision, our models, and our experience with others.

The Community Relationships

We cannot design a strategy for positive community development, if we ignore some of the destructive relationships going on in our community. Our positive values and negative behaviors cannot peacefully coexist. Our commitment to eliminate discrimination and racism and to get access has ignored a corresponding commitment to eliminate inconsistent behaviors inside our community. People push drugs, others use them; people rob, steal, and hurt to support a habit; prostitution and various sorts of racketeering persist.

I made an observation recently after I had delivered a graduation speech for a Head Start program in Lower Roxbury. Directly across the street from this visible example of community development that took ten years of hard work to realize, there was a hot spot for drug traffic. Within view of these children, our future, there persists obvious signs of community destructiveness.

Part of the destruction in our community arises from an overwhelming belief that the system is impenetrable. In spite of positive evidence around them, evidence which may not quite fit white-style evaluations, some people give up and pursue destructive paths, convinced we cannot change the state of things, and that we will not ever be admitted into the white world.

Just as we have to stand up to violence against people of color elsewhere in the city, we must oppose violence by our own people against members of our community. It is dangerous to concentrate solely on external problems. We must make up our community mind that we will deal with these difficult internal issues, including sexism and exploitation by some of our own people.

The stuggle to overcome racism, exploitation and the denial of access is important, but it will not deal with the criminal element which works against us in our community. We have got to reach out, involve the folks on the corners, the undecided who are participating in destroying our community, as they destroy themselves. We cannot consider them outside our community and our responsibility. We have to be committed to driving out those who will not respond; we will have to exact from the police the services that will eliminate destructive behavior. At the same time we must eliminate negative behavior in each other by confronting the way that we unthinkingly reinforce, encourage and support the malignant element in our community.

Believing that there is no way to get access to the existing system creates much of the subversive behavior in our community. There is no statistical evidence that I know of, but there are reports that during the peak of the Civil Rights Movement—school stayouts, marches, demonstrations—that there were fewer incidents of crime within our communities. The increasing use of drugs can be directly related to the reduction in the amount of access to resources and the lack of change in power relationships.

The result of the civil rights activism was momentous: people got so energized and became so effective at articulating the radical changes which they perceived as necessary to realize the American dream, that the entrenched powers were terribly threatened. A number of institutional changes were made, i.e., moving the anti-poverty programs from under the control of city halls and dismantling the Office of Economic Opportunity (OEO) and now the Department of Health, Education and Welfare (HEW). These moves were designed to undercut this momentum and new community power.

Some of the tactics used to stop the movement were more direct: the murders of Martin Luther King, Malcolm X, the Panthers and others who dared speak too clearly, and too loudly about the inevitability of change. Vincent Harding sums up this period of community involvement and personal development,

> In other words, we can actually say that the sixties ended when Black folk, joined temporarily by hundreds of thousands of white people—especially young ones who had created their own version of "The Movement"—joined themselves against the limits of this country's liberal vision of itself. We can say that the sixties ended because we had begun to sense the cost of creating a just and "beloved community" out of an unjust, racist and deeply fearful society.

Along with the intense involvement of those days that took us beyond self, toward community, we began to see more clearly that whatever we do to change our society and its structures will also change us and demand that we change our own habits and our interpersonal relationships. The role we play as social activists, as leaders of social and economic change, will demand new roles within our community, within our families, within ourselves.

The changes we need to make in our community relationships are not limited to the obvious "destructors" we can observe at work. Each of us, and each community organization, needs to examine the way we work together or against each other in the course of our community development efforts. This is a competitive society, and many members of our community are no exception to the American rule of competition. But if we intend to make significant change in the way the institutions of this country work, we should start with our own behavior which prevents cooperation, sharing of resources and work.

Black people have provided America with some extremely important examples of people taking responsibility for liberating themselves and, therefore, others. One of the most important events in our lives took place when Rosa Lee Parks, living in Alabama, decided that she was as important, and as deserving as other people. She decided not to continue to accept oppression, and to play the victim role. So she sat down in a seat customarily reserved for white patrons and said very clearly that she expected her rights to be honored. The history we have lived tells us what an impact her decision made on our world. That decision has to be made over and over again. It has to be made by or Asian or Native American, whether we are women, elderly, handicapped, gay or lesbian, tenant or worker, elderly or youth—every one of us, every group, has to make that statement. But that statement cannot be made in isolation. Our history ought to tell us that if those in power can deal with us one by one, issue by issue, they can play one off against another. If we share the vision about what is possible and what we want to see in our country and our community, we can work in unity as a community, resisting the isolation and separation that makes us vulnerable.

The changes in our community relationships must begin internally, from there we can build the kind of group relationships to develop our vision. We cannot reach other people if we have not first changed ourselves. So many times when we are in the process of organizing and confronting, we don't listen. Father John Harmon, in an article called "The Cycle of Silence," said, "that to listen is to be willing to change." What good does it do us to feel we know what is right if we cannot understand why others do not share and join with us? We need to develop the sensitivity that allows us to identify with the pain that other people in our community bear, but have not been able to work through with us, or we with them, so that they share the new vision, and a new perspective on what is possible and how to stop the pain.

In conjunction with our efforts to build relationships of empathy and sensitivity, we must also establish principles of unity—the " bottom line" that we all agree with and relate to. We need to learn how to bring each of the potentially allied groups into a room, put all their issues and concerns up front and then get the commitment from all of us on the bottom line—the basis from which we can move forward. Working out this sort of baseline means talking to a lot of people that we may not be comfortable with at first. Having drawn the bottom line from which we can relate to people will help make it more possible to negotiate some difficult and painful points of difference. Alliances can sometimes be built around common problems and issues which require common action; but we also need to be clear about the underlying, common commitment to internal democracy and citizen involvement, and a common resistance to racism, sexism, classism and exploitation.

At the same time we must not be afraid to confront difficult issues on which alliance members have differing feelings. The alliances we try to build will fall apart if people are not willing to struggle over the issues which divide us, and not simply come together over those items which natually unite us. We have got to relate to the issues providing support for the members of the alliance, in terms of their own needs, and simultaneously try to get people to erase those lines that separate us.

If Black people continue to say that our issue is the only issue, and if women do the same, and Chicanos and elderly do the same, then we are not going to be able to move. We have to figure out a way to erase the divisions among us so that people are comfortable with saying that all the issues are our issues, allowing themselves to put as much energy into that total process as they would if it were their very own total concern that they were working on. If we cannot learn to reach beyond our own narrow community boundaries, we will never be able to reach the larger community of our vision. Once we have wired the bones of a community able to struggle together, to confront difficult feelings and even differences with compassion and caring, we will have the network of "kinfolk" —the new family—which can be the supportive structure for our continuing work.

The Community Development Plan

The next step in Black community development is to build upon this "kinfolk" network by bringing the Black community together through a Community Development Plan consisting of two key components: decentralization and education.

Decentralization

The overall approach for the Black community and for the city in general is decentralization. There has got to be power in every unit, whatever size, clearly authorized so that people know how and when to use it. Each community has got to have a base of power delegated on the basis of need. We cannot continue to have a city government in which some people outside the specific geo-political area who have no identification with the community, make decisions for those inside who have to live with the consequences of those decisions.

The empowerment of the Black community can take place through the development of Ward Councils which can serve as models for the other Boston neighborhoods. There are eight wards in Boston which have a substantial Black population. In each one of these wards, the development of a Ward Council would be a natural extension of our understanding of community beyond our families and neighborhoods to all the neighborhoods in a ward (approximately 25,000 people in Boston). The Ward Council would be made up of representatives from all the neighborhoods and community organizations in the ward, providing a way for the community to grow through joining everyone's efforts together. The Ward Council would be the decision-making and advocacy body for matters which directly affect the communities within the ward. In particular each Ward Council will be responsible for several important on-going functions: 1) a regular community audit to pinpoint problems and provide data for setting priority action areas; 2) continuous community education about problems and possible solutions; 3) facilitation and coordination of the distribution of resources and support services to the ward, via the programs of member agencies and institutions; 4) contracting for certain development services within the ward if necessary; and 5) coordination of fundraising within a ward.

Each Ward Council will in turn send representatives to a Black Community Council, made up of representatives from all the Black wards, and eventually to a Boston City Council, made up of representatives from all the wards in the city, if the other neighborhoods in Boston develop the same form of community representation through Ward Councils. The Black Community Council, which would include all Black elected officials, would help keep the local objectives of each ward council in harmony with the needs of the Black community as a whole, resolve disputes and assist with difficult decisions of resource distribution. This group could also provide support services and problem solving assistance to the local ward councils as needed. In addition, it might want to sponsor an Institute of Community Development to combine local resource groups, and to provide skill training in a variety of areas crucial to the on-going work of the ward councils, including: leadership, group and community psychology, fundraising and grant writing, labor organizing, collective bargaining, crisis intervention and conflict resolution, problem-solving, planning and evaluation. Existing institutions such as Roxbury Community College could take the lead role in providing these support services.

This plan is designed to maximize the resources that are available in every segment of the Black community in Boston. In particular, these are the churches and social welfare agencies such as the NAACP, the Urban League, Community Action Program agencies and the settlement houses. The goal of the plan is to pull together these resources in a geo-political framework using the methods of coordination and cooperation to further internal development while at the same time building in a structure for on-going community organizing and cohesive community politics. We should be able to build accountability into the delivery of community services, significantly increasing the quality of life.

One important function of the Ward Councils is to measure how the quality of life is changing in our communities. The growth process is quantifiable as well as qualitative, and it is critical to establish some basic units of change by which each ward council can check its progress. Without these criteria there is no way to know whether efforts expended on various community projects is producing any results. Change for people in the community should be measured by their evaluation of the conditions that they live under and their ideas about how they want their community to be. To facilitate the measurement process you've got to know where you started, so the first undertaking by the development center should be a thorough audit of the community to assess its "rating" on vital issues. These basic units fall into many categories including attitudinal and psychological, physical and environmental, economic and political issues.

Every Ward Council should be acutely aware of the vital role that information can play in the process of organizing. Too often people involved in problem solving never quite manage to explain the urgent reasons for widespread and continual participation by community residents. With posters, video tape, cable television and radio we can broadcast information to the community preparing it for action. The need and rationale for participation could be displayed, block by block, to rouse the power of knowledge and begin the priority-setting process.

These displays should not only develop a heightened awareness of problems, but also help people to take action by focusing their efforts on specific problems. The immediacy of a "Community Scoreboard" would make it nearly impossible for people to avoid or ignore a problem ostrich fashion. With the base of information about the conditions in their ward, people will be able to raise pointed questions about the reasons for their community's better status on some important issues.

The Community Scoreboard:

For comparative reasons these common issues should be assessed in all wards.

ATTITUDE AND IMAGE:

Skill Level

Education Level

Participation in Community Affairs

ENVIRONMENT:

Housing Code Enforcement (lead poisoning, unsafe, unsanitary housing)

Grime (garbage in streets, alleys, and on sidewalks)

Air Pollution (noise, emissions)

Open Space Development

Recreation

Alternative Energy Sources

Gardening

CRIME AND SAFETY:

Adequate Police Protection

Reduction in Crime Rate

Fire Hazards (abandoned buildings, housing conditions)

Lighting and Sidewalk Repair

Arson Cases

GROSS NEIGHBORHOOD PRODUCT:

(all neighborhood salaries combined and profits from neighborhood businesses)
Multiplier Effect of Investments and Business
Leakage of Black Money from the Black Community(imported goods and taxes with no return)
Excess Savings

HEALTH:

Infant Mortality
Mother Mortality
Elderly Care
Rates of Stress, Heart Attacks, Hypertension
Malnutrition
Lead Poisoning
Sickle Cell Anemia
Mental Health, Self-Image

EMPLOYMENT:

Number of Employed, Unemployed, Underemployed
Range of Skills
New Jobs Developed
New Business Development

COMMUNITY INVOLVEMENT:

The Number of Groups Working on Community Problems

POLITICAL PROGRESS:

The Number of Black people, Other Ethnic Groups, and Women in Office
Mileage (legislation they've achieved)

EDUCATION:
Number of Persons of Colors Who Are Teachers
Quantity and Quality of People of Color
Parent Involvement
Teacher and Administrative Accountability
Level of Student Skills
Number Going to Higher Education
Adult Education Programs

Another critical ingredient of the Ward Councils and this entire Community Development Plan will be roles that neighbors are willing to play for each other. The key is to make the concept of "Kinfolk" real. In order for the Ward Councils to be fully effective, each street must have designated public people, residents who are willing to be community contacts and the key organizers for activities on their streets.

These public people can help to implement the audits of community conditions street by street and take an inventory of local resources. The presence of such an identifiable person on each street will help offset some of the disrupting mobility and change and change in our lives by providing some sense of continuity. The public person on each street will need to be trained through the Institute for Community Development in survival skills of all kinds, from organizing local buying clubs, to starting community gardens, and protecting people from being displaced from their homes, to encouraging energy conservation and recycling, setting up community skills exchanges, voter registration, training and education workshops on a range of topics, and more.

These Kinfolk would be constantly developing new ways to involve the people of each street in providing for their own basic needs. In the process, they express the values of caring, sharing and cooperation which are basic to the Community Development Plan and to survival of our community of color. Their actions should also be oriented toward the future, providing for future needs by planting food bearing trees and bushes, helping people sow seeds that will root the values needed if our communities and families are going to survive this decade.

The "Kinfolk" concept is not just another variation on the old Ward Boss model where people did things for people for a political price. The patronage machines were based on top-down control of the city's neighborhoods through a hierarchy of city, ward and precinct bosses who passed the patronage crumbs out to their constituents. The idea of the Kinfolk system is to work with people to provide the basis for personal and community development through communication, caring and working together. The whole Community Development Plan that has come out of the experience of the Black community is based on the empowerment of community residents through developing supportive community relationships, and through the development of participatory democracy in the Ward Councils. The Ward Council's power would be based on its ability to represent and mobilize the Black community, not on personal power brokering and patronage.

The Community Development Plan is built on the experiences of the past twenty years. It redefines "service" to denote a process which empowers, strengthening the individual and the home as basic building blocks of community development. In this context those who work in service agencies are "servants" to their clients. It is their job to increase the independence and selfsufficiency of these clients, not to foster dependency. It is their role to facilitate personal, family and community development.

Education

Education is the other leg of the Community Development Plan. It is essential in two ways. First, it is clear that if the future requires us to work together in cooperative, coordinated ways that are largely foreign to the American way of life, then we all need to learn new skills relevant to the building of coalitions, conflict resolution and cooperative problem solving. The community itself can undertake some of this education as it has on a number of occasions when groups share their work and experience with others. But informal sharing is not enough. The second element of education that is crucial to the survival of the city is the public school system. We have young people who are not only unable to read and write, but also completely uninformed about the ways in which they can work on solving the problems of their neighborhoods. The lack of skills and information that relate to their own street experience, the lives of their families their own frustrations and the feelings caused by the sight of dilapidated buildings, out-of-work people, and exposure to the anger generated by helplessness, guarantees that these kids cannot play a constructive role in the community. They are easy prey to the destructive forces in the community that counteract all the good work being done. The schools have to change and change drastically to teach students how to build communities.

The approach we have in mind for revising education to support the process of decentralized government is one that was tested at the Massachusetts Experimental School System during the early seventies, particularly in the Model High School. It is a dual approach to teaching people skills related to both their individual needs and to their role in a larger community. Based on some old social work concepts, the two aspects of this educational process are case-work and group-work. Each student is assessed and an individual program of learning is charted based on the student's needs, learning pace, interests, and strengths and weaknesses. Special contracts were possible for students who wanted to learn a skill outside the school itself through apprenticeship or "shadowing" a skilled person. At the same time, however, each student was programmed to participate in some group projects designed to teach cooperative process and to apply skills to community problems. Each student was in this way able to see how his or her personal needs and interests tied into something larger. The case-work usually focuses on technical skills; group-work transfers political-social skills.

This approach ties directly to the process we have suggested already for coalition building where each group puts together its own program, then returns to the whole to see how it fits in overall. Up until now, group work in our public schools has been extracurricular, thereby depriving students of skills vital to survival in the coming years. Although some community groups have been developing these skills in the course of their own work, it has not always been a very conscious or deliberate process. The group work has been the missing dimension in our community efforts; that is why it has been so difficult to solve many problems, and why there has been so little headway in building bridges among groups with like interests and concerns. The search for community is based on the fact that individual needs include the need to relate to and participate in a whole. No individual can survive alone; cooperative skills are essential to solving problems the individual cannot cope with alone. The point is to design the individual role to meet individual needs, then fit the individual program into a total program to fill larger needs. Like cells forming an organ and then a body, people must group together to fulfill various functions for the survival and growth of the commonwealth.

Decentralization and education are the two legs of the Community Development Plan. Together they can provide the power and the awareness to politicize the Black community to take control, to develop its fullest potential.

The plan also shapes service, organizing and institution-building toward the critical missing point: accountability. Only by building accountability into the service system at all levels can a system survive and do its prescribed job. The model focuses accountability toward the smallest possible geopolitical level, seeking to empower the individual as he or she relates to home, street, block, neighborhood, city and beyond.

Facets of the plan, including the Communtiy Development Institute, are based on the idea that we need continuing education for all ages and that problem-solving experience is the best teacher. The emphasis on political affairs is deliberate, to build on the strides we have made so recently, to continue the process of building unity through organizing and awareness.

In Summary

The Black community is in a natural position to take the lead in developing this Community Development Plan. Ultimately, a city-wide coalition must be developed to reach beyond the community of color. A city-wide coalition can utilize the model provided by the Third World Jobs Clearinghouse which, when faced with the need to set priorities, chose a process of representation which assured the Puerto Rican and Asian members, who are fewer in number, equal weight in decision-making. The priorities were set on the basis of need, not just numbers in the coalition. The Boston Jobs Coalition made a point of settling on affirmative action as a basic part of its agenda.

This is a hopeful example of how many different groups have gone through all the stages of developing consciousness and competence, and have come to the point where they are prepared to enter into coalitions. They must join such alliances in order to deal with overall development issues. Separation is required in those early stages, as each group steps back to view its own identity, and to identify its purpose and goals.

If as a community we are prepared to lead others through the experience of learning to cooperate, dealing honestly with the painful prejudices and tensions built into this society, and learning to bend enough in times of need so that the whole is more flexible and resilient, we will be able to do more than control our own community . We will be able to influence larger sections of the city, bringing together an array of potential allies. It is easy for groups to be played against each other through racist and sexist feelings, and through competition for resources to meet basic needs. It is time to analyze issues in these terms and refuse to be set against potential allies.

Further movement within the system around us, so laden with conflict-producing tensions, cannot happen without an alliance. People must come together, moving out of their isolation, to challenge conditions which exploit us. Alliance, cooperation, coalition: those are the only paths to follow if we are going to make it into the next century.

What we have described is changing relationships, between people of color and white folks; between have-nots and have-a-lots; between men and women. While all these changes have been going on within the community of color, similar changes have been occurring to many other groups: women, the young, students, the elderly, handicapped and gay people.

The chain of change is still being forged. If during the

Eighties we move in the direction of coalition-building, and we work out our most basic values as the basis for unified action on a widening array of issues, the chain will lead us in one of several directions. Those people who have been exploiting this society are the weakest link threatening to destroy the product of our struggle. Our own changes could free those people, bound by personal greed and the hunger for power. Or, it may become clear that we have to take drastic action to wrest control of institutions and resources from them if we are going to return sanity to the society. We have been patiently trying all the storybook approaches—alliances, coalitions, self-help, electoral politics. We will play that thread out to its inevitable end.

Once a truly decentralized system is in place, the hardest work, in some ways, remains. Decentralization means that the community must become more unified. Decentralization leads inevitably to community control. If we use this control to develop the community we will have to ask whether this society is capable of meeting the needs of us all. If we find, from our new strength and skill base, that we can salvage the basic structure and improve it, we will be ready to do so. We will have experience within the community and with the methodology to apply to such an effort.

If, on the other hand, we find that the system is incapable of responding to our changes and that the needs of people cannot be met even when we have reorganized local political structures, then we will be prepared and skilled to go on to the final work.

We will find that our suffering and our growth through the process of change we have shared has convinced people of their right to change what does not meet their basic human needs. It is best said, and guaranteed, in the Declaration of Independence. The chain of change will lead us, quite naturally, to revolution.

EPILOGUE:
Interviews
with Black Community Activists

I taped the following interviews with Black community activists in Boston in 1974 and 1975. I asked each of the people I interviewed the following six questions:

1. What was the catalyst to your political involvement?
2. What have you learned through your involvement?
3. What do you think we as a community have learned?
4. Do you see us making any of the same mistakes now?
5. Does our community have skills now that were not in evidence in 1960?
6. What do you think our short and long run goals should be?

These questions were asked of nineteen persons who were involved in all the different aspects of Black community development in Boston in the last three decades. Many of the quotes in the text of *Chain of Change* were taken from these interviews, but the following passages provide a much more insightful understanding of how members of the Black community perceive the development of the Black community in Boston. The *Chain of Change* is made up of these Black activists, and all the

Black people who are struggling to take control of our community. Prior to the interviews there are brief biographies of these activists which highlight some of their community efforts, but are by no means a complete listing of all their accomplishments.

Biographies

Alajo Adegballoh was a member of the Boston Tenants' Association, the Roxbury-Dorchester APAC, and the co-chair of the Black United Front. He is involved with the Republic of New Africa.

Ruth Batson was the first Black person ever elected to the Democratic State Committee in Massachusetts, a member of the State Advisory Board to the U.S. Civil Rights Commission, started the Lenox Street Nursery School; and currently works at the Boston University School of Medicine and Mental Health.

Dennis Blacket was a member of CORE, part of the successful effort to stop the inner city beltway, a founder of CIRCLE and the Black Housing Task Force, a member of the Board of Massport. He is currently director of Housing Innovations, Inc.

Melnea Cass was President of the local chapter of the NAACP, of Action for Boston Community Development, and of the Women's Service Club. Melnea Cass was a powerful woman whose business was the Black community.

Noel Day helped train SNCC workers for work on the front line in Georgia, was a member of the Northern Student Movement and BAG, and ran for Congress against Speaker of the House, John McCormack in 1964 to raise the issue of the Vietnam War. He is currently working with citizen groups in Oakland.

Leo Fletcher worked at the New Urban League as a job developer, helped found UCCW, and worked on the rehabilitation efforts on Blue Hill Ave. in Roxbury. He is currently involved in solar energy training and alternative energy development.

Ellen Jackson was a parent coordinator for the Northern Student Movement, a social service supervisor for ABCD, a founder of Exodus, director of the Institute on Schools and

Education at Freedom House, and a member of the Board of Trustees for State Colleges. She is currently an administrator at Northestern University.

Elma Lewis has been director of the Elma Lewis School of Fine Arts for the past 30 years: and has worked with the Museum of Afro-American Art, and the National Center of Afro-American Artists, Inc.

Marion McElhaney was chairperson of the People's Elected Urban Renewal Committee, director of the South End Tenants Corporation, and a member of the Black United Front. He is currently an assistant clerk of the Boston Housing Court.

George Morrison was a detached youth worker at Dennison House, in the housing program of AFSC on Blue Hill Ave., and a leading force in the Roxbury Action Program in Highland Park. He now runs a consulting firm in housing and economic development.

Paul Parks was involved in the Citizens for Boston Public Schools, the education committee of the NAACP, in the effort to pass the Racial Imbalance Law and METCO, director of the Model Cities Program, and Mass. Commissioner of Education. He currently runs a consulting firm on education and economic development.

Ted Parrish led sit-ins against United South End Settlements, worked with the South End Tenants Corporation (SETC) to form the South End Tenants Management Corporation and the Tenants Development Corporation, and worked in the rural health care program in Mound Bayou. He now works in public health, and is a member of the School Board in Chapel Hill, N.C.

A. Robert Phillips was coordinator of the Massachusetts Freedom Movement, worked with METCO and the New Urban League, and was an adminstrator of the Roxbury Action Program. He currently heads the Boston Media Council.

Byron Rushing was a member of CORE, worked with NSM in Harlem, helped set up St. John's Information Center, was director of the Joint Center for Inner City Change, and taught at the Commonwealth School. He is now director of the Afro-American History Museum of Boston.

Sara Ann Shaw was involved with the NAACP Youth Council, Stop Day, the Bag Boycotts, and the school stay-outs. She was a director of NSN, worked for ABCD to organize the APAC's, and helped to start the "Say Brother" television program. She is currently a television news reporter.

Chuck Turner was a member of NSM, worked at South End Neighborhood Action Program on welfare rights, was co-chair of the Black United Front, and was involved in the South West Corridor Coalition. He was director of CIRCLE and of the Third World Jobs Clearing House. He currently works as educational director of the Industrial Cooperative Association.

Rudy Waker worked with the Bridgewater Lumber Co., and the King-Bison Housing Development Corporation, where he instituted training programs in construction rehab skills. He is currently executive director of Low Cost Housing Corp., which is developing extensive training in constructin skills.

Archie Williams was Chairman of the Labor and Industries Committee of the NAACP, a member of the Ad Hoc Committee on Poverty, and helped to found NECDC and CIRCLE. He founded and continues to direct Freedom Industries and Freedom Foundation.

Virgil Woods organized the Massachusetts Chapter of the Southern Christian Leadership Conference, the Roxbury Peoples Movement, and the Black Expo. He was Southern Regional Director for OIC, and now is director of the Afro-American Institute at Northeastern University.

QUESTION 1: What Was the Catalyst to Your Political Involvement?

Alajo Adegballoh: "I think it was personal; I found out about myself. I'm still finding out about myself. What can I achieve? What can I do in this whole area where I see problems? I think that's what got me involved. The constant of Black people getting wasted, broken up, ripped off; constantly seeing that happen. And I know it's not supposed to happen. It's happening to some people like me, so it's happening to me."

Ruth Batson: "What was happening to my kids in school. That's what started it all. That's how I got involved. I might have gotten involved in some other ways, but that was how."

Dennis Blackett: "I don't know. I just wanted to do something. I guess I started picketing back in 1958 and 1959 at MIT. That's interesting; I wanted to do something, but I wasn't ready to go south. I wasn't ready to join SNCC. Maybe I was just a little too old. I don't know what it was, but I wasn't ready to do that. But I did want to do something. I got very pissed off on the inner belt thing 'cause they were moving out so many low income families. I thought MIT was one of the things that might be behind it."

Omar Cannon: "By refusing to be *Fucked Over* in plain language..."

Melnea Cass: "Just a dedication to help my fellow man whenever I can."

Noel Day: "Three white social workers in Brooklyn, New York. When I was program director of an agency and the first sit-ins started, and we had this agency in Brooklyn in a community that was 85 percent Jewish, 5 percent Puerto Rican, and 3 percent Black and the rest was just sort of white and mixed. These three guys, all sort of radicals, all said our children's program for the next whenever will be to take the kids on our buses down to the Woolworth's in Flatbush every afternoon and picket. I was pretty apolitical and I said, 'Like, what's that about?' That was just before I came to Boston—the year before I came to Boston. I was not into politics and they kind of really pushed me on my values. I'd come up in a middle class home where picketing and that stuff belongs to the working man and you had your white collar and you didn't get into that. I remember my mother, the changes she went through on the sit-ins. The first thing was 'Those kids are crazy and trouble-makers and they don't know what they are doing.' Then she went through a thing about 'They may be wrong, but they are kids and they can't treat them like that.' And then she came out with 'They are doing something we should have been doing a long time ago;' and was proud.

"...I remember going down on that picket line and being scared shitless right there in Brooklyn, being scared. Nobody ever said a word to us, but I was scared, I was just exposed. Then around the same time, we started trying to organize public housing tenants; our centers were located in public housing. And the housing authority was happy for us to organize the few projects that we were in to have tenants councils, 'cause their official policy called for tenants councils; but when we started trying to organize on a city-wide basis—that wasn't too cool. And Mor-riss, our director, he was out after trying to get a million and a half people together. And the city stomped the shit out of us. (Laughter) We showed up to work one morning and—we had our dollar-a-year arrangement to use space in the housing pro-ject—found it with a board and padlock. We broke in and slept inside for ten days and the community—we were all working on 40 percent salary 'cause it was a grass roots agency, very grass roots—and the first two days we'd only had what we had left in the refrigerators for lunches, and we set up bull horns and we were running the programs from the lawns through bull horns 'cause when our part time staff showed up they couldn't get in—we were surrounded by police— saying take the kids over there and play volley ball, and then we mimeographed up every-thing we could to tell the story—with all the mimeograph paper, right? And early on the cops were letting anyone who wanted to come out to come out, but nobody could come in. We sacrificed two of our staff people with all of the mimeograph stuff to distribute and organize. And the cops would come around and count us every hour and wake us up in the middle of the night by hitting us with billies. And on the third day we hear about a hundred housewives—Jewish housewives—walking around the...building we were locked in. By that time you couldn't come in or out and they had chained the doors and they stormed the building and they started throwing food through the windows until we had about a ton of food, and some of those cops cracked a couple of heads of these women who shouldn't have brought in all that. That was my 'radical' education. It was out of that that I was in Boston saying, 'They shut down this bus line, we'11 shut down their thing!' It was interesting, 'cause all those cops were doing was creating radicals."

Leo Fletcher:"Penn Simon. It was probably a lot before that... like a lot of the things before that had brought me to that point, you know. But that was the main thing that took me and put me into the whole labor scene."

Ellen Jackson: "I would say my kids, and their school. One kid particularly, my son....I see why some people who I used to read about doing certain things, now I do some of those things myself; I understand why they did. But I would say that it was basically my family."

Elma Lewis: "I heard it (community development) at the knee of my parents. I can't remember ever hearing anything else. I was raised in Garvey and the statement I remember is 'Up you mighty people; you can what you will.'...I was three when I first heard Garvey; but since I was 13 I worked myself in the community."

Marion McElhaney: "...there were two things that made me get involved. I had been living and working in this community ever since 1946....I finished law school...but I didn't take the bar because I had a kind of emergency situation because my father died. I became in a sense a kind of sole support of what I call my family (I had to raise some nieces and nephews that my older sister died and left in 1939...). So I went out to the Watertown arsenal and worked and just kind of lost contact with the community. In the meantime I also worked a second job that was a fraternity house, a part of MIT. As the whole Civil Rights movement began to grow up and blossom, the fellows would come back from school and tell me this that and the other. Well, I knew no more than what I read in the newspaper or saw on TV. And suddenly I said to myself, 'Mac, how in the hell can a white person come in and tell you more about your community than you know?' And that was one thing that kind of woke me up. Alas, one day, this may sound strange, it was on a Friday...there was the hearse, the family car and one man sitting in the back of that family car with a huge straw hat in his hand. I don't know who the person was one way or the other, and I stopped and I said, 'God, can a person live and die and not have touched any more lives than this, that people do not stop an hour at least and mourn his passing?' ...It's not that you want a big funeral, but you like to feel like you touched somebody's life, because in a sense this is what life is all about."

George Morrison: "I don't think there was a catalyst; I think there was just something there. Maybe it was the fact that I grew up in the South and sort of knew which way the wind blew and the lay of the land. I had a positive growing up in the South; I could do pretty much what I wanted to do. There were things that were off limits to me—I didn't bowl until I came to Boston. I had a healthy childhood, but knew there were laws for whites and laws for Blacks. That's the basic thing that created the inner drive—to do as much about changing that as possible."

Paul Parks: "It probably goes all the way back to when I started in college and realizing that particularly for Black youngsters— and that was back in 1941—that out of a student body of some 12,000 youngsters there were only eight of us who were Black and four of us in engineering with an engineering school that said it gained its reputation on being able to place its graduates, and that I ought not to be and none of the four of us ought to be an engineer because there was no place for Blacks in engineering. They had nothing against us, except that it would destroy the track record of the institution. I'll always remember the dean saying, 'Now we have a good school of agriculture, and there will always be places for folks to farm.' At that point- ...none of us could stay in the dormitories at Purdue University, 'cause that was for white only, and so we lived in some rooming houses out from town... we lived in some fairly interesting kinds of places. So my first real involvement was when I led the protest and demonstration to integrate the dormitories...This was before the war, before the Brown decision, and it started before the war, and I was drafted immediately because I was causing trouble on campus by my activities in integration. So they recommended against their own standards saying that anyone who had a B average or above would not be drafted, that they would be given an automatic deferral. I didn't get that; they told me that I had to go into the army 'cause they recommended that I was a troublemaker on campus. So four years later I came back and picked up where I left off with the integration of the dormitories and that year—in 1946—we got the dormitories integrated. Because somehow or 'nother, the only hope that I felt most of us had was getting a decent education And education was the only way out of our poverty...so when I came to Massachusetts in 1951, I had been through this whole thing of tutorial and all the other kinds of things to try and change the way that education went—I'd been involved in trying to desegregate the schools in Indianapolis—and came here and got involved immediately in tutorial programs and trying to help youngsters 'cause I found they had the same kinds of problems."

Ted Parrish: "Being Black and oppressed like everybody else; knowing and perceiving that something could and should be done. I remember as a kid, really, being on Tremont Street, Columbus Ave....looking at what folks were doing to themselves—I think I was about thirteen—and at that time I made the decision that if ever I could get involved, I would do it. There were a lot of breaks that helped me get involved."

A. Robert Phillips: "I believed...I now realize I was and can still be a damned fool for that."

Byron Rushing: "When I was in school, I was sensitized by the civil rights movement. I had this vision that in two or three years it would be all over and what was I going to say to my grandchildren when they said, 'Where were you?' and I'd say 'I was in school.' You had to be out there."

Sara Ann Shaw: "My mother and father were people who were involved in the church; they were also NAACP members 'cause that was kind of the organization at that time. I guess part of it...I remember very vividly every Sunday when we were kids, a little lady used to come every Sunday morning before my father went to church and brought the *Daily Worker*, and she and my father used to have discussions about what was in the *Daily*

Worker and it used to be around the house. My father was involved with a group of men who tried to found a Bay State Democratic Club. And I've seen around my house post cards they used to have addressed to Senator Bilbo about anti-lynch laws that they tried to get people to fill out in the same way that we were trying to get people to fill out cards to send urging support for the Mississippi Freedom Democratic Party. And I guess once I got into it, once I got involved in the Youth Council and discovered that there were ways that people could work together to make things change, I've just been at it. I guess I'm committed to it...and that's that."

Chuck Turner: "Being Black in white America. What can you say?...There's another piece to that. I grew up in a situation—in Cincinnati—where I was usually not with a lot of Blacks. I went to a grade school system with whites, went to Harvard where there were a lot of whites—the reality of the experience convinced me that I am not of that world...That wasn't my world—the only world for me was working with Black people...I know the high price—I almost didn't make it. I...almost did not survive the torment of trying to figure out why there was all this—why everyting was so crazy."

Rudy Waker: "The basic belief that the priority for low income families is food, housing/shelter and clothing and upon examination, I found the greatest need in HOUSING."

Archie Williams: "I guess if you got down to the bone, the catalyst is that I wanted to make it. I never kidded myself that I'm some kind of saint and had an urge that my fellow men be elevated, but I—it's a very practical statement to the effect that I can't make it unless the general populace can make it. If I could have somehow have opened the gate and ended racism, I would have been off and running; I probably wouldn't have had a career that reached around me so broadly. That was my incentive for getting into it. After having gotten into it I guess the humanness of it, the kind of 'rapture of the deep' that you get if you're any kind of human being: you cannot talk to a guy who can't write his name, got ten kids and just lost a job that wasn't worth having in the first place without wanting to do something. You cannot go into homes where the roof is falling and the walls are falling and there's no heat and the kids are hungry and not want to do something. After I got into it, I became much more committed to the human characteristics of it. My basic motive was, 'I want to get this damn thing 'cause I thought a good ten years of hard work would open the damn road wide enough so that the rest would be just a matter of erosion' So I committed myself to that: Once I got into it, I saw that it was a lifetime job."

Virgil Woods: "I come out of a family that's always been involved, always been able to take care of its own business...and then be involved in the broader community—that's my daddy, that's my mama."

QUESTION 2: What Have You Learned Through Your Involvement?

Alajo: "Well, I've learned a lot about organizing, about myself—what I'm supposed to do; oh, man, just what is necessary for us to get out of the diabolical fix we're in as a people...I've learned a lot about government; my relationship as a human unit to all the world events—you know, like something happens overseas and I didn't know how it related to me—I could walk down the road and know how it's going to affect me tomorrow, my children, my grandchildren. I've learned how to relate my personal agenda with the group and the need for that...I learned how to function in the area of human rights, rather than just the more local thing like talking just about civil rights. You can't have civil rights until you have human rights, that's for sure."

Ruth Batson: "What have I learned? (Sigh) I think I've learned some intangible things; I think one of the intangible things I've learned is that the most important thing about living and doing and working are the relationships that you establish and they are more important than jobs and appointments in high positions and acknowledgements and accomplishments that other people can impose on you. I've learned that the appreciation and the respect of your peers and the people you work with in your community—for me, this is what I've learned for me—are far more important than an honorary doctorate, degrees or awards or so forth. I...really had to learn that, 'cause I went through a period where I wondered, 'Well, why isn't this happening to me? Why am I not recognized this way?' And so I had to learn where to put my values and so forth. I learned a lot about tangible things—I've learned some real techniques, I've learned how to use the system in certain kinds of ways...and I've learned a lot about how to do some things. I haven't been able to use a lot of things I've learned because of the necessity to earn a living and take care of myself and things like that. So I know the injustice of the system better than I know anything else. An unjust system imposes on people the kind of barriers that make it impossible for you to fulfill yourself completely...I think sometimes if I were to start my life all over again, nobody would know the name of Ruth Batson...and I would just go in my house and be my husband's wife in just the ordinary sense of the word as people describe it—you know, in the 'square way' as my daughter says—raise my children, and not get involved in all of this. I *just* really think that's the way I would live my life over if I had it to do all over again. It has not been easy to put yourself out there, you know; it's not easy for yourself, it's not easy for your mate; and it's not easy for your children. I *sometimes* think that's what I would do. I won't have the opportunity to try that out!"

Dennis Blackett: "I think one important thing...(is) that Black people have to be very hard with themselves and they can't deal with people who can't be dealt with...One of the things that I've learned from all the organizations is that Black organizations have a lot of trouble and I would rather set up an organization— I think we *do* need organizations—I'd rather set up an organization on as informal a basis as possible at first. People get to know each other, get to respect each other, like to see if that thing is going to hang together. If it doesn't hang together, there isn't a lot of bullshit. And if it does hang together and has some important purposes and will continue to meet around those issues, then you can begin to formalize and put the structure in. So like this informal group of housing developers has been very effective although it has no name, no president, no regular meetings, no by-laws, nothing. We just every once and a while get together around what's important."

Omar Cannon: "(Laughter) What have I learned? Not much, I guess...Going back to my beginning involvement in the community...I helped set up a group in Schenectedy, New York, called the Schenectedy Action Committee in 1967...That's when I started getting involved—around the time of Martin Luther King's assassination. There was a riot in Schenectedy, small as it is, and we tried to give the young peple there some kind of direction, tried help the community get some kind of organization together...When they seen that the community was moving, the federal government stepped in and put their program in. They funded a community service program where there was none before...so what I learned...is that we're still slaves. I say that because...there was a time when I thought that we could free ourselves; if we pushed and pulled and confronted the system and tried to get legislation passed, we could better our lot...As the system goes down, which I think it's going, Black people will *have* to depend on each other more."

Melnea Cass: "Too much to explain here; the gains that we made by civil rights, etc. are *working*."

Noel Day: "Well, I learned that social change is a hard thing to bring about; that there's not only opposition to it on the part of the people who would be hurt by it, but a resistance to it on the part of the people who would be helped by it...I've learned that there are some people who can commit their lives to it and get their sustenance continually; that most people get into it, get burnt out, may come back to it, may not come back to it, but that's something that constantly attracts new people, and that's OK. Oh, I guess I learned that a lot of that can be fun and exciting; I think what I looked at at this time as just being really hard work, in retrospect was a lot of fun. I don't know; I have hopes that there will be some more times like the early sixties, but I think there was a kind of excitement, hope, at that point that really doesn't exist now."

Leo Fletcher: "Ho-ho! That's almost...just the knowledge and experiences over the last years, and if I really look back through my life, there's just been a vast amount of knowledge that I've been able to assume, being that I've always had a very kind of open mind—when I say 'open' it's because it *was* empty, 'cause I didn't get any real formal kinds of education and formal kinds of indoctrination 'cause I only went to the eighth grade of school and six months in high school. But I never was what you call a student. .That's probably the reason that during the latter part of my lifetime, my after school years/school age, I acquired most of my knowledge...A lot in human relations, a lot in just every-day living, seeing what's happening. I know I'm very highly politically aware to what's goin on...I'm still learning of course-...that makes it even better, 'cause I get a feeling inside that I'm worth something..."

Ellen Jackson: "I've learned a hell of a lot of strength, determination, and I think that we still have a hell of a lot of hope. But I think we are also very, very aware that we have to begin to be aware of what the future of Black people is going to be in this country. I think that many people are looking to a Third World kind of coalition which is going to become more significant—which we don't see. I...I think some people are slowly trying to move out of their isolation; however, one of the things that's very obvious is that we are moving very much away from racial unity—and that's very frightening to me, because I don't understand the dynamics—moving into a kind of class/economic stratification.

Elma Lewis: I have learned a lot about corporate structure. I have unfortunately learned something about cynicism—I hope not too much. I've learned not to expect that the oppressor will dignify me—that I must dignify myself. I wasn't brought here to be dignified, so if dignity will come, it must come from me. I have learned that things take a lot longer than I originally thought. They are not hopeless, but they are a *lot* slower. I have learned to be satisfied to see a tree put its roots down in my lifetime. I may never see the height of the tree, and the flower of the tree. When I was a girl, Mrs. Eleanor Roosevelt came to talk to some of us in Boston and she told us about the horrible experience that the Jewish people had just suffered in Germany, and I was a very sensitive girl and I really suffered in my teenage life for Jewish people. I remember in *Life Magazine* lampshades that were people and bars of soap that were people and—it was really mentally destructive. She told us to run around and collect money for two reasons: one was to plant trees in Israel, and the other was to institute Brandeis. And I have seen all of the Jewish kids who were running around with me at that time collecting money to put down those seedlings go back to see full-fledged trees. And I have seen Brandeis come from the gift of two raggedy buildings like these to a campus where the bulldozer is always going. And when I would become faint of heart, I get in my car and ride out there and look at Justice Brandeis with his robes flowing back in the breeze and I come back here and get started again."

Marion McElhaney: "That working in the community you set goals, but you also set somewhere in that a goal...certain steps, recognizing that you may not attain the total thing but you may attain a great portion of it—not necessarily being willing to give up your goal, but realizing the realities of the situation and sometimes being able to take all of the pieces and put those pieces together and still come up with something that benefits those people you are working for or serving."

George Morrison: "Be cautious. (Laughter) Listen, talk, don't get committed, don't say anything that would imply commitment until you're certain. There was a time when we all ran around shooting from the hip: 'Let's do this...Right! Let's go!' I'm saying 'No!' more often now than I ever did in my life before; 'I'm not interested; I don't have the time; it ain't my thing;' you got to be able to say, 'No.'"

Ted Parrish: "One of the things I learned is that the establishment put a requirement that folks really get involved in it and expend fantastic energy to get a piece of the pie and they make it so difficult that you can almost bet that substantial numbers of folks are going to get tired over the long run...It seems as though that's a clearly thought out pattern from above—maybe I'm cynical—that we have just so many dollars to spend on housing, just so many to spend on this...If we make the rules of the game so tough that only those groups with massive will can make it, it's a way of continuing to neglect these folks. It's really a way of whipping us."

A. Robert Phillips: "To limit myself and to establish contractual relationships."

Byron Rushing: "I think the thing I've learned is the thing about not being able to predict people, and that you have to open to all kinds of stuff and take chances. You don't know who's going to produce. You can't write people off.' I'm not sure I do it; but you got to hang loose. I've become a little more diplomatic in my old age. If I was going to do it all over again...I would do a lot of things differently. I learned a lot about running places with a lot of different people with a lot of different ideas and expectations."

Sara Ann Shaw: "I guess I've learned that it takes a lot of time, it takes a lot of commitment on the part of a lot of people...And that you've really got to do some planning, you just can't jump out there 'cause you want to jump out there; that you've got to be able to clearly define the issues, you've got to be able to communicate those issues to a broad segment of the people and if you don't get them to understand that it's their battle as well as it is the battle of the organizations who are funded or in existence to work around these issues..."

Chuck Turner: "I've learned that hurrying doesn't get the job done...that I have to have tolerance for my own weaknesses and the fact that I'm not able to do everything...so that's patience...and tolerance—we all have to have tolerance for each other. Also humility...I've learned things I thought nobody could shake me about five years ago are incorrect...Another thing is wisdom...Leadership necessitates wisdom...not learning...that comes of understanding yourself and understanding of people. If you don't have wisdom, you don't develop out of your experiences...Schools can teach organizing and other kinds of things, but a leader has to have wisdom that comes out of their evaluation of their experiences, and what it taught them about their own strengths and weaknesses, tolerances, intolerances, capabilities, noncapabilities and then use that knowledge to understand other people more effectively and how it can all be put together. If you don't have a philosophy that...talks about how we live day to day as we are going to our goal, if you haven't come to grips with the means, then you are not going to reach the end. To me, that's wisdom—if you understand that you can't separate the means from the end."

Rudy Waker: "If anything I've learned not to spread myself too thin. I've learned that I have a slow burning intolerance that's developed—I didn't have it then, but I have it now—I can't go to a Model Cities meeting and hear in 1975 the people saying the same thing they were saying in 1964...I get physically ill; I have to leave. I've learned that critical to any success is the day to day work, the nonglorious work. In terms of technique I've learned that staying out of the limelight is much more beneficial than staying in the limelight because when you're in a business like this, nobody knows what you're doing and therefore they don't shoot you down for whatever motive they have. I've learned to work better. I guess that out of all the things I've experienced, I'm becoming more color blind in that I see more human negatives and human positives across the board. I reject Louise Day Hick's position or any other racist position about Black people, just as I reject Black people's position about white people-...Maybe that doesn't sound significant, but coming up in my formative years in North Carolina people were only white or Black to me; they weren't Jewish, they weren't Irish; they were white or Black;...now...it's what type of people they are. I view that as a minor success, because for me in my heart I've settled that question. But you can't live according to it—not yet."

Virgil Woods: "If I took the 12 years I've been back in Boston and tried to quantify...it's been a library full of learning for me...My family and I talked and we all felt..that the things I've learned in Boston, the experiences, just would not have been possible in the other kind of setting (i.e. a well-to-do parish in the South). But...if I had to summarize it...I did a paper...on the journey from XA—high mistrust between groups, a real closed system—to YB, a system that is built on cooperation and trust where the goals you seek can be shared by almost the total group that helps to bring them off...My greatest lesson is that either it's going to be the YB development in Black communities, or there is going to be destruction—they're just going to go down...As long as we stay on the XA path, that mistrust, and petty throat cutting,...it's genocide (suicide), Yeah, fratricide...It's every dimension of death, but most of it is not age. The thing that could get us moving as a community is not government dollars, at first it's not white brain power, but it's almost a spiritual thing among ourselves: the determination to work together, to share resources and what we have to bring about, a result that is big enough so that everybody who helps to bring it off can share in the fruit."

QUESTION 3: What Do You Think We As A Community Have Learned?

Alajo: "The community has learned that we have got to stick together and we've got to support each other. I think the community has learned that they have got to be aware of issues on every level; that people who work on employment have got to be aware of the people who have problems in education, if you work in housing you got...to support the other groups in order to support yourself. I think that's one of the things that the Black community in Boston has learned."

Ruth Batson: "I think we've learned that we have to—that anything that we attain is going to have to come from ourselves. I think that's why it was right that we had to say to white people, 'Alright let's do it ourselves—even the mistakes.' It's just like at one point in your life you have to say to your kids, 'You know, you just have to go it yourself, make the errors; you got to do it yourself.' I think that we have to learn that we have to do some things for ourselves, rightly or wrong, that we have to have some fights with each other, but I hope that we have learned that these are not lasting things; what should be lasting is our concern for each other. And it sounds kind of schmaltzy to say it, but I really believe that's where it starts. And I think that we've learned a little more about looking out for each other."

Dennis Blackett: "I don't know. It would be good if we had learned something about political power; I'm not sure we have."

Omar Cannon: "I think we've become more conscious in every aspect of our lives. I don't think that we've become what you call 'sophisticated' to deal with those realities."

Melnea Cass: "That we need to work together, believe in our causes, and give of our means to support our causes."

Noel Day: "I don't know; you know, I really don't know. I think maybe as a community we've learned that some people can make it. I'm not sure that's a useful lesson."

Leo Fletcher: "...as a community it's hard to say. Just when you think they are coming along, they do something (laughter) that'll blow your whole mind. The responses that they give...like in this whole busing thing."

Ellen Jackson: "I think we've learned that no one...no Black person or Black group has really had control to decide the destiny and future of the Black community. I think it has always been in the hands of outside whites—the structure of power or the business and political structures—and even as we increase in numbers, we notice the little power that we have. I think we ought to dwell over that. The problem is how do we move to gain more power?"

Marion McElhaney: "That would be very hard to say...I would hope that through our experience in the 1960's here in the city of Boston, that Blacks have learned that they can get it together if they will take the time and will listen and can stop...See, the unfortunate thing is we developed so many people who want to lead and few who want to follow. If we can begin to develop a voice, or two or three voices in our community so that when those voices speak the people know we mean business..."

George Morrison: "We're still naive in terms of politics—we're not real political animals in terms of understanding the process... Economic development—I don't think we understood that...What we understand as a neighborhood and as a people is hard times and the fear of it...can make us do all kinds of crazy things...Education may be something that we learned. OH YEAH! I think that a good number of people in this city—non-white—learned how racist this god damned city is. I don't think that has been all that understood before."

Ted Parrish: "...the SETC community must have learned that if you expend enough energy and you hang together long enough you can set a goal for yourself, and you can attain it...Several of the groups in the South End have failed for a whole variety of reasons, some of which I think were manufactured. Even if it's on an intuitive and unspoken level—though I've heard a number of people speak it—they must have learned that there is a limited amount of bread in the first place and...a small and insufficient amount of support is going to come in and that's all. It's not going to be enough to meet your needs. These resources that are put in are, I think, a device for dividing and conquering folk. I hope the bigger community has learned that..."

A. Robert Phillips: "That the style and ways of the powers that be are more attractive than would be a program or concept that we can be a self-directed community "

Byron Rushing: "I think the main thing is that we have to rely on ourselves. I don't think they know how to do it and that causes a lot of frustration; but that we have to do it is so clear! I think all that propaganda about other people doing it is gone.

Sara Ann Shaw: "I think that in different parts of the community there are different things we learned. I think as an overall community we've learned that urban renewal was not in our best interest. I think that we have learned as a community that we are not as accepted as a part of the city as some people would have liked to have thought we were accepted. In the past I think there have been events that have shown us that we aren't—that we're still niggers."

Chuck Turner: "...that we can value our identity. It's hard to put it in words that are as inclusive as I'd like it to be. But when you look back in 1966 and think about people in 1966, and then you think about 1974, probably up and down the economic scale and various social scales Black people by and large can exist more comfortably with their identity now than we could as a people before. There are a lot of hang-ups, lot of problems, a lot of things we're working out, but it's—we've learned we don't have to sacrifice a part of ourselves in order to survive materially, that the price people ask us to pay materially—the renunciation of our identity—is not a price that we are willing to pay."

Rudy Waker: "In housing, the community must control the action, even appointments to such organizations as Massachusetts Housing Finance Agency and Massachusetts Home Mortgage Finance Agency."

Archie Williams: "I feel an increased number of people have learned a lot of the things that I've learned. I think there are all too many people moving into positions who are as naive as we are and will learn. I think the community has learned in some unspoken way the power that we have; we just don't execute it. I don't think that the young people would be as self-assured if they didn't have a sense that they have a great deal of power that comes from the effort and a kind of subtle thing, and the power may be abused or not abused. But I feel that this community has *enormous* power, much more than it had in the sixties. I don't think it has been clearly defined or effectively used, but I think it's being felt."

Virgil Woods: "I think that's not a question for an individual...the community in session would have to answer that. That's an excellent question...a professional question."

QUESTION 4: Do You See Us Making Any Of The Same Mistakes Now?

Alajo: "Yeah, I see us making the mistakes we made in the 1940's, I see us going back to that. Not of our own doing, but we are being directed back to that...we're headed for assimilation...the whole integrative concept as the correct way. I see us heading back to that, and it's going to hurt us..."

Ruth Batson: "Yeah, I see it all the time, because I think that one of the things that we *haven't* learned was really...how to examine the past with a look to the future, that we continually have to go the same road. Well, I'm not going to do that; I mean, if anybody wants to start to do the same things that I did 20 years ago and make the same mistakes, I don't intend to do that. But if other people want to do it, they can go ahead, but I won't participate in that anymore."

Oman Cannon: "There's one mistake that I know we made in the past that I hope we won't make again and that is letting people because they have degrees or because they are recognized by the establishment to speak for us and to sit down and negotiate for us...Another mistake is that when all the taxation money was being put into the community in the forms of grants to organizations that the people were too wrapped up, too involved in their own individual program or projects to not see the end of the tunnel...the way I see things...is that if somebody gives me enough support to get on my feet, I'm supposed to be able to go for myself and not be dependent on this person for ever and ever or I'll fall. We didn't set up no institutions, we didn't set up no way of financing community programs."

Melnea Cass: "We are always subject to mistakes. As long as we are of different opinions we can make mistakes."

Noel Day: "Sure. Well, for one...not to make people who the community has helped in whatever way feel that they have a responsibility back into that community. We still haven't broken through to the youth so that the youth feel a part of that community, who are hungry, whose interests are survival. Revolution and concern with long range goals are still the province of people who are eating out there, who have a certain amount of education and a certain ability to deal with concepts and theory. And there's a separation between us and the people in the community. Revolution is still the property of the marginal man."

Ellen Jackson: "No, I wouldn't call them mistakes. I think there has probably been growth...I think that though we do have differences we still try to...I'm not saying we always succeed, but we attempt in a way to get together to resolve or communicate, and I think that's very important. Before, we would pick, we would go off into our own little groups and operate, and stay there. I mean, for years, people would stay in those little groups and if you didn't agree with their posture and their policy, then, you know, you just weren't in it...I think that we do go in with a higher level of consciousness when we get into the Vault meetings or whatever as opposed to before."

Marion McElhaney: "...We are making some of those same mistakes and perhaps that is why we quite frequently have a tremendous amount of leadership and then there is a vacuum. Right now we are in a vacuum. Secondly, I think we have no single spokesman for the community, that the community rallies behind, and that becomes very meaningful for us. "

George Morrison: "Yeah, I think we are going to keep on repeating history until writing it, living it, researching it, and some planners someplace can say, 'Oops, that happened in 1926, no need to do it again...look at the results.' Until we become that sophisticated, I think that we will continue to...The schools ...Hell, if you've been in Boston ten years, and you've covered that span of history, it's repeated!"

A. Robert Phillips: "Yes. Educational planning at the state level is still controlled by our adversaries, yet we continue to support that; ditto consumer services. Political education and planning still remain a discussion, not an actively attended process. "

Byron Rushing: "Schools: I think Black people have painted themselves in a corner on this one: too many egos involved and this is the final acting out. Crime, of course, is still something we haven't learned anything about. It would be interesting to see where we'd be if we'd spent the kind of energy on the crime thing that we spent on the schools. "

Sara Ann Shaw: "Um Hmm. We still are not writing stuff down and passing the information on; we're still not trying to find out whether someone else is in fact doing the same thing and how can we in the broad sense dovetail, get together with them and collaborate with them. I still see some people thinking that it doesn't affect them, so there is no need for them to be involved in it. There has not been that kind of communication to them to make them understand that it does in fact affect them and they do in fact have to be involved."

Chuck Turner: "Mm Hmm. I'm not sure we have developed enough tolerance for each other."

Rudy Waker: "We are not pooling our money and restricting the use of same to the community for housing, food stores and manufacturing of basic garments."

Archie Williams: "...Organizations don't coordinate; there's a lot of hostility between them; the leadership has been essentially unyielding and in too long. A yielding leadership can stay forever, but an unyielding leadership cannot stay long. The schism between the young people and the old people isn't so much that they don't communicate, but they aren't able to send back to the younger people information, re the mistakes that we've made...Therefore the young people will take the same route that we took...we are duplicating the white community all too much."

QUESTION 5: Does Our Community Have Skills Now That Were Not In Evidence In 1960?

Alajo: "Yes, we are able to communicate; able to analyze things that happened in the community; we're able to analyze the whole educational thing. There are now people able to go to different agencies and ask so-and-so, 'What do you think about so-and-so?' They can tell you, but they *will* tell you. They'll say 'Look, how many of us?' If there's a white person out there, they say, 'Look, will you come in the office, bring some coffee and come in the office,' if they feel they can't talk there. 'Look,' they'll say, 'look, I'll take you to lunch,' if they think their office is bugged; 'meet me for lunch.' And they'll run it down for you. There's UCCW. You can go up there, or send a youngster up there and you get some training; I don't know how much, but it's there, there's something you can get there. There's OIC; there's something you can get there. There's community schools. There's something they can get there; I don't know how much, but you can get it. There's advice you can get; you can go to CIRCLE and get some business advice if you want; free, too."

Ruth Batson: "No, I don't think we have developed any more skills. I think we have more people doing some things and we have more outlets to wow them. Well, I think that it's cause there are more people in Boston—more Black people in Boston. It's easier for people to become elected; but I think that the same skills that people have now, and enable them to serve, were there. I think the opportunities weren't."

Dennis Blackett: "I think so, there are certainly a lot more people who know more about housing. I think there are a lot, for example, more lawyers to do stuff, an awful lot of, particularly Black women who got all kinds of skills. You know, in 1960 they were secretaries or clerks or whatever. I just see an awful lot of Black women who seem to have done that. One of the great things I know folks learned—I remember people talking about it in 1967-68, saying (guys coming from a meeting with a bank president) saying, 'Damn, that man's a fool and he's president of a bank!' So one of the things we've learned is that the white people who run things are not very bright, not necessarily very bright, and that they're certainly no brighter than we are. And that was something very important."

Omar Cannon: "One thing is that the young student at the university level is more community conscious or will have the tendency to be more than in the past when they went to school basically for skills...based on what they can earn as a salary...not what their skill could do to help the community. I think that the new student is more or less looking in that direction now...what can he do with his skill to help the community?"

Melnea Cass: "Many skills—trained workers in many fields—jobs being performed in new service areas where we never functioned. "

Noel Day: "Yeah, I think some of the different political skills, a *lot* more political power if you look at the community nationally—in fact Black politicians are now part of the establishment and women are now the new thing. I just don't know enough about where it's at in terms of job skills, vocational skills, and things of that sort. A lot more Black college students, professionals trained in the businesses, things of that sort. Lot more Black capitalism, but again, what has happened is that instead of—or if Blacks have changed the system a little, the system has opened up and absorbed a lot of Blacks."

Leo Fletcher: "I think we got a whole lot more going for us now than we had in the sixties...and I think that in the seventies and eighties we are going to be even more up on what's happening and probably be sophisticated enough to know how to deal with it once we cast away the illusions and we're really prepared to struggle."

Ellen Jackson: "Oh, hell, yes. I think we've got a lot of people who aren't even being tapped who can be contractors, educators, business types. I think we've got a lot of resources that are just not surfacing either because there is no place for them to surface in the community and they take their talents and go work for somebody. We've never really done a community inventory to the extent that we know what we do have. I'm amazed every day I meet somebody and the stuff that they're into."

Elma Lewis: "Oh, yes, Fifteen years ago to be a Black architect was an amazement. I know at least thirty kids in architectural school. Right now, this minute doing fabulously. To be a Black business person that was not on the corner store or an eatery was really amazing. But now it's not particularly spectacular. I find my brother went to Harvard to college and he graduated Phi Beta Kappa and they didn't take him in medical. They got two hundred of them. And in my lifetime—isn't that beautiful? I wanted two thousand...the community has broadened, you know what I'm saying? Once if you were saying the community, you were talking about a lot of little store front operations on Bluehill Avenue and so I would say there is a level of sophistication because when I look at Roxbury Medical Technical dental group and I look at the comprehensive health program being conducted by Black people, and if I look at Octavisu Rowe running a school to bring little people up to go into that, and if I look at all of the other things and then I think there is a degree of expertise at work here."

Marion McElhaney: "I think we have some skills now. Just looking at CIRCLE...in 1960 I don't even know if CIRCLE was in existence. But the staff that is with CIRCLE now in terms of its venture capital fund, I have a tremendous amount of respect for. I look at the number of Black people getting off at John Hancock getting off to work. I look at the number of Black people who work at the new insurance building next door to the court house...If I do that, then I have to multiply that, within reason, in other buildings; I look at the number of Blacks that are now employed at Boston City Hospital in a reasonable decision-making position. Assuming that carries itself in many areas throughout the city, then I have to say that we have made some progress as a result of the kind of activity, training, the kind of awakening... we have given some people who never would have had the courage to go out and get a job in...John Hancock...We have also through that kind of activity made businesses aware of their responsibility to the Black community, so much so that the little white girl on TV from South Boston is aware of it because she says that when you go to get a job now, we can't get jobs anymore because they tell you it is for a Black person...There's a greater political awareness on the part of Blacks now; they do not necessarily participate as they should in voting, but I think that awareness is there...There have been some changes, some meaningful changes. I don't think we will slip back, I don't think that there will be a kind of lethargy that sets in, there are too many Blacks who now know or feel 'I have a right to do this.'"

George Morrison: "I think so. It's a whole 'nother question about whether they are being used for anything, or used for the community generally. I know that there are some professional and blue collar professional people that I know now, that I didn't know then. And they're in the neighborhood. Some of them, you don't have to look for; they come to you and ask how they can help."

Ted Parrish: "Obviously, as opposed to a Mindick...and a lot of other landlord bloodsucker types occupying the units or the land where we live, *we* have learned to live and control some of the houses, elect some officials...all those efforts of involvement have helped us learn to control our lives a little bit better."

A. Robert Phillips: "Yes; building and construction skills— economic, teaching, legal and a high potential for political skills."

Byron Rushing: "I think we have a lot of organizing skills; Black people are more formally educated now; and practical skills. Social worker-minister-education has decreased proportionately. I don't think a lack of skills is a problem with Black people. Most of the skills Black people have go to aiding the white community. We have the skills to run things; if white people vanished from Boston, we could run Boston just fine."

Chuck Turner: "We have a tremendous number of administrative skills. What we don't have now is organizing...we have people who have the skills, but they are not organizing."

Rudy Waker: "Yes. In housing the Black community has developed all of the skills necessary in the construction field."

Archie Williams: "Oh, Jeez, yes. Everwhere I look. Everywhere I look. In fact, in 1960 to be able to pick out ten people who could be significant in negotiations or in a political position would have been difficult. Today I could pick out a hundred and still be going. No question but what we've developed the kinds of skills of group management, business management, social management. We've developed more skills in economics, both personal and across the board;...more skills in politics. On every level I see we've developed more skills. That's why I'm a strong advocate of coordination, because maybe now we're approaching the zero point of being able to effectively coordinate. We don't have to pull a guy in and educate him...We've been down the road of urban renewal, model cities, the poverty programs. I don't think the Black community will accept that format anymore."

Virgil Woods: "Absolutely, absolutely...we're much smarter. As a whole community we're much smarter, we've learned a lot of things. I think we're doing things more effectively, more efficiently.

QUESTION 6: What Do You Think Our Short And Long Range Goals Should Be?

Alajo: "The short range goals should be for creature comforts. The long range should be for a scheme of living where our grandchildren can decide for themselves what's going to happen to the schools, in their schools. That is, as long as we remain an identifiable group of people...I want my grandchildren not to have to fear the police, not to have to worry about what the children are going to learn in school today, not to have to worry about a job, not to have to worry about any of the things human beings shouldn't have to worry about...Not to have to worry about the basics of life: food, clothing, shelter, medical care, and security. Those basic things. They should live in an atmosphere so that what they will create as a group will provide that. They should have some say in the provision of that. It shouldn't be dependent on another group to say how much of this they are going to get or whether they are going to get it."

Ruth Batson: "Well, I think our short range goals should be to try to support immediately the families who are involved in this desegration thing, because, you see, I look at the desegregation issue as a racist issue. And so I—we are all going to be subject to the most racist kind of activity and I think our short range—and I guess it has to be long range—but immediately we have to develop techniques and mechanisms for the families that are involved in this situation. Our long range goals should be to build up this community, build up this neighborhood, clean it up—physically—I have a thing on that. And then start from there to be involved in unity and pride—really, real, honest-to-god pride, not the false kind of stuff where you talk about sometimes but really involve our community in a pride about where we live. I think that helps in moving us towards that other kind of pride that people talk about."

Dennis Blackett: "Long range I'm worried about what I call this underclass that has been created and is still with us, and how we deal with it ourselves, and I'm not sure how we straighten that out. Short range, I suppose we've got to worry about a depression; we've got to worry about this school shit. Maybe we've got to put ourselves in the position to take control of the city and to figure out how we are going to do that, what the timing should be on that. We've got some very short range problems like foreclosures from HUD, things like that. "

Omar Cannon: "...Short range I think we should be trying to identify the vehicles whereby those things can come to fruition ...Knowing how the food industry is set up, you got to start from somewhere and we can only start at the retail level because that's the only thing we are into at this point. The next step to that is the wholesale level where basically it's what controls the retail level...So I think that what we need to do on a short range basis is try to organize the retail food merchants into...some sort of union or organized group that would then be able to set up wholesale back-up systems...in construction and all along the line that should be done. That could be done over a period of time...a minimum of 2% of their yearly gross...so it doesn't hurt them financially would be able to set them up—just the retail grocery outlets—a fairly good size wholesale outlet that would back them up. Then the other backup process to that is contacting the farmers throughout the country—there are farm co-ops now—they should be made available... the canning industry is another way to plug in there somehow. Blacks have to start from where they are and then build on the support systems that they need right on back down to the land and from there comes everything. Much as we like clothes, there ain't no way somebody's supposed to be making our clothes for us!"

Melnea Cass: "Immediate action on school situation. Political action with new state administration. This will be long and short."

Noel Day: "Well the long range goals would be, you know—I'm

pretty much where I was ten years ago—should be to change the society in such a way that people have basic rights and that those rights are respected and there aren't people who have the power to trample on other people or use other people for their purpose—a power structure that makes decisions that fuck other people's lives up in a way that tends to happen in this society. Short range goals would be not only to get some people who don't have power into power, but to help them that wants to get into power not to identify with the oppressor. I don't really know how to do that. I would also like, I guess, something that really kind of short range dealt with Black kids. I just have this fear that there is a whole generation or two of Black kids that's going to be essentially wasted, and that the society, ultimately, is going to pay for it in destruction; but... I'm much more concerned about the lives of desperation, pain and so on, that those kids are going to have to live. I don't know what to do about that; I don't know how to break that cycle."

Leo Fletcher: "I think our short range goal is to establish the means—the basic means—it takes Black folks and poor folks to survive—that's control of food, clothing, and shelter...Nonclassical, nonconventional, innovative kinds of approaches to taking control of those things, using the total sum of our culture to be able to create those kinds of systems that are going to be vital to Black people. For instance, farming—inner city farming, manufacturing cloth and sewing, taking folks—welfare mothers and unemployed mothers and setting up factories where folks can start to turn out clothes and start to make garments and shoes, those kinds of things. It has be about producing our own goods for our own needs. Shelter, of course, we're working on that every day so in the next five or ten years we will probably have some kind of hold on that where we can deliver to folks the kind of housing that Black people deserve...That's like short and long range goals all in one."

Ellen Jackson: "Short range goals should certainly be instruments to inform the community—developing instruments to inform the community ahead of time, preparing the community ahead of time, looking into the total ball...We got to expand a whole lot in terms of seeing what's happening to other Black communities, what's working there and how if it's at all possible to get some of those things—maybe not the *whole* program, but parts of it. We need a blueprint; I think we need to develop a blueprint for existence: where it's feasible for us to be looking economically for new housing if we want to be looking into places that are not already used and messed up; the types of education we want for our kids; where do we see ourselves going politically, and is it a new party altogether, or is it still continuing the two party system? A whole new blueprint. Those components have been sorely missing in all our activities."

Elma Lewis: "...If you live in a society, you want to alter some things about that society, but you cannot live on barter if the rest of the system is living on capitalism. Now any major institution in America is supported by the community in which it exists, so that if you look at Harvard one of the reasons they survive is because they run shops in Harvard Square and they own the real estate in which the people live in Harvard Square, and they invest money in stocks and bonds in Wall Street and they do a multitude of things...You have to think in terms of controlling the real estate in Roxbury and running the shops in Roxbury or elsewhere and investing some of that money in Wall Street. If in fact somebody else owns Roxbury and I try to conduct a supportive institution here I cannot...I think most of us are seeing this..."

Marion McElhaney: "Short range should be trying to achieve some kind of financial independence. And through that financial independence developing a political base with people with political know-how of operating. Then I think at that point we should dedicate and delegate ourselves to work to making this society work for us like it is supposed to work for us. That to me seems to be the ultimate achievement as a people in any society."

George Morrison: "...In the short run we need to mobilize and flex our political strength. That's also maybe the long run, too. We've done a couple of things wrong—the potential for registrants is not at its climax, but even those that are registered to the degree they should be...have to be entwined with politics. Some people have gone around the barn; there was a time when some folks—myself included—said we should not participate in electoral politics, be involved in a system that eats you up. Then I tried to do other things, housing development, for example. You realize that while it ought not to be the case, that ain't nothing but politics and you got to go down and deal with those bureaucrats to get your license, permits and so forth. Understanding that, I created relationships with all the ones I could, ..but that ain't the way either. It's always good to have relationships, but a thing ought to just happen and I think the only way to get that squared away is through real political power. So I'd say that political and economic development ought to be our long range goals. I got some other feelings, too, but I just don't think they are going to work. Maybe the time's never going to be right for planning, think-tanking, eliminating some of the schedules and burdens that some people are carrying."

Paul Parks: "Okay, the long range goals, as I see it, is still to gain a quality of education for all those youngsters out there. And I guess you've heard my definition of quality education. My definition—one is that there are a variety of ways in which one can learn his cognitive skills—his reading, writing, numbers and all the other things that one has to be able to manage his language... those things that sort of give us that learning discipline. The second piece of that is learning where my rights stop and yours begin, being able to understand what I'm about and what my worth and value is, and being able to understand and appreciate what somebody else's worth and value is. Those kinds of things work directly hand and hand; if you put those together you begin to arrive at a quality system of education."

Ted Parrish: "Our long range goals should be about realizing that the system as we know it is well calculated to keep certain major portions of the people not only in our community, but in the rest of the world in a dependent and oppressed position. In the short range, every form of involvement that we have should be directed at helping us understand how to get handles on the system—how to communicate: Roxbury, Soul City, Mt. Bayou, Miss., with one another in this country and with the mother country to help anybody who is about changing the capitalistic system. That's what we've got to be about in the short and long range: understanding it and trying to get handles on taking those steps. They say that every mile begins with the first step; we ought to take some small steps to understand the system and to begin to move in the directions to change it."

A. Robert Philips: "Ours is *not* a relationship about which I would generalize."

Byron Rushing: "The long range goal has to be acquiring as much land as possible immediately...turn people around on that. We must literally say that we have to own this community. The larger context is doing that to get the power to negotiate with the outside community. We need to get in a position like the Jewish peoples are in where we can make some real demands on the foreign policy of this country. Internally, we have to make Black people positive about each other, to get Black people reacting toward the negative influences in our community rather than ignoring them. So when Black people are working negatively, that they be rehabilitated or dealt with. We must work internally to make this community look positive, make it beautiful—spend a lot of time at that."

Sara Ann Shaw: "Long range goals, I think we've really seriously got to think about the whole education picture, the whole housing picture, employment, political and the involvement of as many people as possible so that they understand all of these issues and are willing to become involved with it themselves. I think short range we got the whole organizing effort that is going to go with doing the research ...and going to bring people to the long range goals. Because we can't have one without the other. We cannot in fact talk seriously about doing something about housing, employment or economics or anything if we do not have the kind of pressure that we need to effectuate those things. And the pressure is not going to come until we do that kind of organizing effort, which is both short range and long range. The short range piece is keeping people interested initially; the long range piece is keeping them interested."

Chuck Turner: "I can't answer that question. I really can't ...whew!...For me the problem is that...man can't live very long the way he is living in this society. I really believe there's a breaking point—like around integration...There are three goals that we should have as a community—general goals—and those should be the framework of everything we do. One goal is the encouraging of stability in the Black community. At CIRCLE we define stability as any community where the majority of people are living there by conscious choice rather than by necessity. That's a long range goal...and the short range goals are the things that we think will create the kinds of attitudes and the kind of development that will create a community where people are living there by choice rather than by coercion. The second long range goal...is to...struggle to find the balance between human development and material development. For example,...to put before us the goal of human potential so that when it comes to that kind of critical point the question isn't just the efficiency and how do we get it done, but...how do I balance the need to get something done over here that this person has to grow and develop. It's a calculus that makes it harder to be a manager, but...if you can't, you aren't managing in the interests of the Black community. You can't sacrifice the human development for the short term...our means have to be our ends...our end is the development of a community where you have free standing people, right? The third is the industries. It's something that you and Willard Johnson keep coming back to and that is that we have to constantly seek the opportunities to maximize the effectiveness of what we have. Build on what we have... Those are the three long range goals. There's one other; that's the racial one. I guess my position on the race issue-...moves around. I think an integrated society is what we are moving toward, but it's a...the definition has been shaped by the majority of people. We misdefined, we incorrectly defined integration. Ironically enough, Malcolm had the best definition for us when he talked about how can you integrate with anybody if you don't have a basic respect for yourself? If you don't have something that *you* feel you are bringing into that relationship. Then don't talk to me about integration if you have a subservient kind of situation..."

Rudy Waker: "Short range: creation of a list of low income families interested in home ownership. Long range: creation of a people's bank that will grant mortages for home ownership regardless of location. Every home is worth something and could be improved a little bit."

Archie Williams: "Short range...improvement of the Black community by dealing with Black problems. By that I don't mean problems from the point of view 'We got to make whitey change so we can be better,' but dealing with such problems as crime in our community, the lack of any coordinating organizations, the lack of any way of communicating on a mass basis in any way other than like a political campaign.. WE got to work on ourselves, get our home in order. The minute we begin to get a good handle and functioning in that direction, we ought to go back to eliminating the symptoms of racism that cause problems for us...If I separate the racism from the awareness of law enforcement, I knew that a cop was going to do something if I got too far out of hand...I was conditioned by the time I was 17 to be highly aware of that. Now the kids, by the time they are seventeen, are aware of the fact that the cops have abandoned Roxbury, and the symptoms and signs that they see are the general disregard for the law. If I were to address myself to criminal reduction I would start by enforcing the everyday living law...go after the major crimes by way of public relations...I would need money for at least one year of contract billboards, radio, picketing walking the streets...Long range: economic development...in which we can support a sufficient number of functional organizations to carry out given tasks. With those two things I don't think the fight against racism would be so tough...I'd see that as the long range...to support yourself; the short range is making an environment that you want to support yourself in."

Virgil Woods: "Our long range goal ought to be economic independence, educational self-reliance, political empowerment, cultural development and exchange, institutional development—the networking of those institutions...In the short run we've got to learn how to survive economically; but survive in the short run in such a way that we don't sell our souls for the long run."

NOTES

Preface

1. Frantz Fanon, *The Wretched of the Earth* (New York: Grove Press, 1963), p. 167.

Introduction

1. William Ryan, *Blaming the Victim* (New York: Pantheon Books, 1971).

Part I The Service Stage

1. Lerone Bennett, Jr., *Ebony* (February, 1963), p. 81.

2. Black Voters v. John J. McDonough, U.S. District Court of Massachusetts (1975), p. 19.

3. *Boston Chronicle,* 16 July 1932, p. 1.

4. Steve Thernstrom, *The Other Bostonians* (Boston: Harvard U. Press, 1973), p. 194.

Chapter 2

1. Ryan, *Blaming the Victim,* p. 4.

2. Greater Boston Chamber of Commerce, "Boston Renewal" (Jan. 1964), pp. 22-23.

3. *Ibid.*

4. Herbert J. Gans, *The Urban Villagers* (New York, The Free Press, 1962), p. 287.

5. Greater Boston Chamber of Commerce, "Boston Renewal," p. 5.

6. Tahi Lani Mottl, "Black Community Protest to Change Boston's Public Schools" (Ph.D. diss., Harvard University, 1978), pp. 10-11.

7. Thernstrom, *The Other Bostonians,* pp. 198-199.

8. *Ibid.,* p. 202.

9. *Ibid.,* p. 207.

Chapter 3

1. *The Boston Globe,* 16 August 1963.

2. *Ibid.*

3. *The Boston Globe,* 5 June 1963.

4. *Ibid.*

5. *Ibid.*

6. *Ibid.*

7. *Ibid.*

8. *Ibid.*

9. *The Boston Globe,* 28 August 1964.

10. Dr. Steven S. Schwarzchild, Chairman, Commission on Social Action, New England Region, United Synagogue of America (speech delivered February 20, 1964).

11. *The Boston Evening Globe,* 26 February 1965.

12. *Ibid.*

13. Also see *Blaming the Victim.*

14. Massachusetts State Board of Education, "Interim Report of the Advisory Committee on Racial Imbalance and Education" (July 1964).

15. *The Boston Globe,* 19 May 1965.

4 Economic Development

1. *The Bay State Banner,* 16 October 1965, p. 7.

2. *The Bay State Banner,* 3 June 1967.

3. *The Bay State Banner,* 29 June 1967.

4. *Report of the National Advisory Commission on Civil Disorders* (New York: Bantam Books, 1968), pp. 26-27.

5. *Ibid.*

5 Housing

1. The Boston Urban Observatory, "Organized Citizen Participation in Boston" (October 1971), p. 150.

2. *Ibid.*

7 Community Controlled Education

1. Massachusetts Advisory Commission to the United States Commission on Civil Rights.

2. *The Christian Science Monitor,* 22 July 1968.

3. *The Boston Globe,* 22 June 1969.

4. Kozol was fired because he had refused to desist from using in his fourth grade class a poem by Langston Hughes.

8 United Community Construction Workers

1. *The Bay State Banner,* 9 November 1967.

2. *Ibid.*

3. Simon was even convicted of attempting to bribe the Governor of Maine!

4. Charles Curl, Jr., "An Analysis of Racial Discrimination in Boston and National Industries" (Roxbury Joint Center, 1972).

5. *The Christian Science Monitor,* 5 December 1967.

10 Tent City

1. Mayor's Office, Press Release, May 22, 1969.

2. The Boston Urban Observatory, "Organized Participation," p. 129.

11 Student Power

1. *The Bay State Banner,* March 1971.

2. *The Record American,* 11 November, 1971.

12 The New Urban League

1. Paolo Freire, *Pedagogy of the Oppressed* (New York: Continuum Publishing Corporation, 1970).

2. *Ibid.*

13 Court Ordered Desegregation

1. *The Boston Globe,* 7 January 1973, p. 57.

2. Boston Bar Association, "The Boston School Busing Order—What Does It Mean?" (14 December 1974).

3. *The Boston Glober,* 6 September 1974.

4. *The Boston Globe,* 9 October 1974.

5. *The Boston Glober,* 16 October 1975.

14 Racism in the Unions

1. It is also interesting to note that the largest single contributor to Mayor White's campaign was C. Vincent Vappi.

2. *The Boston Globe,* 16 June 1968.

3. *Ibid.*

4. Herbert Hill, "Racism and Organized Labor" (N.Y.: New School for Social Research, Feb. 1971), Vol. 28, no. 6.

5. U.S. Commission on Civil Rights Hearings, p. 346.

6. *Ibid.,* p. 356.

7. Alan Clark, "Fairplay," *Survival (Feb. 1970), Vol. 1, No. 3.*

8. *The Boston Globe,* 23 October 1969.

9. *Record American,* 7 November 1969.

10. *The Boston Globe,* 11 November 1968.

11. *The Boston Globe,* 12 December 1969.

12. Hill, "Racism."

13. *Herald Traveler,* 13 January 1971.

14. Associated General Contractors v. Alan Altshuler, U.S. District Court of Massachusetts (1973), p. 6.

15. *Ibid.,* p. 13.

19 Power to the People

1. Black Voters v. John J. McDonough, U.S. District Court, District of Massachusetts, 1975.

2. *Ibid.,* p. 53.

21 A Strategy for the 1980's

1. Vincent Harding, *Black Collegian (Dec./Jan. 1979-80).*

INDEX